Advance Praise for
REAL PEOPLE

"I have just finished reading a very interesting manuscript by Roberta Chromey, detailing her experience on the second Sherborne course (1972–73), a magnificently ambitious and impressive Gurdjieffian ten-month training program created by J. G. Bennett. Chrysalis for Fourth-Way caterpillars determined to become butterflies. The people who have emerged from this course have proved their stuff over the years, not only as leaders in the Bennett line of the Work, but as powerfully conscious and quietly forceful human beings. Roberta is no exception. I've come to know her a bit through my own association with the Claymont Community, where she has been a linchpin for two decades, and her manuscript did not disappoint me—in fact, it was everything I would have expected of her and more. It's a lean, crisp, to my mind riveting account of the training course I have always been curious about and would have loved to be on if I'd heard about it before Bennett's death in 1974 and if I'd had the nerve. But it's also not the usual starry-eyed disciples' book. Trained early in her Work years to 'write your experience, not ABOUT your experience,' she does just that. It's a transparent, compellingly constructed 427-page manuscript which held my interest from beginning to end and taught me a lot, not only about the Work but about my own self." —**Cynthia Bourgeault,** author of *Eye of the Heart, The Wisdom Jesus, Mystical Courage,* and other titles

"I enjoyed reading *Real People* enormously. It's fresh, and open, and honest, and earnest—and very respectful towards Roberta's teachers. I loved how Roberta built the descriptions of Work through time. It had a very real sense to me. It is great that Roberta spends the time that she does on Mrs. Popoff. Not enough has been said about her. From the descriptions of Mrs. Popoff I got her dedication to spreading Gurdjieff's teachings and to the development of each person and to herself, manifesting in the moment. Mr. Nyland always showed her great respect. The descriptions of doing Movements resonate with my own experience. Roberta focuses on the effort to move to a pattern in the moment and discusses whether that pattern might have higher meaning. It comes through that they take focused attention and are not easy to execute. What Roberta's experiences were in the program are very clear and honest. I have a lot of admiration for her willingness to describe that, and I think they would be helpful to readers. The book does a good job of showing how one's experience builds as one struggles. The practice of Gurdjieff Work is an effort of a lifetime. This book recounts the story of an energetic and questioning young woman and how she confronted that challenge, laying the foundation for a lifetime of the honest application of Gurdjieff's teachings. Those who have also worked with Gurdjieff's teachings will resonate with Roberta's story. And those who are new to Gurdjieff will find here an interesting account of what it was like to take part in the 10-month course at Sherborne House with J. G. Bennett."— **June S. Loy**, Associate Editor, *Gurdjieff International Review*

REAL PEOPLE

AT THE PINNACLE

WITH IRMIS POPOFF

AND THE SECOND BASIC COURSE

AT SHERBORNE HOUSE

WITH J.G. BENNETT

A Memoir

ROBERTA J. CHROMEY

Red Elixir
Rhinebeck, New York

Real People: At the Pinnacle with Irmis Popoff and the Second Basic Course at Sherborne House with J.G. Bennett: A Memoir Copyright © 2022 by Roberta J. Chromey

All rights reserved. No part of this book may be used or reproduced in any manner without the consent of the publisher except in critical articles or reviews. Contact the publisher for information.

Paperback ISBN: 978-1-954744-70-7
eBook ISBN: 978-1-954744-71-4

Library of Congress Control Number: 2022935586

Cover design by Jack Chromey / Colin Rolfe
Book design by Colin Rolfe

Red Elixir is an imprint of Monkfish Book Publishing Company

Red Elixir
22 East Market Street, Suite 304
Rhinebeck, NY 12572
(845) 876-4861
monkfishpublishing.com

I wrote this for you— Jackie and Chris—just so you know.

CONTENTS

Preface xi
Prologue: Getting from There to Here xiii

PART 1: MRS. POPOFF—FINDING REAL PEOPLE

1. The Game Changer 3
2. The Master Game 5
3. The Trip 9
4. Winter Blues 12
5. Meetings 16
6. The Pinnacle 21
7. Impressions 25
8. Atmospheres 30
9. Fall Semester 33
10. Carlos 39
11. Negotiations 43
12. Learning to Work 46

PART 2: INTERNATIONAL ACADEMY FOR CONTINUOUS EDUCATION

13. Sherborne House 55
14. In the Beginning 62
15. Settling In 69
16. Secret Rendezvous 73

17. Something's Cookin' 78
18. Those with Eyes 83
19. Me, Myself, and I 87

PART 3: THE SECOND BASIC COURSE

20. Entering the Stream 95
21. Inaugural Address 98
22. Now It Begins 104
23. Burnt Toast 108
24. Theme Talk 111
25. Dark Horse 115
26. Material Objects 118
27. Stepping Out 122
28. Work on Oneself 126
29. Gratitude 130
30. Noticing 138
31. Mayvor 143
32. Gerald 146
33. Surprise! 152
34. Exeat 156
35. Hermeneutics 162
36. Lataif 169
37. Decision Exercise 174
38. Thanksgiving 177
39. Movements Practice 184

PART 4: JOURNALING: DOWN THE RABBIT HOLE

40. Slip-Sliding Away 189
41. Reversing the Flow of Forces 194
42. Higher States and Changing Stations 201
43. My British Christmas 204
44. Shifting into Mesoteric Gear 210

45. The Two Georges	214
46. Fire Drill	221
47. Long-Term Decisions	225
48. Religion	229
49. March	234
50. Easter Break	237
51. Mad as a Hatter	242
52. Now	247
53. Edith Wallace	251
54. Judy	256
55. The Great Prayer	258

PART 5: FINDING BALANCE

56. Tiptoeing towards Chief Feature	265
57. Essence and Personality	269
58. Chief Feature	273
59. The Key to the Kingdom	275
60. Bhante	279
61. Spring Groups	283
62. Morris On	289
63. Jack's Decision Exercise	295
64. Spring Outing	298
65. Digging Deeper	304
66. The Work at Play	307
67. Looking Ahead	314
68. Nature	321
69. Where's the Love?	323
70. Washing the Walls	326
71. Re-entry	331

Epilogue	335

PREFACE

Memory and imagination are cousins in the same family. Sometimes they play apart quite independently, but sometimes they can't help but join hands and dance together on the written page. This memoir has blossomed over time, starting from bare journal entries. In the act of casting back—thirty, forty, fifty years—dialogue and scene were necessarily recreated to bring alive incidents remembered as benchmarks in my experience. I've tried to be careful to footnote dialogue taken from documents but have also used "remembering" what a person sounded and looked like to relay what they likely would have said. If I have misrepresented anyone, I am truly sorry. I mean no harm. My sole intent is to share, as best I can, the experience of being on one of J. G. Bennett's Basic Courses at Sherborne House and the magic that took place there.

PROLOGUE
Getting from There to Here

May 1971—Cranking down the window in Herby, my leaf-green Volkswagen Bug, isn't even an option, between the fumes of lumbering diesel trucks and the putrid air of north Jersey refineries. Besides, the rumbling road noise would drown out Simon and Garfunkel's "The Sound of Silence" wafting out the dashboard speaker. These lyrics—riding their sweet, rich, melancholic tune—stir me. They speak to the way I feel about the status quo of the materialistic society I grew up in, about the ease of not speaking out, of ignoring cries of frustration expressed on subway walls and in tenement halls. These lyrics make me wonder where Reality lies. They make me a part of a generation that is looking for answers, some in the activism that leads to politics and some in the quiet inner depths of our beings.

The mournful melody coupled with foul fumes reflects my mood. Just look at me, a hypocrite. I want to feel close to God but then go back and forth between sex and drugs. Is that the way to get close to God, with no control?

I can't even resist piling donuts on my plate in the campus cafeteria. It's like I'm being tempted, but no one is there to tell me not to be a glutton. Whenever I give them up, they show up back on my plate. I seem to be all at loose ends, like there's no one in charge. Is it "free love" to sleep with Jack at school, or am I being unfaithful to Carlos while he's in Vietnam? I don't like getting stoned, but I still do it. I see these inconsistencies but can't seem to do anything about them.

I go to church with my parents when I'm at home but not when I'm at school, yet I love God. The Episcopal church I grew up in was part of my life, the pastor a friend of our family. One of the ladies I'd talk to at coffee hour got me thinking about finding kindred spirits. She seemed so real to me, so familiar. Now I look for "real people" like her.

I pull out into the passing lane and stomp down on the gas, inching past a sixteen-wheeler, one with a capped diesel pipe poking up by the cab. I stick my arm out the window and pump it up and down. He blows his horn and a puff of acrid black smoke billows out from the pipe. I quickly crank the window up.

Do I love Carlos? I thought so before he left for Nam. My first electric love, short and compact with dark curly hair, wearing wire-rims like me. His free-flowing drawings and flair for guitar and songwriting made my heart beat fast all through my senior year of high school.

Once on the George Washington Bridge, I roll the window down a couple turns to blow stale fumes out. A passing seagull's harsh cry and a barge's low lament float up from the water. I know Carlos really likes me, but I have no desire to get married right away. I want to live first. I figure if Carlos and I get serious, we could still be engaged for a few years before getting married.

Traffic on the bridge is light. I gaze upstream past the barren cliffs and gathering stands of blushing spring trees. Carlos surprised me with a visit last summer. I was upstate helping Grandma at her historic home, Fish House, which was built in 1784 after being burnt to the ground during the Revolutionary War.

When my grandparents bought it, the house came with horsehair furniture still in the double room parlor with pocket doors, a room with a deep fireplace including a big iron pot that swung over the fire, and a root cellar with a trap door leading down to it. My grandfather had found his and grandma's dream retirement home in Fish House after retiring from the Tuttle Roofing Company, known for putting the roof on the Empire State Building in 1931. At Fish House, Grandpa could all but "fish off the porch," and Grandma could walk to the little white Methodist church at the foot of the drive and across the road to the country store.

I imagine the Hudson River running north to the Great Sacandaga Reservoir, with Fish House perched high on its lonely hill, the undulating lawn rolling down to a sandy shore. Carlos had hitchhiked all the way from Maryland, on leave before deploying. I treasured the friendship ring he gave me, a gold band with a little diamond chip. Catching myself straying into the wrong lane, I adjust, then look downstream to see disappearing riverbanks consumed by Manhattan's clutter.

Off the bridge, tangles of highways, confusing green signs, impatient horns, and burnt-out shells of cars warn me not to even *think* about breaking down around here. Sweat prickles up under my armpits: Did I just miss the exit? Relief dries me up, restoring my confidence. On we sail, little Herby and I, his name hand-painted by Jack in yellow, an arc following the line of rear engine hood.

Yes, Jack. The closest thing I have to a best friend in New Jersey. Where my parents' new home doesn't feel like *my* home. Where Jack, his friends, his town, are becoming my friends, my hangout. Jack, in the seat next to me, quiet and reserved, like an alter ego to my bouncy, busy self. Content to listen to the radio, especially now that it's Dylan playing, he's happy to let me drive and worry about the roads, about our relationship. He doesn't worry about stuff like that.

I glance over at him, his long delicate features obscured by silky dark-blond hair falling straight to his shoulders. All I can see is his tall, wide forehead—eyes cast down in thought. He's probably contemplating what he'll say at the meeting about the Theme we were given last week:

How long is my *now*?

Well, mine is finally over the Throgs Neck Bridge. It's clear sailing ahead. Yes, sail boats swaying and pulling at their moors or floating past with taut canvas. Long Island stretches out before us with grassy greens, wide sweet skies, scents of salt and fish and gasoline engines. Hints of summer. Towns streaming past, each exit closer to the goal, closer to Sea Cliff and Mrs. Popoff. To creating a unified "I," one that knows what it wants. An "I" that makes a decision and sticks to it with discipline. That lives inside a millisecond as long as eternity, as natural as breath. That loves God.

Yellow, then red, traffic lights slow my progress. We still have a way to go through thickening townships. Herby sputters and coughs, refusing the green light. I'm stuck at the intersection.

PART ONE

MRS. POPOFF—
FINDING REAL PEOPLE

> Life is real only then, when 'I Am'
> —G.I. GURDJIEFF

With Mrs. Popoff and Rigi.

CHAPTER ONE
The Game Changer

December 1970—I dangled my feet over the side of Jack's bed in his narrow college dorm room and watched him rearrange various piles of detritus. All I could see of his slender face was the nose protruding through a curtain of straight dishwater-blond hair. That oversized nose with the flared nostrils and an off-kilter bump had caught my attention at orientation. We'd been crowded around a table in the lounge, and I'd stared across the donuts and coffee, wondering if I was glimpsing the ugliest girl or the prettiest guy I'd ever seen.

Now, I watched his long fingers move thoughtfully, picking up a piece of paper, slipping it into a dresser drawer. His roommate had complained that he wasn't doing his share of cleaning. At least he was making an effort.

"So, Jack, what is it about you? What're you into?" I asked, peering out through wire-rimmed glasses, my head cocked to one side. I wanted to know where the sense of mystery about him came from.

He stopped shuffling his textbooks and papers and looked at me, a small-framed young woman with too much thick brown hair falling around a petite oval face perched on his bed. We had ended up at Livingston College, part of Rutgers University, from different ends of the social universe.

Like other baby boomers coming of age in the 1960s and 70s, we were searching for a deeper meaning to life than the rampant materialism engulfing America and Western Europe. Drawn to spiritual teachings that provided pathways to higher consciousness and inner growth, Jack and I were no exception.

"D'you really want to know, Bobby Jo?" he asked.

It was December and the air was crisp, the New Jersey sky outside his dorm window was laced with scudding gray clouds.

I was dying to know.

Jack moved to a corner of the cluttered room and rummaged through a pile of pants and T-shirts, disengaging a book with gentle hands, a paperback with a bright yellow cover. "Read this," he said, handing it to me.

Red letters inside a black circle spelled out, *The Master Game*, and below that, at the bottom of the yellow cover, "by Robert de Ropp, author of *Drugs and the Mind*."[1]

"Isn't de Ropp one of those UC Berkeley guys who discovered LSD?" I asked, scrutinizing the cover. A name linked to Timothy Leary, Stephen Gaskin, and Alan Watts—names resonant in the recent 1960s drug culture. I looked up at Jack for confirmation.

"Yeah, they were all into exploring psychedelics and how they affected people's minds," he confirmed, glancing around at his dresser, now tidy with collections of papers and personal artifacts. Like the Osmiroid calligraphy pen sitting on top of his black hardbound book of unlined sheets—the one he sketched, doodled, and scratched thoughts into—opening to random pages with no thought of sequential order. Like the black felt hat sitting on top of his reading lamp, with a broad enough brim to hide his eyes and most of the world when he wore it. The juggling balls collected into a cloth bag. His older brother's light brown, short-sleeved sweatshirt from Memphis State U, which he loved and said the MSU initials really stood for Mighty Strange Universe.

Voices could be heard out in the quad as kids headed back to their rooms. His roommate would be arriving from class. It was time for me to go to mine.

"But this is different. When you finish *The Master Game*, tell me what you think," he said as I hopped off his bed.

I took the book with me, wondering what I would find in it.

---

[1] Robert S. de Ropp, *The Master Game* (New York: Delacorte Press, 1968).

CHAPTER TWO
The Master Game

A few weeks later, we were sitting at Jack's kitchen table in West New York, New Jersey. The New York Daily News sat on the red-checked vinyl tablecloth along with his mother's leftover piggies. I could still smell the hamburger, onions, and rice in her spicy tomato sauce, rolled into boiled cabbage leaves. The piggies tasted good, despite my unfamiliarity with Slovakian food.

I had brought back Jack's copy of *The Master Game* and was flipping through it. What I had found in its pages was the idea that we could be the masters of ourselves, that life was a game one could choose to play but could not win by taking psychedelics. That this game wasn't easy and that one would need a teacher. What the book didn't say was how to find one.

"So, what did you think of it?" Jack asked, gazing at the table.

"Yeah. Well, I thought the ideas were interesting," I said, looking up from the book. "Especially where he says you don't need to do drugs to play the Game. But now what?"

I squeezed around Jack and began washing the dirty dishes left in the sink, feeling sorry for his mom, with five boys and hating messes. She liked me and was always trying to give me stuff like packets of sugar or tea she'd brought home after work at the hospital, where she delivered and retrieved food trays.

Jack sat back in his chair, thinking about my question, about what came next. The front door opened and two of his young brothers bustled in. They carried large plastic stacking trays of Tasty Cakes and cream-filled Moon Pies. Dishes clattered aside as they set them down on the table and kitchen counter. "Wow, good haul today," Jack commented, knowing they could bring home outdated products after unloading delivery trucks on Sundays.

The boys disappeared into the living room to join their dad, who had a football game on, confections in hand.

"So, what about *The Master Game*?" I asked again, looking for something to dry my hands on and ending up using my bell bottoms. "What happens next?"

"Hang on." Jack said as he disappeared into his room. He strolled back out a minute later and handed me another paperback. "This is next," he said. "If you really want to know." The title of this one was, *In Search of the Miraculous*, by P. D. Ouspensky.[1] He sat back down and popped open the cellophane on a Twinkie.

"Ouspensky was de Ropp's teacher," he said, putting the spongy cake down on the table, his eyes serious. "And G. I. Gurdjieff was Ouspensky's teacher."

"Who's Gurdjieff?" I asked, losing the thread in all the weird names.

He stood up and came over to the kitchen counter. He leaned over my shoulder, looking at the blue and white cover on *In Search of the Miraculous*, a more substantial read than *The Master Game*.

Jack picked up *The Master Game* from the counter where I'd placed it and sat back down thumbing through pages. "Here," he said, listen to this, "Self-observation leads to self-knowledge, self-knowledge leads to self-mastery." I felt a thrill go through me. Yes, this is where de Ropp was coming from. Replacing the book on the counter behind him, he pushed back from the table, the metal legs of the chair scraping the linoleum.

As he disappeared again into his room, I sat down at the table brushing crumbs away and folding up the newspaper to put it aside, feeling a bit like we were following a trail, unravelling a mystery, like Sherlock Holmes. Jack emerged and sat down on the vinyl seat, tossing hair out of his eyes. This time he held a worn, oversized hardback book with a brown cover, entitled *A New Model of the Universe*.

[1] P. D. Ouspensky, *In Search of the Miraculous: Fragments of an Unknown Teaching* (New York: Harcourt, 1949).

"Ouspensky wrote this before he met Gurdjieff," he said, holding the book up to show me. "He was already exploring altered states and working with dreams in Russia," he explained, handing me the book. "He experimented with drugs too, like de Ropp. He was a mathematician and into metaphysics but much earlier, like in the early 1900s. Then he met Gurdjieff." Jack was speaking in earnest now.

"Oh yeah," I nodded, remembering de Ropp had said something about the Gurdjieffian System. I was curious, peeking inside the book, wondering where all this was going, yet distracted by the clutter of wrappers and food on the table.

"Yeah, well, when de Ropp talks about the Psychological Method, he gets that from Ouspensky, who kind of developed the idea in *New Model*." Jack reached around and lifted *In Search of the Miraculous* from the counter again. He held it in both hands, reverently. "And this," he said, looking very solemn, "tells how Ouspensky met his teacher Gurdjieff, who was way ahead of him in all this stuff."

I was totally caught up now, feeling invited into something like a sacred trust. The discomfort of alien surroundings I felt when visiting West New York were forgotten. Jack sat down at the table. Beyond him on the wall hung his mother's wooden crucifix and a small picture of Christ. Jack looked so beautiful, with his shoulder-length hair, slender build, and soft features—quite Raphael-like.

"And if you want to know what I'm into, it's in here." Jack handed me the thick paperback, *In Search of the Miraculous*, as if it contained the mysteries of the universe and our place in it.

I felt honored at being welcomed into his inner world. An inner world I was beginning to resonate with because, more and more, I was finding myself questioning just who this Bobby Jo person was.

Words de Ropp used, like false ego, self-observation, self-mastery; these were words I had never used but were vibrating within me as if they had a familiar ring. False ego was the perfect word to describe what it was about a person that made them seem phony. Perhaps the lack of a false ego was what made someone seem real to me.

Since high school I had known it was "real people" I was searching for.

I wondered, too, how others saw me. Maybe self-observation was the way to see who I really was. The idea of self-mastery trumped it all. To be able to rid oneself of faults, control one's appetites—be Real.

Was it possible to become a more real version of me? Someone others related to as I *was*? Someone who didn't need to be explained or justified.

Could I find other people who were trying to be real too?

CHAPTER THREE
The Trip

January 1971—Jack's New Year's resolution was to give up getting high on weed or psychedelics. We were back on campus before the spring semester started, and I still had his copy of *In Search of the Miraculous*. Ouspensky had a way of both relaying Gurdjieff's philosophical ideas and telling a good story. I kept finding myself thinking *Yes, yes, this is what I've always thought, I've just never had the words!* Ideas like how we have different little "i"s. One "i" will make a decision one day and another "i" will do the opposite the next. Like making a resolution to give up drugs, then eating peyote.

Someone on Jack's floor had come back from break with a bag of peyote buttons. I'd been hanging out with Jack in his room and was invited to join the group that gathered. The idea of cooking the shrunken brown cactus leaves created action. We lit candles, turned off the light and sat in a circle on the floor, a hot plate with the brewing buttons in the middle. This was going to be my first psychedelic experience. I had only started smoking pot last semester and wasn't wild about it. But having read Carlos Castaneda, *The Teachings of Don Juan: A Yaqui Way of Knowledge,* and thinking this was organic and not a chemical, I decided to give it a try. As the broth began its ritualistic path around the circle, I remembered Jack's stories about how he'd helped his friends get through bad acid trips. I would be in good hands, if needed.

"Ugh!" I groaned, throwing up bitter bile in the bathroom. *This isn't much fun.* Others were having a similar experience. By the time I returned to the room, everyone had left. Jack and his roommate were crashed out on their beds. *Tommy*, the new album by The Who, was playing at top volume. It was too loud and too rock for my taste.

Not knowing what to do, I wandered downstairs, drawn by a dim light in the lounge. There was only one other guy there. A slight, withdrawn kid who always stayed to himself. Distracted, I gazed at him, then all at once saw WHO HE WAS. It was like his face had been a mask and it lifted for a moment. I could see he was gay but either he wasn't ready to acknowledge it himself or couldn't admit it to others. But now he knew that I knew. So he knew. Total recognition passed between us in that silent cold room. That's when I knew I was tripping.

I started running upstairs to tell Jack. It was like climbing inside an accordion. I flew up steps in one moment and then went into s-l-o-w m-o-t-i-o-n the next. Time contracted and expanded. It took a nanosecond. It took forever. Then I was there.

"Jack, Jack!" I yelled through the door, pounding on it. "We're tripping, we're tripping!" The music inside blasting, the door opened. Jack blinked into the florescent light bouncing off the bright white cinderblock hallway. "We've come up!" I exclaimed again. Gary was gone, riding the waves of pulsing music, but Jack followed me downstairs to the lounge.

The little guy had left the room. I felt sorry for him and hoped he'd come out now and be himself. One of the other guys from the peyote circle had realized he was tripping before he went to sleep, so had also wandered down to the lounge. The three of us found a board game, Battleships, where you try to sink everyone else and take over the world.

As we played, I realized the real way to win was to work together. They didn't get it at first, but I knew, and I knew that they would get it. Usually, Jack picked up on things way ahead of me, but this time I was there first. It was as if we were playing from a different dimension. Joining forces, we worked together to win rather than conquer.

I wandered outside. It was snowing, the ground powdered; it was beautiful, soft, and quiet. I started shuffling, pushing my feet through the snow. Looking up at the night sky through the floating white flakes, my heart crying out in aching silence to the universe. When I'd finished moving, my feet had spelled out C A R L O S in big continuous letters in the snow.

Carlos, my artistic, musician, hippy, high school boyfriend, the first love of my life. The two of us discovering the wonders of sex together and losing our virginity to one another. He shipped out to Vietnam and I transferred to Livingston College soon after. I had not been thinking of him until now. Jack had been watching the letters form from the window in his room. I had been watching them spool out from my heart.

Back in my room, Mescalito appeared as a little green image hovering at the edge of my vision. I couldn't discern a figure, but I could tell it was Mescalito. I remembered reading about him in Carlos Castaneda's first book. A book I had read at University of Maryland before ever having met Jack. I didn't talk to Mescalito like Castaneda had, but I knew he was there—a protector, a guide.

Mescalito showed me how peyote lets you see through it if you want to. It doesn't trap you into thinking the peyote dream is real. My big Aha was realizing we have psychedelic chemicals in our bodies already. All we have to do is learn how to unlock them naturally. I had seen little doors in my brain, complete with keyholes. I was scribbling in my journal, hunched over my sliver of a desk as the morning dawned crisp and clear.

Leaning back to think, I felt a smile of relief playing with my face, my solar plexus relaxing. *Cool. I don't need to take psychedelics.* Now I had a reason not to—I wanted to learn how to be high without chemical crutches. *The real trip is here, in our natural world. In my own body. God's the Grand Master of that game. Mescalito is just a messenger. I get it!*

CHAPTER FOUR
Winter Blues

February–March 1971—"What? But why?" I was in the hall, on the pay phone. Jack had dropped out of school. I couldn't believe it. No wonder I hadn't seen him around. "So why didn't you tell me?" *Man!*

"My friends needed a bass player and I decided, that's all. It's my chance and I have to take it." His voice sounded flat. What I didn't know was that he had no money for a second semester.

"Can I still come visit?" I asked. The hall was cold, it was snowing out, and my feet were bare. I shivered, rubbing one foot up against my flannel pjs.

"Sure," he said. Long silence.

"Okay. Next time I'm at my parents' I'll give you a call. I can drive over in Herby." I wanted to fill in the silence, brighten the mood. But I didn't know when I'd see him.

I buckled down into my classes, a double major in English and Education. This way I could support myself as a teacher while I wrote my novels in the garret, like Louisa May Alcott. I loved my English Lit. courses and found alternative approaches to education intriguing in books like Bel Kaufman's *Up the Down Staircase*.

When I drove north to West Caldwell in my VW Bug, Herby, to visit my parents, I parked my bag in the room they had designated as mine after the move from Maryland. It had my horse-show ribbons and silver trophy hanging on the wall, my ballet slippers in the closet. But the heavy mahogany four-poster and matching dresser crowded the space and there was no room for a desk. No matter, I would soon be on my own.

On Saturday afternoons I would jump into Herby and drive east onto increasingly congested roads to West New York, New Jersey. West of the wide Hudson River, across from Manhattan, West New York was different from the small-town feel of West Caldwell. Towns marching along the Hudson from the Lincoln Tunnel to the George Washington Bridge made West New York feel part of a single urban city. Asphalt streets and cement sidewalks left little room for anything green. You had to go two towns up the avenue to Hudson County Park to see a grassy field or trees large enough to climb. But I could smell bread baking from the corner Spanish store and see people walking everywhere.

I was sitting on the spare bed in Jack's room while he looked around for his hat. We were biding time until leaving for his band gig at the high school, waiting to be picked up by a good friend. The Hardy next to his Laurel, The Man with the Van. His girlfriend would keep me company at the dance while they played.

Jack's parents didn't mind if I stayed at their house, sleeping in one of the twin beds in Jack's room. His mom once told me on her way upstairs, "Oh, don't worry about him," nodding her head in Jack's direction. "He's harmless, just like his father." I never figured that one out.

Jack sat down next to me, turning the wide brim of his hat around with long fingers. A late winter glow shimmered in the dust motes through half-shuttered windows. Scents of boiled pierogis mixed with Bud and tomato sauce wafted in from the kitchen.

"Hey man, are you okay?" I led off, wanting to know more about why he quit school and why he wasn't more excited about the band.

"What do you mean?" he asked, his hands still. The laugh track from *All in the Family* floated above the rattle of dishes coming from the kitchen. The house was quiet except for his mom and her TV on the kitchen counter.

"I guess, I mean, you seem so down lately." I looked at his young face, always so serious. "Sometimes I wonder if you ever have ordinary fun. You know, like without being high." I wished I could see him smile spontaneously, as a kid playing ball or skipping rope would, alive in the moment.

"Well yeah, I've been having a tough time." He looked up, straight locks falling away from his high forehead. "The band hasn't been doing much. We're kind of deciding tonight, depending on how it goes. Besides that, I don't have much goin' for me right now." He added, "You know Richard Fariña's book, *Been Down So Long It Looks Like Up to Me*? That's pretty much where I'm at."

Damn, I thought. I'd never seen him like this. Out loud I said, "You know, something's gotta turn up."

"Easy for you to say. And what do you mean, I don't know how to have fun?" Jack stood up, withdrawing inward. "What do you know about my life, anyway?!"

Our ride was beeping his horn out front. I gathered up my coat, feeling put-out. I was trying to be encouraging, and he was taking it the wrong way. I felt my jaw tense. Frustrated, I snapped, "Well, you don't have to get all kowtowed over a huff!"

Jack stared at me, dumbfounded. "What?!" He started laughing despite himself. "Where are you from?" I'm from the DC suburbs, man, I thought to myself. "Talk about accents, you're from New Jersey!" I snorted as we left the house, our friendship restored.

I'd arranged at Spring Break to go home to Maryland, stay with friends and visit schools. After observing in several classrooms, I came away depressed. The public school system was still about keeping kids quiet, not generating excitement and curiosity.

To do any real teaching, I would need to be well-versed in my subject, become knowledgeable in the study and understanding of people, be in tune with myself. A true teacher was a resource to her students, a fellow student on the path of knowledge. Was I together enough for that? What did I know about dealing with people, what inner resources did I even possess?

I wasn't together at all. I wanted to write but thought I needed to be a school teacher. I was sleeping with Jack but still thought I loved Carlos. If I loved Carlos, why wouldn't I want to marry him when he got back from Nam next year? I was just being honest when I wrote him the letter saying

"I have places to go and people to meet." I know it's going to be hard for him to hear that, but please God, help him! Help me! Shit, what am I doing?

My hands shook after I read Carlos's next aerogram. He had gotten in trouble, might lose his desk job, be sent into the field. He was using heroine, trying to quit. *Oh God*, I prayed again, *help him come home safe.*

When I opened the little box Carlos had sent with the letter, I exhaled a low *Ohhhh* from the back of my throat as if someone had hit me in the stomach. My heart pulsed in my neck as a huge diamond ring gleamed up at me. It was beautiful and unusual. I'd never seen a square cut diamond. I put it on. It glittered. But it looked gaudy on my short square finger. I took it off and held it up, turning it this way and that, admiring the sparks of light, looking into its mirrored depths. Reluctantly, I put it back in the box, not comfortable wearing it but not wanting to give it up.

CHAPTER FIVE
Meetings

April–May 1971—"Turns out my friend from the School of Visual Arts was seen on the subway carrying *Search*," Jack said, finishing his story.

It was early spring, grass peeked out through melting snow on the quad. Jack had come to visit. We were seated at a table in the student lounge. He was telling me about Paul, a friend he'd made before coming to Livingston College. They'd both been going to the School of Visual Arts, a well-respected art school in New York City. Jack was interested in finding people who had read Ouspensky's *In Search of the Miraculous*. A mutual friend reported having seen Paul with the book.

"So, I got in touch with him," he continued. "There's a woman, Mrs. Popoff, who was a student of Mr. Ouspensky's in the 1940s. She's teaching the Gurdjieffian system of ideas at Paul's loft in the City."

"Wow, really?" I said, shocked. "You thought Gurdjieff's teaching had disappeared with Ouspensky years ago. There's still someone out there who knew him?"

The background din of student conversations, rustling papers, rattling dishes, dimmed around us as I focused on the import of what Jack was saying, "Yeah, this means there's a living teacher and it isn't up to us to figure the system out on our own."

I felt a pull inside me, a desire to have access to this teacher too.

Jack sounded more engaged than I'd heard him in a long time. "There's a group that meets once a week," he continued. "Paul got me in. In fact, they meet at his loft by Port Authority in New York. It's easy for me to get to."

I could tell by the way Jack was talking, looking at his hands and speaking softly, that he took this development seriously. Maybe this was the break he'd been hoping for.

I was still reading *In Search of the Miraculous* and absorbing the ideas. Yes, I wanted to be free of my false personality, create a single I, learn to "observe" myself and become a human being in the true sense of the word. I wanted all these things so I could become a good person, one without pretense. De Ropp had given me the notion that life wasn't just about having a successful career, or creating a loving family. It was about how we managed ourselves. Ouspensky was relaying how Gurdjieff was teaching him to do that.

Introducing the practice of self-observation, Ouspensky quotes notes from one of Gurdjieff's lectures. "From the very beginning, observation must be based upon the understanding of the fundamental principles of the activity of the human machine. The human machine is divided into four sharply defined groups, each of which is controlled by its own special mind or 'center.' Therefore, before beginning to observe, one must understand how the functions differ; what intellectual activity means, what emotional activity means, what moving activity means and what instinctive activity means. One must begin observing oneself as though one does not know anything about oneself."[1]

It sounded fascinating. But how to begin? What did it mean to "observe oneself?"

Towards the end of the semester, in May, the Gurdjieff group in New York "opened" to new members. Jack brought me. His friend Paul met us at the door. He had a solid, stocky build, a mop of tight, curly dark hair, and an infectious grin. He wasn't grinning when he first saw me, though. He later told us he had been furious, thinking Jack had brought his little sister to a group meeting.

Mrs. Popoff, the leader of the group, was elderly, short and stout—a grandmotherly type with thin white hair and an olive complexion. She was the daughter of a Venezuelan diplomat stationed in the US. At first,

---

[1] Ouspensky, *In Search*, 106.

I thought she had an accent but later learned it was a harelip lisp. She commanded great respect and was accompanied by two middle-aged women, established members of her main group.

During the initial part of the meeting we sat on chairs arranged in a circle, and people took turns asking questions that Mrs. Popoff answered at length. Later, the chairs were pushed back and we stood in two rows, six abreast, an arm's length apart. I could see the utility of the open space of Paul's loft. One of the women pressed the button on a tape recorder and we started marching in a military-like fashion, adding sharp, angular, arm gestures at Mrs. Popoff's instruction. With my background in ballet, nothing about this was appealing. But still, there was something about Mrs. Popoff. The other members of the group, all college age I guessed, were attentive and serious in a way that legitimized who this woman was.

At the end of the meeting, Mrs. Popoff hugged me warmly. Surprised, I hugged her back, wondering if at last I was meeting "real" people.

Not long after I joined the group, an outing with both new and established members was arranged. Mrs. Popoff was taking us all to hear someone give a talk at the Gotham Book Mart. The Gotham was legend in the City, owned by Francis Stelloff, who knew everyone. Authors, artists, playwrights, actors—you never knew who you might bump into there. We filed in, creaking over wooden floors, squeezing through narrow aisles, passing tables strewn with books half-read. Jack said he thought he had stood next to Christopher Isherwood, the novelist, at one of those tables once. The air was redolent with the odor of vintage wood, ink, and leather as we passed through the store.

Upstairs, a large meeting room was already full as we took our seats. A mix of young and old, men and women—all with quiet, intent expressions. I later learned that many had come from the Gurdjieff Foundation. Apparently, J. G. Bennett, a former student of Gurdjieff and Ouspensky, had a reputation within the Foundation for being unpredictable and unorthodox, always trying something new.

Our group sat towards the back of the room. Just before the presentation was to start, two elderly ladies were ushered to the front of the room. Someone whispered, "That's Madame de Salzmann and Madame de

Hartman!" Both had worked for years with Mr. Gurdjieff, before he died in 1949.

In the hushed room, with purposeful gait, Mr. Bennett traversed the aisle between the folding chairs. He was the tallest person I'd ever seen. Untamed white hair and piercing eyes shot out under bushy eyebrows. Quite British, too, with houndstooth jacket, leather elbow patches, and proper pronunciation.

He spoke at length of a ten-month course offered at the International Academy for Continuous Education in Sherborne, England. Students would live and study together, and practice the Thematic Process. Take cosmology and psychology classes, participate in practical work projects, learn dance.

Coming to this presentation as a new group member, I had assumed I was tagging along for the ride. But I was riveted. Mr. Bennett's voice was warm, yet precise. He spoke slowly, searching inwardly for the right words. No sign of notes or memorization. He was talking to *me* as if he had found me out, knew my own unfolding thoughts.

"One must not underestimate the importance of true education. Not what one currently calls education, but learning that comes from within, that continues throughout a lifetime." He said students would work together to become more awake. To develop the potential to become real human beings.

Yes! I shouted inside myself. *That's what I'm into. That's how learning should be.* It was as if little electrical impulses were coursing through my body. The room was crowded and stone silent except for Mr. Bennett's British voice gripping my attention. Without thinking, I turned to Jack and whispered with total conviction, "We're going!" It was clear, like knowing I had to transfer to Livingston College. Excitement welled up in me, I was riding the crest of a wave headed for shore. With no thought for logistics—Carlos, my parents, money. I knew in my soul that Jack and I had to go on the course at Sherborne.

Bennett fielded questions—some skeptical, some excited. He invited those interested to apply for the Basic Course. At last, he stood for a long minute, pensive. Then concluded softly, "Gurdjieff once said, 'No teacher is worth his salt until he's called a heretic by one hundred true believers.'" Lifting his head with the hint of a twinkle in his eye he proclaimed, looking out into the audience, "To Mr. Gurdjieff, the Arch Heretic!" He departed the room with long, sure strides, just as he had entered.

Jack and I came back the next day to be interviewed. I spoke passionately to Mr. Bennett about my interest in alternative education, declaring, "It's the wave of the future!"

We were given prospectuses and told we could apply for the second Basic Course, which would begin next year, in the fall of 1972.

Our weekly meetings with Mrs. Popoff took on new purpose. We were invited to join the regular group which met in Sea Cliff, Long Island. I felt as if I had been initiated into an inner circle. The little green Volkswagen Bug, Herby, that my dad had bought for me to drive to college, now carried Jack and me to Long Island every Monday.

CHAPTER SIX
The Pinnacle

The Pinnacle, Mrs. Popoff's house, sat on a quiet street with mature, overhanging trees next to other houses braced against an incline leading to a cliff's edge, hence the town's name, Sea Cliff. At the end of a narrow lane dappled in shade on the far side of the house, steep flights of rickety wooden steps led down to sparse strips of rocky beach along the southern shore of Long Island Sound.

An aging wooden structure, painted white, the house rambled four stories high with floors of empty bedrooms. Immense porches wrapped around three sides of the old building on the second floor. A tree, three feet in diameter, had grown through someone's carefully cut circle in the painted planks of the main deck. The place had been a fancy summer hotel in its day, complete with a ballroom.

A silent group of men and women sat in a circle on an odd collection of wooden chairs in Mrs. Popoff's dated downstairs living room, which was perfumed with the acrid scent of cat. Most were middle-aged housewives, with one or two professional husbands. We newer, younger students were in the minority. One by one we took turns speaking, describing our experience with the task Mrs. Popoff had given the week before.

Listen to the sound of your voice as you speak.

One lady who owned her own business admitted sorrowfully, "Because I was so busy all week ordering merchandise for my shop, I kept remembering the task after I'd gone to bed."

Jack raised his hand and Mrs. Popoff addressed him, "Jack, no. We already have a Jack. I think I'll call you Juan, Don Juan. Yes?"

Jack melted down into the floor, head bowed. He was certain Mrs. Popoff intuited his New Year's Resolution to give up drugs and a subsequent Peyote trip. In a low voice he mumbled, "Umm, yes—well, I was walking down the block and ran into my friend and in the middle of talking to him I remembered the task and heard myself speaking. That's all."

I was amused at Jack's discomfort. I'd never seen him nonplussed before. But at least he offered an observation. I had thought about the task several times during the week, but never when I was actually speaking to someone. I kept quiet, for once.

The man who always wore a white button-down shirt, was overweight, and looked the part of an executive spoke next, "My boys, who are five and seven, were bringing a dinner tray to me in the living room. I flashed on how our white carpet would be ruined if they spilled red spaghetti sauce on it."

He shifted uncomfortably in his chair, remembering. "The word *don't* jumped out of my mouth and I heard the anger and disapproval in my tone. I saw a look of hurt surprise on my older son's face."

His gaze came up off the carpet and he looked at Mrs. Popoff, saying, "It broke my heart, and in that space, I said, 'Oh, how thoughtful of you!' And meant it. It sounded warmer and deeper than my normal speaking voice. Not only was my negativity gone—but the light shining in their eyes—I'll never forget it."

I'd been listening with polite attention to the first few observations, but now the room held a deep silence. I could hear the cats scrabbling around in the back room where they'd been banished for the evening. For a lingering minute, no one spoke.

Mrs. Popoff sat, short-waisted, back resting straight in her armchair. I listened carefully as she lisped, "Yes Gary, that was a good observation. Your work is beginning to bear fruit."

I gazed at Gary, touched by what he said despite the fact that he looked so establishment with his short hair and business attire.

Mrs. Popoff nodded her white head. "You had a true moment of self-observation and in that instant, there was choice." Her brown eyes were soft, "You chose to act rather than react. To be intentional with your sons rather than asleep." The noise of the cats had receded as well as the closeness of the small room. Her voice was firm, sure of what she was saying. This is how we forge a Real I, how we begin to replace all the little i's that rule us."

The fact that I was in this old house, with suburban housewives and middle-aged establishment-type people, seemed incongruous with the fact that we were being taught by an Elder, one who had known Ouspensky and Gurdjieff themselves. No mountaintop, no pilgrimage to a distant land. Here, in this very room, a direct line of esoteric knowledge was being passed on. The cat smell did not matter to me anymore.

Once we had taken our turns describing experiences with the week's task and receiving comments from Mrs. Popoff, chairs were moved aside. We stood in a row of six across on the threadbare carpet with a second row directly behind at arm's length.

Mrs. Popoff faced us, her feet rooted to the floor, as if she were channeling energy through the ground up into her torso, emanating presence. With purpose, her arms took sharp angular positions, held long enough to seem as if there was a mold she was fitting them into. We mirrored her, striving to be exact. Her right arm faced forward, bent at the elbow, then to the side, then down. To the side, then front, then up above her head went the left arm. Next, she moved both arms each in their own pattern. We followed as best we could. The front row with more experienced students caught on first. Now she was moving her feet, in a kind of marching step.

I had taken ballet and modern dance classes for years and considered myself a dancer. This didn't seem like dancing to me, and I chafed internally, uncomfortable with the asymmetry. I glanced over at Jack, who always claimed he had two left feet. His forehead was contracted in concentration.

"*No*, not that way, *this* way!" Mrs. Popoff commanded above the scratchy tape cassette of music, throwing her right arm out in exactly the opposite position from what she had first shown. There was nothing for it but to follow. Impossible to figure out the pattern mentally before something new was added. Turn right four beats; right foot, left foot. Back one beat; left one beat; left three beats; keep the arms going, the feet marching, relax shoulders, count the rhythm. Don't think. Concentrate on moving with the person in front, the person to the side, now pivot to the back of the room and I'm in front! Let my feet march to the rhythm, one, two, three, four; one; one; one, two, three—

Suddenly the feeling in the room changed. The air took on a luminosity—soft, vibrating. The atmosphere expanded. Inside a giant bubble, we were connected and Jack was grinning. I surreptitiously peeked at the others, the bewildered look on Gary's face confirming my suspicion that it was happening to all of us. This felt like the same expanded awareness I had experienced on the Peyote trip. We were in this together, we were high! Here was the confirmation that I had been right. Drugs weren't necessary to reach a higher plane of experience: we had the stuff within ourselves.

The rhythms from the scratchy tape cassette reverberated in my bones. My body had absorbed the cadence, my feet moving in their rhythm and my arms in their own. For a few moments it was as if all our gestures were connected to our neighbors and we moved as one. My head just watched, amazed.

I had read that Gurdjieff called himself a Teacher of Dancing. What kind of dance was this? The central point seemed to be to keep us so confused we didn't have time to think.

It all ran counter to my experience of ballet, where steps and patterns were painstakingly taught and learned to create a beautiful performance. *What is she trying to do? No one can learn anything this way. What the heck just happened? Wow, cooool, man!* Thoughts and feelings jangled within me as Mrs. Popoff brought the class to an end and sent us home with a new "task" for the week. Become aware of your posture.

CHAPTER SEVEN
Impressions

Concerns about my boyfriend Carlos, still in Vietnam, had faded to a background noise in my head by the time final exams came around. I was busy applying for summer jobs and absorbed with the weekly tasks given by Mrs. Popoff. My mind had no room to worry about the engagement ring tucked away in its little box, out of sight in my dresser at my parent's house. I'd all but forgotten about it and my moral quandary about two-timing Carlos. My new internal struggle was how to justify keeping the ring, which I wasn't ready to give up, but neither did I want to accept the commitment it represented. Better to hide all this in a place I didn't visit that much.

As summer approached, Mrs. Popoff developed a program to prepare six of her students, all college age, to attend Mr. Bennett's first Basic Course in England. The group would be leaving in the fall of 1971 and returning the following summer. Mrs. Popoff's seminars would be open to anyone who wanted to attend.

The residential program utilized the Pinnacle's many bedrooms, large upstairs sitting room, and downstairs sunporch for dining. Mrs. Popoff wanted to simulate the Course in England with physical work in the morning, a long lunch discussion centered on sharing observations of inner work, Movements in the afternoon, and evening lectures or presentations. Those who could were encouraged to stay and participate full time.

With no job or band to tie him down, Jack planned to attend all summer. Since I had a job as a camp counselor for eight weeks, I could only come at the beginning and end of the summer.

On a breezy, sparkling-blue, June day we sailed out to Long Island in Jack's V8 bomber of a car for the first ten-day summer seminar with Mrs. Popoff.

"I still can't believe your neighbor sold you his car for a dollar. And I really can't believe you talked me into letting you drive Herby down to Maryland during Spring break, that was crazy." I munched on a peanut butter and jelly sandwich as he maneuvered the lanes across the Throgs Neck Bridge, the tartness of the jelly playing against the sweet sticky goo of the peanut butter. I handed him his half across the wide front seat. "You never said you hadn't actually driven in traffic or on a highway before."

I remembered the jerky starts and stops in Herby that got us out of New Brunswick that morning and onto the Turnpike. Luckily, once we got going on the highway, he could stay in one gear and concentrate on learning how to look over his shoulder before changing lanes. "Got to admit though, you're a pretty fast learner. We made it and you drove all the way."

Jack looked like he didn't appreciate my critique.

"Bobby Jo, I don't know why you keep saying you taught me how to drive. I knew how to drive. Dave Shaw taught me. Besides, I drove a motorcycle, remember?"

"Yeah, but you only drove around in Palisades Park in Dave's van. Driving a motorcycle isn't the same."

"Well, in any case, I got my license and I'm legal now." Jack was closing the case.

We reached the Pinnacle in time to settle into our respective rooms before the first meeting of the seminar. Jack went up to the fourth floor and Mrs. Popoff showed me my room on the third floor, the women's floor.

The room smelled a bit musty, of old wood and metal. But the window was open and a salty breeze ruffled the muslin curtains. Two iron twin bedsteads, one wooden dresser and two chairs made up my accommodation. The bareness of the room did not matter. The seminar schedule was full and only left me time to gratefully fall into bed at night after making brief entries in my journal.

Meals were communal. Mrs. Popoff and her older women students did the cooking. There were big practical work projects for the men, like painting and repairing the big room on the ground floor called the Russian kitchen. The rest of us younger women would be set to sweeping the common areas, clearing or setting the table for meals, or cleaning the many litter boxes.

The midday meal reminded me of stories about Hemingway, long interactive affairs that went on for hours after the meal, many of us sipping on hot cups of tea or hot water, as Mrs. Popoff did. Instead of discussing literature we would share how we'd fared with a given task or continue a discussion of an aspect of Gurdjieff's teaching, which Mrs. Popoff referred to as the Work[1].

One morning, halfway through the week, I came downstairs to the ground floor and out through a narrow entry into the sunroom. The room took half the length of the house and was full of rectangular wooden tables and chairs, all painted a matching pale green during one of the practical work projects. Banks of windows looked out to the lawn with wide doors leading outside to a level area of grass and graveled parking.

The usual quiet sound of early morning voices was absent as I found a place at the long table. Cutlery clinked in subdued tones as everyone sat with heads bowed, concentrating on their food in studied silence. The schedule by the door had Silent Meal written in large hand lettering.

A small bunch of weeds with cute pink flowering heads sat perkily in a juice glass by Mrs. Popoff's place-setting. She hadn't arrived yet, so I looked around and reached for the orange juice before settling down to the business of eating silently. She came in shortly after and I felt her pause by her chair before sitting down. The limp apron she wore when working in the kitchen was still on, the bib up over her white button-down blouse. Wisps of white hair were held off her face with a bandana. A babushka, she called it. I caught her out of the corner of my eye gazing intently at the little pink flowers perched on slender green stems. She held her coffee cup with pinky extended in a genteel manner which seemed incongruous with the apron and bandana.

---

[1] Gurdjieff's teaching, referred to by Ouspensky as The Fourth Way, has also been called The Great Work, or simply the Work. In the *Dramatic Universe*, vol. 4, J. G. Bennett notes the term refers to the human contributions made to the Magnum Opus of world creation, with the entry of creative energy into the human mind, about thirty-five thousand years ago.

The next morning the weeds were still sitting in front of her place-setting and again I caught her gazing at them, seemingly entranced. On the third morning they were still there, fresh as if newly plucked.

During the discussion at lunch Mrs. Popoff brought up the flowering weeds. "You have heard me speak of the First Conscious Shock?" She stopped talking and took a long breath in through her broad nose. "Air is our Second Being food, and taking in impressions with the First Conscious Shock allows us to fully digest air."

I inhaled deeply, catching a whiff of strong tea and hot buttered toast rising up in front of me. At the same time, I felt my body sitting at the table, noticed the aromas of creamy potato soup and ripe tomatoes entering my nostrils and stirring my stomach. I exhaled as Mrs. Popoff continued speaking.

"The First Conscious Shock is taking in impressions consciously."

It seemed to me she was gazing with affection at the little juice glass sporting the tiny pink blossoms by her plate.

"For the past three days I have been conducting an experiment." She looked down the long table with all faces turned attentively to her, no clatter of silver on plate or movement of cup to lip.

"Without the conscious shock of 'eating' impressions, life energy, including man's energy, is simply food for the moon." She paused and let that piece of information sink in. My stomach tightened. I was put off by the notion that in the cosmic scheme of things Bobby Jo was just compost and like those weeds, "food for the moon." This was my first sense of disquiet at the consequences of embarking on a quest for consciousness.

Ignorance might have been bliss, I mused. I paid closer attention to what Mrs. Popoff was saying next.

"Every day I have given special attention to these little flowering weeds, taking in every detail. Normally they would have died in a few hours. I fed them my loving attention and was conscious of the impressions they in turn gave me. My Second Being Body has been nourished. Their life's energy has been transformed for a higher purpose and look—they continue to live!"

As people around me thoughtfully returned to their soups and salads, I paused a moment, buttered toast in hand, gazing at the weeds, their delicate stalks holding plump pink blossoms handsomely aloft. I raised my hand timidly.

Mrs. Popoff had just taken a sip of soup, a thin drip falling back into her bowl. She put the spoon down, acknowledging me, "Yes, Bobby Jo?"

In a small voice, sure I was the only one who didn't know, but wanting to understand, I asked, "So how do we nourish our First Being Body?" I had no idea what a 'Being Body' was, but feeding it sounded important.

She smiled at me, "We are doing that now. When we eat the food on this table consciously, we are feeding our physical, or First, Being Body."

"Oh," I said relaxing. "So that's why we've been eating our breakfasts in silence?"

Her wide face broadened as her smile expanded and her eyes held the hint of an inner memory, "Only if you are remembering yourself as you eat in silence." She paused a moment, then decided to say more, "When we eat consciously, we are also transforming the lives we eat. As we evolve, so too will they."

Another hand went up, emboldened by my question. "Mrs. Popoff, can you say more about Second Being Body?"

"Yes. As I understand it, Second Being Body has to do with the formation of a *Kesdjan*, or Astral, body, which is the vessel for the soul. We grow this body within us through our efforts, our Work." Mrs. Popoff picked up her spoon, and said, "We'll continue our discussion at lunch if you have more questions. Now, let's eat in silence, consciously."

CHAPTER EIGHT
Atmospheres

Jack took me back to New Jersey after the ten days were over. I had a list of Mrs. Popoff's inner tasks to take to Maine where I would be a camp counselor for eight weeks. I planned to continue working inwardly to bring intentionality into my day. My list included: avoid saying no, do something you don't like to do, speak with as few words as possible, listen to the sound of your voice, give up something you like. I was sorry to be missing the next seminar, afraid of falling behind Jack in changing myself and becoming more conscious.

My time with the Youth Conservation Corps that had recruited counselors from my college campus did not go smoothly. Half a dozen canvas tents were set up in a field. I was assigned a tent with six or so junior high-aged girls who presumably would widen their horizons by learning about the great outdoors. It seemed the counselors were more interested in their romantic relationships with each other than in interacting with these inner-city girls from New Jersey, who were wild, or the Native American boys from Maine, who were aloof. At one point the administrators had to round up two counselors who had wandered off during a beach excursion. Then they had to deal with the histrionics of a woman counselor who was cracking up under the strain of camping. I thought she had made her issues worse with inner-considering and identification, and I was thankful I had the Work to lean on. But it turned out that my practice with the tasks made everyone think I was distant and unfriendly. Then the black girls from Newark, whom I thought I had a good relationship with, all told me I'd offended or irritated some of them through things I'd said. And I'd been thinking I was getting on better than anyone as far as tensions and problems like that by conserving energy and controlling my emotions! The only thing I learned that summer was how to use an axe to clear forest trails on our daily outings.

In the end, the camp experience brought me back into a more ordinary part of myself. It had been impossible to keep up the effort at inner change without the support of others around me. Luckily there was still time to attend the final seminar at the Pinnacle before school started and I returned to Livingston College as a junior.

The older members of Mrs. Popoff's group were becoming familiar to me. They would come to evening lectures as their lives allowed. All except for Richard, who rarely showed up, although his wife was an involved member. Richard was an architect, carpenter, and house painter and had given Jack a job as his assistant when Jack was between seminars. He did so to help Jack earn the money to go on the course at Sherborne. I was curious that Richard didn't come to meetings, since Jack said he often used Gurdjieff Work ideas when they were on house painting jobs together.

One day, Mrs. Popoff announced that Richard was coming to give a group presentation on the nine-pointed esoteric symbol Gurdjieff referred to as the Enneagram. Apparently, Richard had made quite a study of the Enneagram.

The meeting began well enough with us sitting in a circle on chairs in the upstairs meeting room, quiet and collected. I gathered my attention into my hands, resting them palms down on my knees. I sat cross-legged on the floor as younger members of the group had been encouraged to do, in preparation for the course. The glass-paned French doors at the back of the room were open to the porch. A spring breeze stirred the gauze curtains with scents of lilacs and honeysuckle, somewhat mitigating the Pinnacle's pervasive Eau de Cat.

Richard presented a carefully wrought diagram showing the Enneagram circle. Its inner lines divided the space into geometrical figures that he had filled in with bright colors. He had obviously worked long and hard on this project and was explaining with great authority the significance of his conclusions.

I didn't understand a word of it, never having seen this figure outside of Ouspensky's brief references in *Search*, and those were mostly obscured with numbers and musical notes, as in do, re, mi. I spent the time sensing my hands and trying not to wander off into random thoughts. Inner Chatter, Mrs. Popoff called it.

But I did wander off, thinking about how hungry I was. I hadn't allowed enough time to eat before the meeting. My attention drifted down to my pinched stomach. I reeled it back to focus on my hands, aware of their warmth on my thighs through my jeans.

A sharp note in Mrs. Popoff's voice brought my head up. The atmosphere in the room was tense—the curtains at the door, still.

"No Richard, you don't see it!" Mrs. Popoff raised her hand, dismissing Richard with a flick of the wrist.

"Yes, Irmis, I *do* see it, and I can show you if you would listen to me for once," came the heated retort.

The breeze stood shocked, the honeysuckled air gone rancid.

Mrs. Popoff held her ground, implacable. She had risen, feet planted on the rose-patterned carpet.

Richard gathered up his display with pressed lips and an exasperated shake of the head. After he was gone, Mrs. Popoff turned to us and said tightly, "Excuse me a moment while I go clear my atmosphere."

As she moved to leave, I blurted out, "Can I go get a carrot while you cleanse your atmosphere?"

Mrs. Popoff stopped. Turning slowly, she replied, a rare laugh erupting from her generous mouth, "Yes Bobby Jo, go get your carrot. But hurry, I no longer need to cleanse my atmosphere."

CHAPTER NINE
Fall Semester

August, 1971—At the end of August Richard offered Jack a full-time job as his assistant house painter and carpenter.

Mrs. Popoff invited Jack to live at the Pinnacle, and I was to come on weekends. The two of us were the first ever to live at the Pinnacle in order to participate in Mrs. Popoff's group. She was throwing her support behind our intention to go to Sherborne for the Second Basic Course. We had a year to prepare.

One evening Mrs. Popoff began speaking about Gurdjieff's cosmology as Ouspensky had outlined it. On a large pad of paper propped on an easel in the middle of the upstairs meeting room, Mrs. P had Essie, one of her senior students, draw seven circles one under the other.

"Now Essie, draw a triangle, pointing down, under the bottom circle, good."

Essie, a middle-aged woman with a ready smile and curly red-dyed hair, nervously did as she was told, aware that a reprimand from Mrs. Popoff could come at any moment.

"These circles represent worlds," Mrs. P explained to us. "Essie, put the number of each world inside each circle."

With the marker, Essie wrote a bold 1 inside the top circle, a 3 in the one below it, and continued filling in the circles in descending order: 6, 12, 24, 48, 96. She turned to Mrs. P, waiting.

"Now the notes," Mrs. Popoff instructed. Essie looked confused, hesitating. "The notes!" Mrs. Popoff repeated. Essie raised the marker, hovering over the first circle. "No, no, start at the bottom!" Mrs. P said sharply. Essie moved the marker towards the bottom of the paper. "To the right of the triangle, start there with 'do,'" said Mrs. Popoff in a stern voice. Essie quickly complied, writing 'do' to the right of the downwards pointing triangle. Then moving up the page next to each circle: re, mi, fa, sol, la, si, and again 'do' next to the top circle.

"Very good. Thank you, Essie." Turning to the group, Mrs. P asked if we could name the worlds in descending order. Hands went up. As Essie wielded the marker and wrote to the left of each circle, group members called out the names: Absolute, All Worlds, All Suns, Sun, All Planets, Earth, Moon, and finally, Absolute, next to the downwards pointing triangle.

Mrs. Popoff explained that this diagram represented the Ray of Creation. She asked Essie to sit down and handed Ruth, her other most senior pupil, Ouspensky's *In Search of the Miraculous*. Ruth, a stately woman with short silver-grey hair, turned to the marked passage and began reading in a clear voice.

> The ray of creation like every other process which is complete at a given moment can be regarded as an octave. This would be a descending octave in which do passes into si, si into la and so on.
>
> The Absolute or *All* (world 1) will be do; all worlds (world 3)—si; all suns (world 6)—la; our sun (world 12)—sol; all planets (world 24)—fa; the earth (world 48)—mi; the moon (world 96)—re. The ray of creation begins with the Absolute. The Absolute is *All*. It is—do.
>
> The ray of creation ends in the moon. Beyond the moon there is *nothing*. This also is the Absolute—do.
>
> In examining the ray of creation or cosmic octave we see that "intervals" should come in the development of this octave: the first between do and si, that is between world 1 and world 3, between the Absolute and "all worlds," and the second between fa and mi, that is, between world 24 and world 48, between "all planets" and the earth. But the first "interval" is filled by the will of the absolute. One of the manifestations of the will of the Absolute consists precisely in the filling of this "interval" between the active and the passive forces. With the second "interval" the situation is more complicated.

Something is missing between the planets and the earth. Planetary influences cannot pass to the earth consecutively and fully. An "additional shock" is indispensable; the creation of some new conditions to ensure a proper passage of forces is indispensable.

The conditions to ensure the passage of forces are created by the arrangement of a special mechanical contrivance between the planets and the earth. This mechanical contrivance, this "transmitting station of forces" is *organic life on earth*. Organic life on earth was created to fill the interval between the planets and the earth.

Organic life represents so to speak the *earth's organ of perception*.[1]

Mrs. Popoff indicated to Ruth to stop reading. She then went on to speak about each successive World being under a greater number of laws, or influences, as represented by the numbers 1, 3, 6, and so on. The world of the Absolute was influenced by the least number of "laws" (1), and the Moon was under the most (96). Therefore, world 96 represented the world of the natural order under the laws of World Maintenance. The life of unconscious man, as with all other organic life on earth, was therefore compost for the maintenance of the cosmos, nothing more.

The 'Law of Accident' was much more likely in lower worlds where there were more laws. Conscious Man, however, had the possibility of living under fewer laws, and thus changing the meaning and purpose of his life by ascending in the octave of world order.

We left the meeting that night with much food for thought and a renewed interest in rereading those impenetrable chapters in *Search*.

My junior year at Livingston College started. I arranged my class schedule so I could drive to Long Island on Friday afternoons, attend Group meetings Monday nights, and get back in time for class on Tuesday. Besides seeing me at the Pinnacle, Jack visited periodically at school.

"Jack, I need to talk to you about something." We were sitting in my new private dorm room at Livingston after Jack had painted a gnome figure on

---

[1] P. D. Ouspensky, *In Search*, 137–138.

the wall in the hallway. It was a likeness of the book plate I had glued inside my copy of *In Search of the Miraculous*. A friendly, plump, little dwarf in profile striding through a wood with peaked cap, spectacles, and walking stick, carrying a book under his arm. I took off my wire-rim glasses and set them carefully on the bedside dresser.

"Uh, hmmm, here," I stammered, not sure how to broach this subject. "Just read from here to there." I handed him my journal with the page open. I waited nervously while he read, his fine slender features bent over the book, fair hair falling forward past his face so I couldn't see his expression.

He looked up, puzzlement in his eyes. "So?" he asked.

"I just don't think we should have sex anymore," I blurted out. "See, I've been going back and forth about it in my head. That's why I wanted you to read what I'd written. It just doesn't feel morally right to be working on ourselves and abstaining while we're living at the Pinnacle but then sleep together when we're not. It's like if we do, aren't we being deceitful to ourselves as well as to Mrs. Popoff?"

I'd been leaning forward, trying to look into Jack's blue eyes. Miserably tight in my stomach at the whole idea, I reminded myself it had seemed like the right thing when I was working it out in my journal.

Jack handed back the small book, black with a red spine and RECORD stamped in gold foil on the cover. He sat on the bed next to me, thoughtful as usual, waiting for me to speak.

Abstinence was easy at the Pinnacle. Our rooms were on different floors, and we really didn't have much time to hang out together there. But now I could feel him sitting next to me. I sensed the warmth of his body, my heart thrumming. I had been longing for him to hold me, missing his touch on my hair, his nibble at my ear. But wasn't that the point?

"If we can say 'no' at the Pinnacle, then that same 'no' should apply here or anywhere, right? Isn't that the point of having a single I? Of being Master over ourselves?" I said, my resolve less sure now.

Jack responded to this reasoning, "Those eight weeks that you were in Maine proved to me that I can be abstinent. But being abstinent now doesn't make sense."

"Well yeah, I was abstinent all that time too."

I remembered I had not been drawn to any of the guys at Camp. Hadn't even thought about sex outside of missing Jack's company. We had both proven we could give up sex when circumstances demanded. So maybe it wasn't the same. Perhaps sex didn't have to be all or nothing.

Jack was right, we could choose. He had demonstrated he was not ruled by his physical desires. Besides, wouldn't it be a more legitimate struggle to discern when it was right and when it was wrong for us to sleep together? I relaxed, snuggling up to him, happy to feel his arms around me, welcoming his feathery kisses.

One day at the Pinnacle I brought the subject of sex up with Mrs. Popoff. We were cleaning the half dozen litter boxes strategically placed about the house, accessible to the twelve or so cats, but out of the way of human traffic. I scooped and she poured new sand into the plastic rectangular boxes. She wore her usual ankle length denim skirt with an apron tied up under her breasts.

"Mrs. Popoff, is there a basis in ancient knowledge for religions to discourage premarital sex?" I asked, standing up from the last box, blurting out what was hanging in the front of my mind.

"Well, yes," she replied, holding the sack of litter in one hand, seemingly unsurprised at my question. "But it wasn't based on morality."

She stood, her weight resting slightly backwards over her heels. "It was to discourage young people from having sex before responsible age, at least until eighteen. It had to do with keeping the energy of the sex center from being depleted before giving birth to one's astral body."

For the first time ever, an argument against casual sex that made sense. I was glad I had asked.

"No, Bobby Jo," she said now. "Discouraging premarital sex in those days had nothing to do with morality."

I noticed she was holding the bag of kitty litter slightly away from her side, in what must have been an awkward position to maintain. It struck me that she was doing this with intention. I felt my own hands responding, filling with sensation as I held the paper bag of dirty litter in one hand and the plastic pooper scooper in the other. We stood there, carrying on the conversation, but my attention rose, as if tuned to a higher channel.

"Not having sex at an early age was about conserving the energy needed to give birth to one's inner child, our Second Being Body." She sighed. "Of course, as in so many things, that knowledge has been lost in institutions like the Catholic Church."

CHAPTER TEN
Carlos

A few weeks later I received a letter from Carlos. He was safely back in the States. I thought he had accepted the fact that we were breaking up and hoped he was handling it okay. But he still expressed the wish to see me again.

That night I dreamed about Carlos. He had short hair, was strange and sort of removed, like he was out of place. He lived in a ranch house next to me, but Jack lived in the house on the other side of him. So, I couldn't exactly ignore him but I couldn't go with him since Jack was nearby. Then things morphed and Carlos was going back to University of Maryland, and I was going back to Livingston College with Jack. My mom showed up and wanted me to be nice to Carlos. I wanted to be nice to him too but felt I must act restrained because of Jack.

Then I woke up. Mulling over the dream, I realized I still felt protective towards Carlos. And yeah, I would like to see him again. I had to admit I was curious. What would my feelings be if I saw him in person, would the old magnetism still be there?

Inner growth had become so important to me that I was set on pursuing it wherever it led. I didn't think that path led back to Carlos. Jack, on the other hand, was equally committed to this quest for self-knowledge. He stimulated me intellectually as we studied the Gurdjieffian System together—something I was sure I couldn't do with Carlos.

Thursday night, ensconced in my dorm room, the high-intensity lamp cast its bright warm circle over my textbook. I concentrated, quite content in this cell-like cubby of a room. Jack had helped me paint the walls a golden yellow to warm the cinderblock. Bright posters and multi-colored Indian bedspreads draped across the window and bed transformed the sterile space into a cozy retreat.

A helium balloon, that's how my head felt in curlers. I'd suffer through tonight but be all set for the weekend in Long Island. Someone knocked on my door. One of the girls down the hall, I supposed, wanting to borrow my curling iron. She'd need to give it back tonight. "Hang on!" I called, marking my place. Pushing back from the desk I shuffled over to the door in my fuzzy slippers, tying my bathrobe around me.

I opened the door to say so—and there stood Carlos, almost the same.

He looked good, really straight and solid. Like a soldier, only not in uniform. Tight dark curls, like a mop, were growing back on his head. I could smell the leather of his old fringed jacket, which I'd always loved, but which now seemed out of place, outdated.

He was short, not much taller than me, so I didn't have to look up to him. And I could be mad at him, face to face. "Oh, Carlos—why didn't you tell me you were coming," I groaned. I must have looked a fool to him, in my frayed bathrobe and curlers. This was so embarrassing. Heat swept up my neck into my face as my solar plexus played ping-pong across my middle.

He'd come with a friend whom I'd never met. Must be an army buddy, I thought. Since I didn't slam the door in Carlos's face, the buddy politely bowed out, saying he'd just wait outside. I stepped aside to let Carlos into the room, but kept the door open to the hall.

Carlos sat on my only chair holding the guitar he'd bought in California with Army-issue travel money. A few feet away, perched on the bed, my feet were glued to the floor. Luminous hands ticked on the silent face of my clock radio. I'd given up feeling embarrassed. Now I was curious, aware of Carlos's presence in the room and myself on the bed. I watched as reminiscent feelings of mutual attraction collided in my chest with a new feeling, I wasn't quite sure of what.

We sat and talked. He told me how hard Nam had been, with all the Vietnamese wearing pajamas and looking like everyone else, you just never knew when you might get blown up. He'd found God in his darkest hours, Christ his port in the storm. He'd read the Bible every day, had concluded that the real stuff was in the Gospels and Revelations. He'd even written songs.

He began to play soft pleasing melodies on his guitar. His voice wasn't great, but he'd written his own lyrics—about loss, about fear, about finding Jesus when there was nothing else to turn to but drugs.

I was impressed; he'd really come to something. The ping-pong game in my belly died down as I directed part of my attention into my feet, a practice Mrs. Popoff was teaching us. I could feel them pulsing inside my slippers, leaving my head void of commentary, my emotions quiet, ready to be open.

The music he played was sweet, but by the third song his lyrics bounced off the cinderblock walls, falling flat on my heart. His message rang hollow in me. He'd looked for Jesus and found Him, all black and white. His verses were real and poignant, but he'd hung his hat on a literal Bible, not looking for more in the depths between the lines, which was where my search was taking me—to subtleties of perception and experience that could not be found in black and white.

A sense of regret, as at the inevitable loss of summer's golden heat, tiptoed into my waiting heart. Carlos's last song was over. I felt my answer. What I felt was a sense of wanting to protect him, of feeling sorry for him—of knowing I would always feel like it was up to me to make his world right. It wasn't that way with Jack.

I stood up, saying, "Carlos, I'm really glad you made it home safely from Vietnam." I gave him a hug and pulled away. "Thanks for singing your songs for me. They were great, and I hope you do well at University of Maryland." I walked to the doorway of my room.

He followed, stepping out into the hall. "Do you think I could see you again?" he asked, without much hope in his voice.

"I don't think that's a good idea. But I'll always remember you, Carlos. Take good care of yourself." We parted in the hall, both of us knowing that I was breaking his heart.

Weeks later, my mom called me on the phone. I hadn't known it, but her brother worked at the same company where Carlos's father worked. The message had gotten through to Mom that Carlos's dad was expecting me to return the ring, which I had not known what to do with, not wanting to part with the beautiful diamond. I thought maybe since he had mailed it to me, instead of formally offering it in person, it was mine to keep. At least that's what I was telling myself. Apparently not, with a big NOT. When I did mail the ring off to Carlos's dad, it was my first taste of the meaning of closure.

I realize now that in the ripening wood of my life I had come to a fork and had taken the divergent path, from which I would never look back. Unencumbered, I found myself running to catch up with Jack, wanting to match his stride.

Determined, I directed myself towards Sherborne, where I thought the answers to my internal questions lay; where the real Bobby Jo would stand up and come into her own.

CHAPTER ELEVEN
Negotiations

"Hey, Dad—did you get a chance to read the prospectus for that school in England I told you about?" I asked as I came upstairs from the basement, having come in through the garage with an armload of schoolwork for the holidays. I'd arrived home the night before and dropped the "Prospectus of The International Academy for Continuous Education" booklet on the old wooden tavern table in the living room.

"I'm looking at it now," Dad replied, standing by the antique tavern table flipping through it with his strong square fingers. He was a practical man, although he had dreamed of being an English major and had dabbled in oils. His modest still life paintings still hung in his study downstairs. For all that, he had acquiesced to his father's insistence that he study business and had found success in sales and marketing. "What do you know about this place?" he asked me now, looking up from the prospectus.

"Well, it's a ten-month residential course, so the tuition includes room and board. The course is held at Sherborne House, a Victorian manor house about eighty miles west of London in an area called the Cotswolds. There's only about one hundred students per course, so I'd like to enroll now, to make sure I get in," I said earnestly.

I had taken the booklet out of Dad's hands and was flipping through it to the back. "See?" I showed him the page with the tuition printed. "It's less than $2,000, so it would cost about the same as Livingston and could be my senior year abroad."

I was giving Dad the full "please Daddy, please" treatment, looking up at him with hopeful and innocent blue eyes—hoping he wouldn't read the prospectus so closely he'd realize what the "course" was really about. I wasn't sure he'd go for the idea that the school was based on an eastern mystic's teachings.

Mom came out of the kitchen drying her hands on a towel, her apron covering her button-down blouse and red slacks. She came over, looking over my shoulder at the picture of a sprawling stone building with peaks and chimneys sitting on a snowy field with bare trees.

"Would you get enough credits to graduate next year if you went?" She asked, always cutting to the chase.

"Yeah. That's the best part," I said putting down the prospectus. I heard bacon sizzle and pop in the kitchen, my mouth beginning to salivate. Good ol' home cooking! "I'll only need ten credits to graduate next year, so that won't be a problem."

What I didn't say was that I'd been working on my favorite creative writing instructor, and he seemed interested in helping me swing the Livingston College side of things. He'd help me create a bogus independent study with a fancy title worth ten credits. The real deal was, I would keep a journal and share it with him after the course. He had heard about Gurdjieff and was fascinated with the idea of inner freedom.

"Well, as long as you can graduate on time and it doesn't cost more than a normal year of school, I think it sounds like a wonderful opportunity," Mom said, heading back to the kitchen.

Dad and I moved towards the dining room, where I'd set the table earlier. He wasn't going to be that easy. "Just who is this Bennett fellow, the Director of Studies?" he demanded as he took his place.

"I understand he's a scientist and mathematician," I countered as I stepped into the kitchen to help bring out Mom's proportioned plates of bacon, fried eggs and toast, buttered to the edges, the way Dad liked, the way I thought everyone buttered toast.

I served Dad and sat down with my own plate, shaking my napkin onto my lap with a soft deft snap. "I think at one point he invented some kind of device to capture coal emissions and turn them into fuel so they wouldn't pollute the air." I reached for the marmalade, sedate on its serving plate with the scalloped jelly spoon next to it.

"He's also really into education, which is what got me excited," I continued, spooning pale jelly with floating bits of orange rind onto my plate. "Besides the Academy, he runs The Institute for the Comparative Study of History, Philosophy and the Sciences. I think he's really well known in England," I concluded, biting into my toast.

"I'll talk to your mother about it," Dad closed the conversation as Mom joined us, bringing an aroma of freshly perked coffee to the table.

CHAPTER TWELVE
Learning to Work

Winter, 1972—The job Mrs. Popoff helped me find was just down the road from the Pinnacle. I worked weekends as a bus girl at the Harbor View Restaurant, a small family-run place on a private pier jutting out into the harbor. Mrs. Popoff knew the family. Dad had agreed to pay the tuition for my senior year abroad, with mom's encouragement. I still needed to earn airfare and spending money. Students were encouraged to pay their own way.

Jack's job as Richard's assistant was barely earning him enough money to pay for the course and airfare. Mrs. Popoff was letting both of us stay at the Pinnacle for free, which we never thought to question. Our aim was to get to Sherborne, and anything that moved us in that direction was a welcome sign that it was meant to be.

One Saturday morning Mrs. Popoff started talking to Jack about a project she had in mind. "Jack, I'd like you to construct a moveable partition to block off the third floor this winter." She had come out of her little suite of rooms onto the main-floor landing as Jack and I rattled down the stairs.

"We lose so much heat up there." All three of us climbed back up past my floor to the top of the stairs on the third-floor landing so she could point out, "I'm picturing something that would cover the stairwell. You'll have to arrange it so you can lower and raise it into place once you're on the other side."

With trial and error, much pounding and some sawing, Jack came up with a make-shift trap door of plywood, crossties and plastic that he could laboriously lower into place each night after ascending to his floor. He went to bed that night with a sense of accomplishment.

The next morning, I came downstairs to the disturbing ring of Mrs. Popoff yelling at Jack. "Idiot! That's not what I asked you to do! Why are you so lazy? Why can't you follow directions!" Spittle sprayed out of her mouth with the lisping tirade. She looked livid, her hands on her hips.

Jack's head was up, glaring back, but he was biting his tongue.

He had worked hard and long to figure out how to build the contraption and had done the best he could. He wasn't a skilled carpenter, after all. I stood there, feeling bad for Jack, my stomach tight with the discomfiture of conflict. Mrs. Popoff stomped off and we quietly slunk down to the kitchen.

We had both experienced "hits on the head" as Mrs. Popoff called her abrupt reprimands. But they had always been in context of working with the group and could come at any time to any of her students. We understood them to be part of our training, much like a Zen master hitting a slumbering monk with a reed to wake him up during meditation. But this seemed a little more personal. It was just an ordinary Sunday morning after all, not like we were on a seminar or anything.

Monday night came, everyone sitting expectantly in the meeting room waiting their turn to share experiences or insights, or to ask a question. Mrs. Popoff began to chuckle, "On Sunday morning I decided to work on myself and do what Mr. Gurdjieff called, 'Acting Otherwise.' That is, acting in a way that is opposite from how I feel in that moment. When our Jack here," nodding with a smile at Jack, who was sitting cross-legged on the carpet in his green long-sleeved jersey and wide-striped bell bottoms, "came stumbling downstairs still half asleep, I let him have it, complaining about the trap door he had made for the third-floor landing."

Brown eyes dancing, she smiled all around, "Oh, you should have seen his face! It was all I could do not to burst out laughing. And the whole time I was really so pleased with what he had constructed."

Jack was studying the rose pattern in the carpet, his eyebrows raised in pleased relief. At the same time, I noticed my own abdominal muscles relaxing. Surprised, I realized I'd been holding them tight from the tension of thinking Mrs. Popoff had been mad.

I raised my hand and Mrs. Popoff nodded at me, "Yes, Bobby Jo?"

Peering up at her from my position on the floor next to Jack, I impatiently brushed the hair back from my face. I needed to see clearly to think. "So, if you aren't really mad at Jack, then why have I felt so tense, thinking you were? I mean, negativity is an energy, right? I wasn't mad at Jack so if you weren't mad at Jack, where was the negativity coming from?"

Mrs. Popoff smiled and replied, "Why, it was coming from you! We all have the tendency to project the source of our negativity onto others instead of observing it in ourselves. You are very identified with Jack, Bobby Jo, so you have been mad at me thinking that I was upset with him."

Directing her attention away from addressing me and out to the room at large, Mrs. Popoff continued, "It is very important that we observe our negative emotions and see where they come from. Noticing one's posture is a good place to start."

As Mrs. Popoff spoke, my attention went to my shoulders, which were hunched, my chin down. I was looking at the floor. My lower back had collapsed, curving my spine. Darn, I thought, that always happens! I straightened up, like a ballerina would, feeling a lift as if an invisible thread were pulling me up from the top of my head.

"We need to be impartial when observing our posture. That is, simply notice the posture without reacting or changing it. So often we observe with one 'i' and then immediately correct with another 'i.' We judge ourselves just as we judge others but never actually see. Nothing changes because each little 'i' does what it wants and hides from the Observer. Before we can ever see who and what we really are, we must develop within ourselves an objective Observer."

At the end of the meeting Mrs. Popoff gave the task for the week, "Observe your posture without changing it. Then observe yourself observing."

That night I snuck up to Jack's room, a sweater wrapped around my night gown against the chill in the air. I was aware of every creak in the floorboards. Jack was in bed, reading. "Hi" I said, as I pulled a wooden chair, skritching across the floor, up beside the bed. "What're you reading?"

"*Witness*," he answered, slipping a piece of paper between the pages to mark his place in Mr. Bennett's autobiography. "What's up?"

"Oh, I don't know," I said, leaning forward in the chair using my fingers to comb the hair away from my face. "I was just wondering about what happened on Sunday with Mrs. Popoff. That was pretty amazing that she was 'acting as if' she was mad when she wasn't. Did you think she was mad?"

Jack sat still, holding the book in his lap, his tall forehead smooth, eyes cast down. He sat that way for a long moment, then looked up, still thinking. "Well, we know from reading *Beelzebub*, that Gurdjieff set himself 'never to act as others do.' Which was his grandmother's advice to him just before she died. So, he would often act and say the opposite from what people expected. That must be what Mrs. Popoff meant by acting otherwise." Jack continued, more thoughtfully, "I read Gurdjieff practiced 'the way of blame.' That would be tough, doing stuff intentionally that made people think you were a jerk, but then in the end it would teach you something about yourself. I guess Mrs. Popoff had her reasons for doing what she did. It sure shocked me." His thin lips held a little smile, like he'd come to terms with the event.

"It's true what she said, though. I could tell you were mad at her afterwards, Bobby Jo, even though she hadn't yelled at you." Jack leaned back on his pillow, his fair hair falling past his shoulders.

I maneuvered myself onto the narrow mattress, the bed creaking, wedging my hips next to his and trying to rest my head on his chest. "Weren't you mad at her too?" I asked as I draped his arm over my shoulder.

He looked down at me and smiled. "Well, yeah, at first. But you know, I did have the strange sense that she didn't mean it, even while she was yelling. Maybe it's true, she was just acting 'as if.'" I'm glad she likes the trap door.

"Well at least I don't think she can hear us up here together," I sighed, snuggling closer.

Winter flowed into spring, wet snow and gray days giving way to soft rains and whiffs of perfumed hyacinth and snow drops. My classes were speeding towards final exams. My days at Livingston were peppered with practicing sensation as I perched on the side of my bed upon awakening, moving the sense of internal aliveness, like low-voltage electricity, from arm to leg around my body.

As I went about my day, I would incorporate the weekly task. Aware of my body sitting in class before the teacher arrived. Sensing my arms as I strode across campus hugging textbooks to my chest.

In my Education 301 discussion class, six of us sat in a circle on molded plastic chairs. I raised my hand, hearing a high-pitched voice coming from my tight throat, "No, teachers can't just be babysitters or entertainers. I really think if we want education to be—*real*—we have to be real ourselves." Something inside me noticed stiff muscles in my neck, a slight forward thrust of torso and set tilt of head. The Something registered, *identified with making her point and being right*. After another student interjected their response, the something in me noticed my pursed lips and furrowed eyebrows, this time registering, *judging another's point of view*.

Back in my room I began to wonder about being identified and being impartial. What had happened today? Was that the observer Mrs. Popoff talked about? Was I seeing 'me' being identified, and did that mean the seeing was impartial? I wrote in my journal, "Impartiality seems to be the opposite of Identification, but I feel it contains *more* than just nonidentification."

In Gurdjieff's large, dense, and abstruse magnum opus, *Beelzebub's Tales to His Grandson: All and Everything*, I came across this passage: "He had very definitely expressed being-manifestations, as, for instance, those called 'self-consciousness,' 'impartiality,' 'sincerity of perception,' 'alertness,' etc."[1]

Okay. It says right here, "impartiality" is a "being-manifestation." That's it! I need to strive to become impartial and to stop being identified so I can manifest more Being.

Little did I know then that being impartial, like not reacting when I thought someone was being mean, was not easy. It didn't just happen because you wanted it to. But contemplating new ideas, wanting something in me to change for the better and doing something concrete,

---

[1] G. I. Gurdjieff, *Beelzebub's Tales to His Grandson: All and Everything*, First Series (New York: E. P. Dutton & Co., 1964).

like bringing attention into my body, were worth striving for. These were the first steps on a path that left the garden gate far behind. Not only did this path lead through woods, but across oceans, down rabbit holes, into deserts, and up mountains. In fact, this path has no end, but it takes a very long time to realize that.

PART TWO

INTERNATIONAL ACADEMY FOR CONTINUOUS EDUCATION

At Sherborne House Gloucestershire, England, 1971–1976
Founded by John Godolphin Bennett (1897–1974)

> Continuous Education is founded on the principle that human beings are capable of unlimited self-perfecting from birth to death and beyond. Self-perfecting is threefold: bodily, mental and spiritual. It gives meaning to our lives as individuals; but there is also a continuous education of the human race to enable us to become truly human—which we are still pretty far from being.
> —J.G. BENNETT

CHAPTER THIRTEEN
Sherborne House

September 1972—Dusk settled as two boxy British taxis bumped down a long country lane. They turned into a short driveway leading to the service entrance of an imposing manor house. I peered out of our taxi's square window at the massive, gray stone walls, irregular peaked roof line and multitude of chimneys as it rose above us. This was to be our home for a year. In reality, it was to become our spaceship. For now, we might as well have entered a time warp.

I clambered out of the car between Jack and Van Carter, a slow-talking, soft-mannered guy from a Gurdjieff study group in North Carolina. My feet crunched onto gravel. Stretching, I took a deep breath of chilly, damp, mid-September air, redolent with taxi exhaust, end of summer fields, and a whiff of sweet decomposing chlorophyll.

My brain felt like cotton candy on a stick, my body buzzing from lack of sleep. Between the overnight plane ride, negotiating train platforms and breakdowns, I could no longer think. I found myself in what might have been an eighteenth-century stable yard. The old pavers by the heavy wooden back door and the octagonal brick meat house centered within tall, thick, stone walls had an ancient, surreal appeal. This was Sherborne House. We had finally arrived, a year and a half after our interview in New York with Mr. Bennett, one month before the start of the Second Basic Course. I couldn't put my finger on it, but it felt familiar, like I'd come home.

The grand estate of Sherborne House had not been in the original picture. According to Mr. Bennett's book, *Witness*, the International

Academy for Continuous Education had been envisioned as a modest experimental school of perhaps twenty-four students. One of Mr. Bennett's group members had even offered him a house in a London suburb. The last chapter in *Witness*, "Life Begins at Seventy," told a lot about how the school had come about.[1]

Two years previously, after a medical crisis, Mr. Bennett had retreated to an abbey in France to meditate and seek guidance about the direction of his life. He felt at a crossroads, needing to choose between spending his remaining years working in the business world to establish Systematics, his approach to problem-solving, or returning to his writing and to nurturing an inner life in himself and others. In the midst of prayer, a voice that had spoken to him before in a time of need quite clearly said, "You are to found a school." When he considered this unexpected answer and wondered why a school, the answer came, "Because people must be prepared for the troubles ahead."

Bennett also realized that the school would be one of the Fourth Way, based on Gurdjieff's work, yet grounded in his own research and experience. It would be a school unlike any that existed, to teach the tools needed for a New Epoch, tools that could be used to develop the latent potential of human beings—beings who could respond to a call for a New Society. A society in which concern for others would take precedence over concern for oneself and become a template for the world. A world in which Bennett foresaw the current social and political institutions crashing down, creating havoc.

This was all well and good, but Bennett had no idea where the money, resources or students would come from. Neither did the members of his Institute for the Comparative Study of History, Philosophy and the Sciences, although they supported the project. He decided that if the Higher Powers were calling on him to start a school, then they would have to provide the wherewithal.

Unexpectedly, a series of circumstances led to Mr. Bennett being invited to give lectures in the United States. In May of 1971, just before the

---

[1] J. G. Bennett, "Life Begins at Seventy," in *Witness: the autobiography of John G. Bennett* (Charles Town, WV: Claymont Communications, 1983), 388–407.

end of spring semester, Bennett spoke at Harvard and Clark universities in Massachusetts; Franconia State College in New Hampshire; San Francisco State, Berkeley State, and Sonoma State universities in California; Washington University in Missouri; and finally at the Gotham Book Mart in New York City, where we had heard him.

The response he received from students thoroughly disaffected with the status quo of the time was so great that he called his wife, Elizabeth, in England and told her they would need a "very large" house. It just so happened that she had been to see Sherborne House, a former boys' school for over a hundred students, and it was for sale.

Upon his return to England, the money to buy Sherborne House materialized, and he ended up with ninety students enrolled for the first Basic Course. Within five weeks of taking possession of the run-down property—with only five staff members, including Bennett and his wife—the first Basic Course was inaugurated on Oct. 15, 1971. Despite everything, the course unfolded successfully even with so little time for preparation.

Externally, the place offered very little. No furniture to speak of, walls in need of repair and paint, broken down heating, intermittent hot water and a derelict kitchen. Bennett utilized these conditions as sources for practical work with real-life consequences.

Internally, Sherborne House was rich with opportunities for "work on oneself." Gurdjieff's teaching was all about people confronting themselves in everyday life situations. Circumstances that were externally challenging were perfect for exposing automatic reactions, which allowed for seeing oneself and practicing techniques to avoid reacting in one's habitual way.

Emerging out of the second taxi was plump, motherly Trudy and her adult, but mentally challenged, daughter Emily. Emily's hands clutched claw-like at her green cardigan as if the buttons were missing. She stood mute, never far from Trudy's side. I was twenty-one and Emily was twenty-eight and operating on the level of about a ten-year-old, I guessed. I wondered what Trudy would do with her in a place like this. But she couldn't have been left alone at home. Trudy was one of Mrs. Popoff's older students, widowed, and this was an opportunity that might not come again for her. So, she had come with Emily in tow.

"Hellu, then," we heard as the large wood-paneled door by a line of trash barrels swung open. Mick Sutton, a tall, lanky Brit, thirty something, emerged looking out at us through golden eyes and bushy flyaway brown curls.

"Where'd you find this lot?" Mick asked the Academy's Secretary, the elderly Olga de Nottbeck, who had been riding with Trudy and Emily and was now paying the taxi drivers. She had introduced herself at the train station in Charlbury, coming back from holiday in Denmark.

"Oh, I spotted them at the train station. They looked lost and tired, but like a Work group, they had formed a chain and were passing their luggage hand to hand off the train," Olga said. "I found they were indeed on their way here, so we came together."

"Right you are. I'll carry on, then," Mick bobbed his head at Olga, who promptly disappeared into the dim interior. "This way, ladies and gents," Mick said brightly as he grabbed Trudy's bag and led the way into a wide, dank-smelling corridor with smooth, worn stone flooring.

A long walk down passageways and upstairs brought us to a king-size dining room with rich mahogany wainscoting and sturdy wooden tables even larger than at the Pinnacle. Oil painted portraits of Lord Sherborne and others, presumably family members, stared down out of ornate gilt frames on pale yellow walls. The darkness of the room was mitigated by the height of the ceiling and tall windows, through which remnants of red-hued light from the day's end filtered in. A large, barren fireplace adorned one wall.

"The library is right through that door," Mick said, pointing a long arm to a high doorway at the other end of the room. "You can wait in there if you like whilst I pop down to the kitchen." Fixing us with a gimlet gaze, he added, "None of you would be ve-ge-tar-ian," drawing out the word with distaste, "now, would you?" We all shook our heads in the negative.

"You missed our proper dinner time, so mind you, I'll have to see what I can do." Tucking in his narrow chin, he looked down his long nose as if to reprimand us for being late, then poof! He was gone, like a genie.

Trudy was peering up at one of the portraits, her soft round face squinting in the fading light. Emily stood close beside her, thin arms and legs poking out from unadorned skirt and sweater, scarecrow-like.

Tugging at Trudy's arm Emily said, "Mom, it's cold in here." And in a high, tired whine, "I'm hungry."

Truth was, I felt like whining too. It had been a long day, starting from last night when we were standing together in small groups at Kennedy Airport waiting to be boarded, our bon voyage well-wishers around us. Mrs. Popoff, my parents, and Jack's mom had all made it out. We'd been full of excitement then. We were tired and hungry now.

Wandering into the library, I sank into a cushioned chair. My soul delighted in the Persian carpet and white recessed shelving sporting colorful book spines that winked at me from floor to ceiling. The sharp tang of paste-waxed wood in the dining room had followed us but was soon lost in a background aroma of old leather and fresh paint. Tall, unshaded windows admitted diminishing twilight, the table lamps casting pools of warm yellow as the outside light faded into dark.

Mick reappeared in the doorway, arms crossed, rocking slightly back on his heels. "Come on then, your supper's in here, for what it's worth," he said, leading us back into the dining room where we gratefully set to as he disappeared again.

"This is good," I said, biting into thick brown home-made bread, still soft and smelling of fresh yeast. Together with slices of sharp cheddar cheese, creamy butter and a spicy bean soup, life began to seep back into my skin. We chatted quietly, reviewing our travel adventures.

Mick popped back into the room. He surveyed the empty bowls and plates with approval. "Leave the dishes in the Servery and we'll take a look at your room assignments," he said, ushering us through a small room adjacent to the dining room.

The Servery had a large double sink with counter space and a window looking out to a garden area. We piled the dishes on an island in the middle of the room. Glass-fronted cupboards filled with white dishes lined the walls.

Mick led us down a wide hallway, past another entrance to the library, and at the juncture where it turned a corner was the largest door I'd ever seen. On the wall next to it was a substantial bulletin board. Everything in this house seemed to be on a grand scale, as if giants lived here.

Scanning a list on the board, Jack and Van discovered they shared a room with four others. Mick looked at the room number and pointed them down the hall, not far from where we were.

Trudy and Emily were next, finding their private room number indicating the second floor where my dorm room was also located. Mick directed us back down the hall to where we had dropped our luggage.

"Just up these stairs," he said, arcing his arm up towards a grand staircase outside the Servery. "Your room numbers will be on the doors. Sleep as late as you like, tomorrow you'll have the day off. Most people take advantage and go to Cheltenham to take care of their banking and such," he said, looking wise. He dismissed us with a tilt of the head as he bustled back into the Servery.

We lugged our bags up the stairs which seemed as long as they were wide. After walking for what felt like miles down an endless plain wooden hallway, we found our rooms, Trudy and Emily's not far from mine.

"Good night, sleep tight, don't let the bed bugs bite," I chanted as we parted. Inside, the room was bare and cold, no carpet on the wide plank floor. A small barren fireplace appeared to be the only future source of heat. Three narrow beds had sheets and towels laid out on foam cloth-covered mattresses. The fourth looked occupied, but the occupant was not there. I poked my head in through an open doorway leading to an adjacent room. Three more beds. I chose the first room and took a bed farthest from the entrance.

Moving around my bed to make it up with tight, square corners like Mom had taught me, I mused to myself, "I can't wait to explore this house with Jack tomorrow."

I stowed my duffle bag under the bed, then padded down the empty hall in my slippers looking for a bathroom in which to brush my teeth and wash my face. No one seemed to be around, and the sense of cavernous quiet was a little eerie. Comforting to know Trudy and Emily were nearby.

I opened a door labeled "toilet" and that was what I found. No sink and no bathtub. *Hmmm.* Finally, I found a room with twelve sinks lined up back-to-back down the length of the room—no mirrors, no cupboards, no counters. I ran my tongue over my teeth, which felt like they had sprouted fur, my mouth and nose involuntarily scrunched together, yuk.

Back in my room, exhaustion pulled me into oblivion as my head hit the pillow.

CHAPTER FOURTEEN
In the Beginning

We slept late the first morning, had tea and toast together in the library, then Mick gave a tour of the house and grounds to orient us. At the back of the property, he warned us, "Mind you, don't go through those woods to Harry's general store and post office." He pointed with a bony finger at a well-worn path, "some use it as a short cut, but it's not our property, so it's *strictly* prohibited."

Among other instructions, Mick informed us that we were to start coming to morning exercise in the ballroom at seven a.m., beginning the next day. He began to review the practice of cold-water ablutions to be done upon awaking.

"Oh yeah, Mrs. Popoff taught us those," I chimed in. "She said to say, 'In the name of the Father, and the Son, and the Holy Ghost' as we splashed each part three times."

Mick looked at me skeptically, head cocked to one side. "I don't know about that, luv. I can't imagine the Bedouins including that bit. In fact," his eyes grew round and his mouth pursed, very serious, "did you know they used sand when there was no water and only the right hand will do?"

"Wow, that's pretty cool," drawled Van, who was part of the group tour with Trudy, Emily, Jack, and me. "Why only the right hand?"

"Because they wipe themselves with the left hand!" There was an unmistakable twinkle in Mick's eyes as he imparted this bit of arcane knowledge.

On the second day, Jack, Van, and I followed up on Mick's suggestion to take a bus to Cheltenham, the largest accessible city, to attend to any banking or shopping we wanted to get done. After that we would be joining the advance work force preparing the place for the next basic course.

The third day dawned gray and cold. After breakfast I went to the bulletin board to see what my first assignment was. It was cleaning the top floor by lunch time, myself.

Someone decked me out with broom, mop, bucket, rags, and scouring powder. I started with the loos, British for toilets, and discovered these were little closet-like rooms. The bath rooms were just that, rooms with multiple tubs. The top floor had four loos and three bath rooms, two with multiple tubs. Then there was the sink room, which I had discovered on the first night.

My task included sweeping down all the corridors and four staircases to the first floor. The long, wide hallways had one radiator but no carpets, which made the sweeping easier at least.

Working as fast as I could, I scoured all the sinks, tubs, and toilets, then mopped the floors with the big heavy string mop and clanging metal bucket. With a thick-handled broom, I swept the long wooden corridors and multiple staircases, some wide, others narrow and winding. The upstairs carried faint aromas of paste-waxed floors and lingering charcoal from dormant fireplaces.

As I worked, I remembered my training at the Pinnacle. Even though this seemed like an impossible task in front of me, I knew that if I let myself start thinking about it, my "inner chatter" would drain my resources with negative commentary. I was going to need all the energy I could muster to get this done by myself. I began a counting exercise Mrs. Popoff had taught us to keep my mind occupied. As I scoured toilets and sinks, I counted: one-two-three-four, four-three-two-one, two-three-four-five, five-four-three-two, up to one hundred and then back down again. When I messed up, I started over.

The lunch bell heralded relief from my first experience of voluntary work during this month-long period of helping to prepare the place in advance of the second Basic Course. I thought I had known what I was getting myself into. Now I wasn't so sure.

"So, what were you doing this morning?" I asked Jack at lunch, gratefully attacking my thick cheese sandwich on its yeasty home-made bread.

"I was working in the Stable Block, taping sheet rock," he replied between bites. "It's nice to put to use things I learned from working as an apprentice with Richard while we were at the Pinnacle."

"Yeah, I was doing a lot of cleaning," I said. "You wouldn't believe how many sinks and toilets this place has. But you know, it's weird, I think I have more energy now than I did when I started this morning." I gave Jack a self-satisfied grin.

After lunch my assignment on the bulletin board directed me to the kitchen down in the basement. The room I stepped into intimidated me right from the start. Alone in its grandeur, I felt insignificant and helpless. Everything appeared larger than life or at least larger than the life I was used to. Tall sturdy wooden worktables and enormous metal pots were overshadowed by ominous looking long sharp knives arranged along the wall. I reflected on the galley-like kitchen at the Pinnacle where we had to squeeze by each other. Obviously not going to be a problem in here.

The day after our arrival, during the tour of the property Mick had shown us the old cast-iron Aga coal burning oven in the kitchen. He explained in detail how oatmeal was cooked overnight. The pot, two feet deep, took two people to slide into the bottom of the Aga oven where it was left to steep overnight.

"At the beginning of the course last year, the kitchen was barely manageable, and we never knew when the electricity or water in this old building would break down next." Mick shook his head in a tsk, tsk, kind of way, then added almost with relish, "Ah, those were the days!"

I gazed at the unfamiliar cooking utensils hanging from the walls as my accumulated energy from the morning's cleaning evaporated. I looked around in bewilderment, wondering what I was supposed to do. The kitchen was clean and organized. A fresh tang of soap and metal lingered on pots and pans still drying on their racks. I felt small and lost in this official looking kitchen.

Mick breezed in and assured me, "Aisha will be here shortly, she's Chief Cook for dinner tonight. Here you go, luv, just wash up over at that sink, aprons are under there, and let's see . . . I know I left the menu plan here somewhere . . . ah yes, here it is."

With that he waved a piece of paper under my nose and set it down by a bushel of fresh eggs sitting in a basket on the tall tabletop. Scanning the menu plan with his finger he instructed, "Right. Just you go ahead and separate out seventy-five eggs for this here soufflé." Giving me a satisfied nod, Mick disappeared before he could hear my feeble, "Wait!" as panic welled up in me.

My cooking expertise growing up had amounted to French toast and, most recently, cranberry bread. But I had never done much to help with dinner. Cooking for fifty in a kitchen of this proportion was a more daunting prospect than I was prepared to contemplate, let alone attempt by myself. Miserably, I cast about and found a couple of bowls. Cracking an egg, I carefully let the white run out into the first bowl while containing the yolk inside the shell and dumping it into the second. Ten minutes later, I had separated ten eggs. Glancing up at the clock, I wondered how this dinner would ever be ready to eat before midnight.

Then the door swung open and a young woman, about my own age, walked in with a cheerful, "Hi, my name's Aisha." Her manner was friendly and easy-going, as was the light-brown, curly hair that breezed about her face.

"Hi. My name's Bobby Jo. Man, am I glad to see you!"

"Forget doing it the way you would at home," Aisha suggested, looking over at my slow progress. "Just use your fingers, like this." She showed me how to sift the egg whites through my fingers into the first bowl and slide the yolks off my hands into the second bowl. It was fast and efficient and unconventionally fun.

To my surprise, the soufflé rose in the big iron Aga oven, filling the kitchen with rich melted cheese aromas. Crispy brown on top, it looked golden and delicious. Dinner was served on time at 7:00 p.m.

I found Jack in his dorm room after the dinner clean-up. He was rereading *Witness*. We had read it together last winter at the Pinnacle, when I would sneak up to his room, sometimes at night. I ducked my head, crawling onto the lower bunk bed in his dorm room and snuggled next to him, flipping my hair onto the pillow, out of my way. I didn't have my glasses on and asked which part he was reading.

Instead of answering me right away he said, "Remember how Mr. Bennett started this school on a hope and a prayer? Well, I feel like we're taking up where the first course left off. The walls are painted, the place is in good working order—I keep being overwhelmed by feelings of gratitude towards last year's students. You can still feel the vibrations of the work they did here."

"Yeah, I know what you mean. I feel it too," I said, remembering warm thoughts tickling my chest as I swept halls earlier in the day, envisioning the Pinnacle people who were here last year with scrapers and paint brushes. It was as if I was standing on their shoulders with my broom in hand, able to reach higher somehow.

"So, I'm reading the part where Hasan Shushud—you know, the Sufi mystic that Mr. Bennett invited to Sherborne last year—" Jack explained, answering the blank look on my face at the mention of the name, "—where he tells Bennett, 'You have been chosen to be one of the rare ones who are destined to go all the way to final liberation.' Here, listen to this," Jack said, moving two fingers over the page until he came to the part, reading out loud, "'Your only home is the Absolute Void.'"

Jack glanced at me and continued, "then Bennett remembers Gurdjieff had told him, 'You can now have Paradise, but you must not be satisfied until you have attained Soleil Absolute.'"

"Wow," I murmured, following Jack's tapered fingers touching the black print. "The Sun Absolute, isn't that like World Number One? So he wouldn't be subject to any laws and would have attained absolute freedom?"

"Well, almost." Jack explained, "He would still be subject to the one law in World Number One."

"Which law?"

"The Will of the Absolute," Jack said with finality. "Remember, in Gurdjieff's cosmology, the number of forces in each world equals the number of laws that world comes under and the farther away it is from God, or the Will of the Absolute. People always think accidents just happen.

But according to Gurdjieff, it's because we're asleep, drifting through life in World 48. At least by working on ourselves, we have the possibility of becoming conscious and experiencing World 24, the sensitive world, the world of the Astral Body. You know, like Mrs. Popoff was talking about."

"Wow," I said again, wondering when we would actually get to meet Mr. Bennett. I'd heard he and his family were away on holiday. No one seemed to know just when he'd show up at Sherborne.

"Yeah," Jack said absently, reading again. "Here, listen to this, Bennett says, 'I was convinced that I had lived before in Central Asia at the time of Khwaja Ubeydullah Ahrar and asked Hasan how it had come about that I had been born so far away from my native land. I have always felt at home in Asia and a stranger in Europe. Hasan said, 'The wind can blow the seed across continents. The wind is blowing towards England now. That is why you were born here.'"

A shiver ran up my spine. Man, Bennett must be something else. How the heck had someone like me gotten here? Reflecting back, I remembered how I'd been so sure I had to go to Livingston College where the first thing that happened was that I'd met Jack. Then Jack had given me *In Search of the Miraculous*, where Ouspensky talked about going through life "asleep" and being a bundle of little i's bouncing around like ping-pong balls, instead of one big "I" that knew what it wanted and acted rather than reacted. It was as if I'd had these thoughts in me all along but had been waiting for someone to put them into words.

When Jack had stumbled onto Mrs. Popoff's group, I'd joined just in time to hear Bennett speak at the Gotham Book Mart in New York. Listening to him, I had suddenly *known* that Jack and I were going on the course. And here we were, where fate had brought us.

"Apparently when Hasan Shushud visited last year, he told Bennett he was wasting his time starting this school. And he didn't think much of the students, either." Jack put a slip of paper in the book and shut it. He turned to face me, kissing me on the lips, softly, his hand moving down my arm.

"Hey, Bobby Jo," came a familiar southern voice from across the room. "It's gettin' kinda late, d'y'all mind if I turn out the lights?"

"Oh yeah, sorry, Van. I guess I'd better go." I gave Jack a regretful kiss and swung my legs down off the side of the bed. "Wow, it is late," I said, looking at the Timex on my wrist. "Okay, see you all tomorrow."

I left the room wondering just what couples did do here if they lived in the dorms.

CHAPTER FIFTEEN
Settling In

The days were taking on a routine. Wake up bell at six, morning meditation in the ballroom, breakfast of oatmeal and toast, then morning assignments starting at nine.

Even though I didn't feel very competent in the kitchen, I found myself back there again the next day. Aisha and I were assigned to cook lunch. Compared to the work I had done the day before, this felt like a picnic. All we had to do was bake fifty-five potatoes with big wedges of cheese hammered into their middles. While the potatoes baked, we made coleslaw, and I learned how to make mayonnaise.

Mayonnaise is like whipped cream, I learned. If you overdo it, the egg and the oil separate out. But unlike cream, by patiently beating a small corner of the mixture, you can eventually pull it all back together again. This became an analogy Mr. Bennett liked to refer to. When faced with something gone awry, by working diligently with what was possible, the whole could be set right. Because we had experienced making mayonnaise ourselves, it made the point even more compelling.

There was time after lunch before our afternoon assignments started. Jack and I walked to town to post aerograms home. I had bought several of the flimsy blue self-mailers on our first day here.

As we rounded the corner to go out the back door by the kitchen, I noticed the hall floor, large worn stones polished smooth from traffic. When I asked Mick, he told me the stone flooring was from the ninth-century monastery the manor had been built upon.

Mick also informed me that gypsies still showed up at the back door on occasion, as it was part of some ancient Romani route. I was used to thinking of the American Revolution as ancient history, but compared to England, American history happened yesterday.

We found our way out to the kitchen gardens and strolled through them, swamped in late summer sunshine and smelling of compost and a tumble of ripening tomatoes. I was loving the rectangular vegetable beds, orderly paths, and the feeling of envelopment within the thick, tall stone-wall enclosure.

"You know, it just isn't as strange and foreign as I thought it would be. In fact, it's kinda neat—almost familiar," I said, looking around and thinking of *The Secret Garden*, by Frances Hodgson Burnett, which I had read as a kid. The calf-length denim bib-skirt I wore felt appropriate in this place. We walked on in silence, enjoying the golden warmth of the September sun in contrast to the cold, dark interior of the house.

Pushing through a wooden door in the far wall we came out onto the back of the property and followed a path through a copse of trees next to the neighboring farm's fields. The leaves were beginning to dry and turn yellow; a few had fallen and rustled underfoot as we walked.

Technically, we were trespassing, and Mick had told us we weren't supposed to go this way. But then it turned out it was safer and quicker than walking down the long driveway out to the winding and sunken roadbed leading into Sherborne Village. It also turned out to be the way everyone went, including Mick.

It wasn't as manicured-looking here, but it wasn't like the wild woods at home with tangled underbrush and fallen logs. No, everything around us felt like it had been tamed a long time ago.

"You know Jack, it's weird, I feel like I'm not all here," I mused, almost to myself. I combed my fingers through my brown hair, pushing sun-bleached strands away from my forehead. Bangs were not a solution, since they ended up growing into my eyes. I was so short-sighted it was hard enough to see, without having hair in my face.

"I'm surprised how much at home I feel here, though," I said. "I always thought England would be dull and uninteresting, all gray and rainy." I looked over at Jack, thinking how much at home I felt with him, too. "But it still feels like something's missing. Like my personality hasn't arrived yet. Like everything is sort of suspended."

He was taking long strides down the path, like he was walking down the sidewalk in West New York. He slowed down and fell in beside me, arms hanging long at his sides. He was wearing his wide-striped bell bottoms, splattered with fresh drips of pale-yellow paint from working in the Stable Block that morning. His faded, green, tie-dyed T-shirt hung loose outside his pants. "Yeah, it feels weird to me too. It's like we're here but our luggage hasn't arrived yet. Today was better. How many days has it been?"

"Four," I answered.

We had come out of the woods at the edge of the village, where another road made a T-junction with the village road. Across from us was the quaint little post office and general store. It was built of the same creamy-gray stone as the Manor House and had a similar dark slate roof.

As we crossed the street and walked up the short path to the front door, I was surprised to see that on both sides the front lawn was awash in bright flowers climbing and bumping all over each other. There wasn't a blade of grass visible. Bees buzzed with industry, the sweet scent of fall blooms perfuming the air. The house reminded me of *The Hobbit*, by J. R. R. Tolkien, a book I'd loved in high school.

Stepping into the cramped interior, I walked up to the postal window and handed the postmaster my aerogram to be mailed. From behind the counter, wearing an apron and his postmaster's cap, we were greeted with, "Would you be new students arriving for the next course up at the big house?" Upon answering in the affirmative, the postmaster smiled and promptly introduced himself as Harry.

"What can we do for you today?" asked Harry hopefully.

"Do you sell aerograms?"

"Yes indeed. Do you see them over there next to the soap flakes? The mail posts every day promptly at 4:00 p.m. You can retrieve your incoming postals from here as well. What else might you be needing, then?"

Between the postal window and the display of candy and various sundries from soaps to stationery, there wasn't much room in the store to maneuver. We looked around the crowed shelves, nooks and crannies.

We didn't recognize any of the brands and had little money to shop with. Jack picked up a long narrow box with a picture of triangular shaped white chocolate. It said Toblerone. I chose a flat rectangular bar of dark chocolate with nuts, labeled Cadbury. We added two sheets of thin self-mailer aerograms and pulled out our British money. The pound notes seemed overly ornate and large, much bigger than an ordinary dollar.

Harry disappeared from the postal window and reappeared, minus the postmaster's cap, behind a larger opening in the wall where a cash register perched on the ledge. We handed him some bills and he gave us back our change in an odd assortment of thick, solid coins. One of them was smaller than a dime. It was a half-penny. A ha'penny, like in the Christmas song. He smiled at us, adjusted his glasses and said, "Good-day, then."

We re-emerged into the gold day. My hand found Jack's, and we headed back, our horizons expanded.

Harry Taylor's Post Office and General Store

CHAPTER SIXTEEN
Secret Rendezvous

I checked the bulletin board when we got back, and sure enough, I was assigned to help with dinner. My first chore was to haul big pots onto the stove and dump water into them to start heating for tea.

Making tea was part of the dinner cooks' job. For those doing hard physical work, tea was a welcome break in the long afternoon. Of course, the highlight of afternoon tea was the "biscuit." This was a plain dry round wheat cookie. Sweet and substantial, it was called a "digestive," which I took to be its nickname. In reality, these were McVitie's Digestives, another unfamiliar brand. It didn't take long to look forward to digestives at tea time. Besides, they were perfect for dunking in strong black tea subdued with milk.

As well as setting out the tea and biscuits upstairs, there were two work crews that had to be delivered to, one in the Stable Block and one in the Orangery. The Stable Block was the closest but still a walk out past the parish church with its tall steeple at the edge of the parking lot, through the graveyard, and up the stairs among the construction that was turning the old stable into apartments.

At first the work crew was all smiles, happy to see me. Until: "So what's this then?" One of the guys asked, eyeing the small pot of tea and the four cups I'd brought.

I looked around at the eight men and women, dusty from taping, spackling, and sanding the walls. "Oh. I guess I brought the wrong pot."

"Yeah, this one goes to the blokes out in the Orangery."

I trudged back to the kitchen, spilling hot tea all over because the pot was heavy and awkward, even if it was the smaller one. The Orangery was on the other side of the property. I would have to go out through the back door by the smelly garbage bins and through the walled kitchen gardens to get to it. My back and arms ached, which didn't help. I felt stupid and dreaded having to retrace all these steps. But then I thought of Mrs. Popoff.

"Inner chatter," I heard myself say, remembering Mrs. Popoff's term for talking in my head. I stopped lamenting my stupidity and told myself, "Okay, pay more attention, be more present, this is a *lesson*." I directed my attention to my feet and started feeling them, sensing. I became aware of my shoulders, noting the tension there and allowing the muscles to relax. Sensing my feet and releasing tensions, I picked my way back through the graveyard and around the corner of the chapel without fueling more inward negativity.

Once I had gotten the tea to the correct crews, I met Mary Cornelius. The exact opposite of Mick Sutton, she was sweet and very soft-spoken. Mary never ranted on about "vegetarians" or looked sage. Part of the staff, she shared responsibilities with Mick for running the kitchen.

"Here, Bobby Jo, take this colander and we'll walk out to the kitchen garden. We need to pick half a stone of carrots." Her white hair and small-boned frame made her look frail, but she had an inner strength. I wondered if that came from having known Mr. Gurdjieff.

Back in the kitchen we scrubbed the carrots in deep metal sinks. Mary came over with a large knife, testing it with her finger as she handed it to me, admonishing, "Do be mindful when you work with this, my dear, we wouldn't want you to chop your finger off."

I was surprised to see Emily industriously at work chopping onions with no concern for the dangers of the knife. Humming quietly to herself, she was quite content. She had discovered the warmest room in the house and assigned herself a permanent position there. The kitchen crews came to appreciate her ability to focus on a repetitive task and never grow tired of it.

After cutting the carrots down into bite-size chunks for stew, I helped Emily and Aisha prepare green beans for freezing. Beets, also from the garden, were prepared for jarring. The smell of blanching beans and boiling beets, giant pots pouring steam into the air, sautéing onions, and the sound of industrious chopping all imbued the kitchen with warmth and a companionable air. The afternoon went quickly and pleasantly, dinner served without incident.

Dinner cooks cleaned up the kitchen, which included sweeping and mopping the floor. What was left of the evening was free. By now Aisha and I were getting the distinct feeling that we had known each other before. A kind of déjà vu as if we had been here together in some other life, an experience that happened with others on the course.

Jack found us as we were putting the mops and buckets away. He was holding three hard rubber lacrosse balls in each hand with his long fingers. "I'm going downstairs to the Great Hall to practice some juggling. Want to come?"

"Thanks, Jack, but I need to go write a letter," Aisha said, peeling the stained apron off over her head. "I'll see you tomorrow," She added in farewell, heading upstairs to the dorm rooms.

"I'll come. We can work on that passing routine you're showing me," I said, happy to spend some time with him. We hadn't seen much of each other in the past couple of days.

We walked down the corridor to the Great Hall. It was aptly named. The largest room in the Manor House, it had a white marble floor with ornate pillars and lintels and a tall deep fireplace. One end of the room had tiered steps ending in a platform, ideal for setting up chairs so guests could watch Movements demonstrations on visitors' weekends. These would be held later in the course, Mick had informed us on our tour.

Standing four feet apart in the cold hall, we juggled three lacrosse balls each to warm up. Then we started our pattern. One and, two and, three and—pass with the right hand and catch with the left. After a year under Jack's tutelage, I was improving and could keep the rhythm going for three or four passes before missing or throwing too wildly for Jack to catch. He was very good at catching, even when my balls went too high or too low for comfort. For Jack, juggling had started as an art form but now was another way to practice working with attention and sensitivity.

We stayed up later than usual, enjoying each other's company. But finding the time and energy for romance was proving illusive. The schedule was just too grueling.

As I snuggled into my narrow bed and faded into delicious sleep that night, I dreamily thought, "Oooh, tomorrow's Sunday, and I get to sleep until 7:30 a.m. Oh, Joy!"

But Sunday turned out to be just like every other day, hard physical work from morning to way past dusk. It was late when I went to visit Jack and Van in their room that night.

"Bobby Jo, come with me," Jack said as he took my hand and led me down the hall away from his dorm room. We went around a corner and halfway along, Jack paused, quietly rapped on a door, then turned the handle. It was unlocked. He stepped in and pulled me in after him. Closing the door softly, he locked it.

The room was dark and smelled musty, with old mattresses and wooden furniture pitched here and there. As my eyes adjusted, I made out one double bed frame complete with mattress. Jack led me to the bed and we sat down.

"What is this place?" I asked cautiously, peering into the corners. It wasn't very inviting.

"I hear it's called the Trysting Room," Jack replied with a grin. "Trilby told me about it."

"Well, let's try it out." I answered back, pulling him down as I collapsed onto my side. It felt illicit. We hadn't made love in forever, it seemed. We fumbled a bit with each other's clothes, then gave it up and kissed, his fine hair falling into my face. Knowing his ears were sensitive, I nibbled and blew into them. In response, his fingers found my resonant parts, playing me like a guitar. Our call and response became more urgent as suppressed sex energy bloomed into full passion.

It was heaven to lie together in a bed, alone. I moaned, and Jack put a soft hand over my mouth. "Shhhhh," he whispered. Someone was banging on the door.

"Hey! Hurry up in there, why don't you. We ain't got all night," came an irritated female voice.

"Okay," Jack called out, "We'll be gone in a few minutes."

The heat of passion thoroughly doused, we sheepishly rearranged our disheveled clothes and slunk out of the room. A woman student and her boyfriend stood by, barely waiting for us to get out of the doorway before pushing their way in.

CHAPTER SEVENTEEN
Something's Cookin'

I was scheduled to make breakfast with Martin. He was a wiry little man, his thick black hair in stark contrast to his gray beard. He had arrived with five young kids and a sweet-looking wife even smaller than himself with lovely soft black hair curling about her shoulders. I mistook their Yorkshire accent for a brogue of some sort. I loved to hear them talk. Martin ruled his clan with an iron will. He was very religious, and I assumed, Catholic. But he was kind and fun too. We were in the big kitchen on the ground floor after the evening cleanup. We had to stay until the bread was sliced and the oats could be left in the Aga oven to slow-cook overnight.

"Hi Martin, have you done breakfast before? I haven't." Tying on an apron, I looked for instructions to tell me how many loaves to cut and how to make the porridge. As usual, I was at a loss as to where to begin.

"Yes, love. I cooked breakfast the other day. I have a good idea of how it goes," Martin said with a lilt in his voice and a smile in his eyes. "See there? The bread we need is on the table under that cloth." He directed my gaze with a tilt of his bushy chin as he washed his hands at the sink.

I took out a heavy wooden carving board and one of the long, serrated bread knives, placing them on the table next to several nicely domed brown rectangular loaves. As I took the cloth off, the aroma of fresh baked bread wafted up from the striped towel, still warm to my touch. I picked up the knife and started sawing at the heel of the bread. It fell flat onto the board, a yeasty smell rising up from the soft interior of the loaf. I started cutting a second slice, resisting the urge to pick up the first, slather it with butter and eat it right on the spot.

"Oh no! Martin, it's falling apart," I yelped as the bread crumbled under my knife in warm moist clumps.

"Blessed Mary, I should have warned you. We're not to cut the bread until the morning. It was just baked and hasn't finished cooling." Martin had put the measuring cup down and was hurrying over to check the damage. "Don't worry about it now, darlin'. Here, let me fix that." Taking the knife gently from my hand he expertly sliced down, severing the ragged piece so the next slice would be even. In a moment of inspiration, he placed the towel back over the loaves, carefully tucking the end in around the cut loaf. Then he picked up the two pieces I had cut, quickly found some butter and jam, and the two of us closed our eyes in mutual bliss, disposing of the evidence.

Martin set me to counting out measures of oats into a ceramic bowl while he clanged a large steel pot into the sink and started filling it with water. With some difficulty he lifted it onto the stove, threw in the oats and banged a lid onto it.

It was fun being in the kitchen by ourselves, the house having gone to bed without us. The kitchen was still aromatic from the day's cooking and baking, the heat of the ovens dispelling the chill of the old stone manor.

Martin bustled about, measuring coffee and water. I helped him set heavy blackened oven racks out on the worktable ready for us to load with slices of bread for toasting the next day. Every once in a while, I'd catch him murmuring something and crossing himself. Imploring the saints for our success, I guessed.

Martin beckoned me over to the stove saying, "Bobby Jo, help me lift this down, please. Mind, 'tis quite heavy."

Together we carefully set the pot down on the stone floor, maneuvering it gingerly over to the door of the Aga oven, careful not to let the water spill out. I opened the wide iron door with a towel. The two of us swung the pot up onto the low sitting rack and pushed it far back into the coal-burning oven, tamped down for the night. It would simmer slowly there until morning.

"Nothing more to be done tonight," announced Martin, looking satisfied and placing his apron on the table ready to grab in the morning.

"We'd best meet down here at five to be sure we have time to get the bread cut and toasted. I'll start cutting first thing."

I thought Martin was being more than generous offering to cut the bread, clearly not my forte. "No problem, Martin, I'm cool with that!"

The next morning my heart lightened as I swung through the kitchen door and found Martin at work in a lighted and warm kitchen. The hollow echo of my footsteps on cold bare wood through dark hallways and down winding stairs had creeped me out a bit as I'd scurried downstairs before dawn.

Martin put the bread knife down as I entered, and I threw my apron on over my head, headed for the sink and washed my hands. The deep quiet of early morning felt sacred with him there and we moved over to the Aga, hauling the heavy pot out together in silence. Martin lifted the lid and I stepped back as steam billowed up. Leaning in, I stirred the thick oatmeal with a long wooden spoon. We both inhaled the rich nutty fragrance.

"Ahhh, this will do," Martin approved. "Why don't you ring the wake-up bell whilst I cut the bread?"

With measured tread I slowly swung the big brass bell, echoing up and down the halls and corridors, the deep resonant *dong, dong,* making me feel like a monk in a monastery. I could hear people stirring in their rooms and no longer felt alone. I hurried back to the kitchen to take over toasting the bread so Martin could get the coffee and tea going.

Making toast, it turned out, was a tricky business. Slices had to be watched, turned over and taken out, while the next batch was quickly placed onto the hot oven racks and slid in under the broiler. Sometimes one slice would start burning before another was finished browning.

By the time we'd hustled porridge, toast, coffee, tea, milk, butter, and jam up to the Servery I felt like I'd been at work half the day.

The next morning my assignment was to work with the construction crew, converting the old Stable Block into rooms. Finally! Something other than cooking or cleaning. From Jack's experience I knew I would be sanding and painting all day. It was hard work, and I was coming down with a cold.

Bruce, an American from last year's course, was staying on until our course started, which would be soon. Until then, he was in charge of the Stable Block.

"When you're working, find your rhythm and relax into it. Not only find the particular motion of the job but discover the rhythm of the tool you're working with." He had an open, intelligent face and a natural leadership quality.

We always worked in silence, so when Bruce spoke it resonated. I started to put more attention on the paint brush, sensing my hand holding it.

"Here, Bobby Jo, like this." Bruce took his brush, dipped the bristles three-quarters of the way into the bucket, and smeared two long streaks of creamy white paint onto the bare drywall horizontally. Then, holding the brush at the base of the bristles between his thumb and three fingers, he spread thick paint out in long smooth vertical lines. He followed again with horizontal strokes filling in the square area and finished the section with delicate strokes from top to bottom, so you could see the little bristle lines all going in the same direction before the paint dried.

I relaxed into the dip and spread back and forth, up and down. My chosen brush fit my hand as I worked the paint, my arm and shoulder opening to the motion. *Okay, I can do this.* It's no longer a chore. It's an art.

The rest of the crew already knew this. We all worked together, paying attention to the paint, the brush, the wall in front of us. A warmth filled the quiet we shared, creating connectedness, a sense of community.

I'd worn my battered bell bottoms, green and black checkered Woolrich shirt, and the babushka Mrs. Popoff had given me. The old scarf kept my long hair covered and back out of the way. It was chilly and dusty in the open Stable Block. I sneezed again, *ker-choo!*

The pace picked up—completing the room was within reach. Energy infused the cold air as if it were breath. I didn't even know their names, yet we were connecting on some deep nonverbal level responding to the acuity of our heightened awareness.

I was again experiencing a change of state, like tripping on peyote, only more lucid. It amazed me that I had heard about Sherborne and gotten myself here. How could I be so lucky?

Lucky. The pleased feeling brought back a childhood memory. The revelation that I was more privileged than many. That everyone didn't live in ease and safety, things I took for granted.

In Gurdjieff's *Beelzebub's Tales to His Grandson*, Hassein the grandson says, "Only now have I come clearly to understand that everything we have at the present time and everything we use—in a word, all the contemporary amenities and everything necessary for our comfort and welfare—have not always existed and did not make their appearance so easily."

Hassein goes on to say, "There has arisen in me, side by side with this [realization], the need to make clear to my Reason why I personally have all the comforts which I now use, and what obligations I am under for them."[1]

Exactly. So how come I get to be here? Why am I so privileged? How and to whom do I "pay the debt of my existence?"[2] I wondered this to myself, an unexpected gravity replacing the pleased feeling in my chest.

---

[1] G. I. Gurdjieff, "Becoming Aware of Genuine Being-Duty," chap. 7 in *Beelzebub's Tales to His Grandson: All and Everything* (New York: E. P. Dutton, 1950).
[2] Gurdjieff, "Becoming Aware."

CHAPTER EIGHTEEN
Those With Eyes

A few days later, a small note on the bulletin board invited anyone who was interested in learning some eye strengthening exercises to meet in the library before tea. Mrs. Bennett had put up the note herself, one of the Brits from last year's course had mentioned, pointing out her scribbled initials.

The rumors must be true, that the Bennetts were back from London to settle in before the course started. I was on p.m. service and setting up for tea, which made it easy for me to go to the talk.

Mrs. Bennett entered the library where we were waiting. Practical looking, she was dressed in a brown wool skirt and white oxford shirt. Her face was framed with light brown flyaway hair, her cheeks were ruddy as though she'd just been out for a brisk walk. Her bright eyes were kind but frank. She wasted no time, introduced herself as Elizabeth Bennett, and welcomed us all.

"And I understand that some of you are interested in the Bates Method of eye exercises." She showed us some exercises that were similar to the ones I had been introduced to at the Pinnacle, holding one finger up in front of her oval face and focusing on it with eyes crossed, then refocusing the eyes on an object as far away as possible. "Out a window, if you can manage it," she explained, demonstrating.

Another exercise was "palming." She had us all cup our hands over our eyes so no light could get in, instructing us to keep our eyes open, allowing them to relax in the dark and warmth of our palms.

"I would be happy to lend Dr. Bates's book to anyone who wants to borrow it, let's say, for a fortnight?" She looked around the room as some heads nodded, concluding the arrangement with, "Please return the book to the library and the next person can sign it out with the paper we shall keep on the shelf, just here." She put a piece of paper and a pen on the ledge of the bookcase. "Well then, I think working to strengthen our vision is a splendid endeavor."

Just then the tea bell rang out and Mrs. Bennett dismissed us with, "Teatime, is it?"

We trooped into the adjoining dining room with its mahogany paneling and high-hung portraits. Remembering that Mrs. Popoff had allowed one of her group members to talk about Bates and to show us some of the exercises, I decided right then and there to work with the Bates exercises. Maybe I could lessen my 20/500 myopia. I was so freakin' short-sighted! If both Mrs. Popoff and Mrs. Bennett encouraged the exercises, there must be something to it.

Holding my mug of tea and a plate with two Digestive biscuits I looked around for Jack. He was coming through the line waiting his turn for the tea pot. I sat down at one of the long wooden tables and waved him over. Wrapping my hands around the hot porcelain, I inhaled the sharp astringent steam deep into my cold chest and felt my hands grow warm. Dropping in a cube of sugar, I poured the milk, watching it swirl and lighten the brew, sweetening the aroma. I dunked my wheat digestive and took a bite of the softened cookie, letting it dissolve on my tongue.

Jack slid onto the chair next to me, tucking his big feet under the rungs and curling his hands around his mug. He'd been working in the Stable Block. The tip of his nose was pink, his shirt lightly dusted from sanding spackle.

"That's Mrs. Bennett over there," I told him, nodding my head towards the table by the recessed bank of windows. "I just met her in the library. She was telling us about the Bates eye exercises." I took a sip of tea and smiled. "Mrs. Bennett seems very down to earth. I like her."

"I ran into Mr. Bennett this morning, sort of," Jack said, munching thoughtfully on a McVities "digestive" biscuit. "I was sitting on top of the framing in one of the rooms of the Stable Block. No one else was working there and all of a sudden he walked in. He was looking around but didn't see me. I wanted to let him know someone was there and thought it was a good moment to make an impression." Jack took a sip from his mug, pausing a long moment before continuing. "We looked right at each other and I said hello or something, but it was weird." A far away, inward look was on Jack's face and he said, "It was as if I wasn't there, like Bennett was looking right through me. And I felt like," he stopped, groping for words, "like he was right, I wasn't there. Like there wasn't anyone real for him to see."

A little shiver of recognition ran through me. Somehow, I knew what Jack meant.

We finished our tea and biscuits, stretching out the half-hour break before returning to our assignments. Cleaning up after tea was a p.m. service duty, so I got up and started bringing dishes into the Servery to wash.

After reading about the Bates Method and getting into the habit of doing the exercises, I also took up Bates's suggestion to avoid wearing my glasses as much as possible. Normally the fog of my myopia would have made me claustrophobic after half an hour. However, since Mrs. Bennett endorsed it, I wanted to give the exercises a concentrated chance.

Lunch time in the kitchen. Every day, there were more mouths to feed, with new people trickling in before the course started.

"Bobby Jo, we need to get the salads upstairs, now!" Aisha looked at the clock on the wall, "It's 12:30 and there's still plenty to do."

No matter how well prepared we thought we were, the last half hour before serving a meal was always hectic. "Don't worry, it's under control." I called back as I pushed one more platter onto the dumbwaiter and started hauling on the thick scratchy rope to pull it up to the Servery.

Crash! The wooden lift jerked to a halt, my stomach feeling like it had dropped back down the shaft.

"Bobby Jo! What happened?" Aisha called from the kitchen.

"I don't know. I can't see," I said despairingly, standing helplessly out in the hall in front of the dumbwaiter, peering in.

Aisha rushed over. "Oh man, you put too many platters on the shelf. We lost one and there's another one stuck between the shaft and the back of the shelf. I wish you would wear your glasses!"

I felt like a fool. "But I was doing so well without them," I wailed.

"We'll have to clean this up and redistribute the salads. Hopefully we'll have enough. Can you manage?" Aisha asked.

"Yeah, sure." Inwardly shaking, I pulled the platters off the dumbwaiter, scraped the spilled lettuce into a compost bucket and reached back to get the last platter. I still couldn't really see what I was doing. As my fingers groped towards the back of the shelf, the stuck platter crashed down, breaking.

Shit! Why do I always mess up in the kitchen? I need to put more attention, or feeling or something, into my kitchen work. I rearranged the salad plates, self-esteem plummeting.

Lunch was late. Sitting next to Aisha, I felt stupid and embarrassed, face flushed, heart pounding.

Damn it, I'm supposed to be working on myself! Come on, take all these dumb negative emotions and transform them! I jabbed my fork into a tomato. *Okay, sense. There—I'm lifting my fork—I'm sensing my hand. That's better . . .*

Hey, this potato soup sure tastes good! I reached for the bread, dipping a piece into the creamy mixture, glancing with appreciation at Aisha who was working on her own soup in silence. *Oh God, I can tell Aisha doesn't want to work with me in the kitchen anymore. Why can't I do anything right!*

I couldn't help but think of Gurdjieff's aphorism: *Roses, Roses. Thorns, Thorns.* Yes, I had become lost in smelling the roses, convinced I knew how to work and was handling all the challenges. And the biggest challenge of all was staring me right in the face. What I couldn't see was that I couldn't "see." What I didn't yet know was that I didn't know anything.

CHAPTER NINETEEN
Me, Myself, and I

I picked up my cushion just inside the giant door to the ballroom and padded down the wood floor in my stockinged feet. Finding a spot along the right-hand side of the wall in semi-darkness, the first strands of light slipped in through the tall bay windows. Settling in on the floor next to the other women, I propped the cushion under my butt. I sat, crossing my legs with palms resting lightly on my knees, muscles taut against the cold air. It was like this every morning, whoever was in the house came to morning exercise, no exceptions. There were more people now, maybe fifty.

Unlike some, I didn't need to prop my back against the wall. Through practice I had learned to sit cross-legged comfortably, thanks to Mrs. Popoff's training.

Mr. Bennett sat at the end of the room farthest from the door, facing us, men on his right and women on his left. He also sat cross-legged, even though he was seventy-something years old. I heard later that he had coined the phrase "morning exercise" for the meditations he led throughout the course. He led the exercise every few days as new students arrived. Today we practiced on our own.

As Mr. Bennett had instructed, I started with my eyes. Gazing straight ahead above the shadowed heads across the room I shifted my attention right without moving my eyes. Once my attention was fixed on the shape of a woman next to me, I moved my eyes to the right, "meeting" my attention. I repeated this to the left, up to the ceiling and down to the floor. Between each direction, my eyes moved back to center, focused on the gray light filtering in through the windows above the men. At the end, I circled my eyes once to the right and once to the left, stretching them to the outer edge of my orbit.

Now I let my gaze fall on the floor, unfocused, a few feet in front of me. Early morning dimness and quietude in the room pulled at my lids, inviting them to drop shut, but I caught myself and blinked them open again.

I put my thoughts on my forehead, trying to feel it, to identify it, to find tension there that I could will to relax. I became aware of the area around my eyes, a pressure there. Was it relaxing? Don't know. I thought I could identify my nose, but the appendage was too amorphous. The mouth, now we were getting somewhere. I felt my chapped lips, and became aware of a tightening in my jaw. I told it to *relax, goddamn it*.

Now for the throat, I could feel that, and the top of my shoulders. *Ooh, that's tension for sure*. Taking a deep breath, I let it out slowly, focusing deep into my shoulders. The room was quiet, sleepy yet alert, the sense of all our bodies sitting together and concentrating created a kind of tension in the air. The silence was deafening. I focused harder, my shoulders alive with pain. Instead of dissipating it, my attention increased the tightening. Sharp stabs seared into my shoulders.

I deflected my attention away, down my arms to my hands. Everything felt tight and tingling and I couldn't tell if it was pain, relaxation or sensation. The harder I concentrated, the more tense I became. I was holding my breath. My stomach was tight. There was a buzzing in my ears. I wanted to scream. Instead, I whined, *Shit, shit, shit!*

Finally, thankfully, we heard Mr. Bennett rise swiftly to his feet and we all stood up, rustling like fall leaves. He bowed from the waist, back straight with his hands on his knees and we followed suit. He stood, we stood. This was repeated two more times in silence. Without a word he strode down the center aisle towering above us and left the room. In silence, we gathered up our cushions, wraps and shawls and slowly filed out.

This was what Mrs. Popoff had been preparing us for—a real teacher in a real school, but on a grander scale than I could have imagined. The structure and discipline of the place seemed familiar, echoing the seminars we'd had at the Pinnacle. Because we were all here to work on ourselves it felt safe despite the strangeness. I was grateful for the students still here from last year's course who modeled how to work and how to sit. The great presence of Mr. Bennett aside, I could appreciate the results of their training in the quiet attention they brought to their work. I hoped I would end up like them.

The breakfast bell sounded as I found my shoes outside the door. I hung back until Jack emerged and we shuffled down the hall together to line up outside the Servery, men and women trailing down the hall. The scent of fresh toast, anticipation of hot tea and creamy porridge temporarily dispelled my tensions.

Later that morning I lugged a mop and bucket into the Great Hall and started swabbing the stone floor. My assignment on the bulletin board had me on ground floor cleaning crew, only I'd seen no evidence of the rest of the "crew." I started pushing the mop around. Anger, like a slow burning volcano, bubbled up. *Where the heck is everyone? They're supposed to be here too! Why am I the one who always shows up? I'm not supposed to be doing all this by myself!* I plunked the mop into the bucket, pulled out my dirty handkerchief, and blew my nose.

The Great Hall was a cavern of stone and marble. Thoughts bounced off the walls, reverberating in my head. *What the hell am I doing here? Who am I kidding?* My hands were red and chaffed, my nose cold and runny, my back and shoulders ached. I was sick and tired of the drudgery. *I don't know what I'm doing here half the time anyway, I keep making stupid mistakes—why am I the only one working here this morning? Dammit to hell!*

Heaving the heavy mop head out of the bucket, I let it fall onto the floor with a plop, puddles of water spreading out around the cotton strings. I didn't care about wringing the thick ropey strands back into the bucket. Heart pounding, hot anger lacing my arms, I pushed the thick wood handle in front of me; sloshing water out of the bucket, not caring how much I left on the cold stones. Gone were my smug thoughts of how well prepared I was to come here and how I would become "enlightened." I was tired of being cold, tired of being sore, and tired of "working on myself."

When I looked at the bulletin board the next morning it was like receiving a gift—I had no morning assignment.

A bemused looking man was standing near me, scanning over the board and watching me look for my assignment. He peered over my shoulder through his glasses and spoke to me in a slight French accent, "Ah, I see you are quite free for most of the day. I'm sure there is plenty of work in the garden that you could turn your hand to."

"Oh, hi, umm, sure. Who are you?" I asked.

"But of course, Mademoiselle, allow me to introduce myself," the man said with a slight bow. "I am Pierre Elliot, part of the staff. Recently arrived with my family." Pierre smiled with thin lips, a close-cropped beard making his jaw appear square. "And whom do I have the pleasure of speaking with?" he enquired of me.

"Hi, I'm Bobby Jo, glad to meet ya." I said, sticking out my hand and shaking his with a firm grip while looking squarely at the nose above his thin mustache like my father had taught me to do, which he had learned from Dale Carnegie's *How to Win Friends and Influence People*.

We smiled amiably at each other and departed in our own directions. I decided to catch up on long overdue personal things, like writing in my journal and practicing my Tai Chi, which I'd had few chances to do since arriving at Sherborne House.

Around 10:00 a.m. I wandered downstairs looking for a cup of tea. As I walked past the bulletin-board I saw a little notice and looked closer. In a scrawled hand it read: "Anyone not on House Duties please join Bobby Jo in the Garden." I made a sour face, went back to my room, donned my work boots and jacket and went out to the garden.

I found Barbara June, my slightly nutty, funny roommate from Chicago, and Emily already in the garden. The sun beamed down warm on our heads as we worked together in companionable silence for the rest of the morning, the sweet scents of ripening tomatoes and fresh-turned earth our reward.

I wouldn't be out here if Pierre hadn't put that notice up, I thought ruefully. Jabbing my trowel into the ground I heard the pop of a young dock root and lifted the weed out with satisfaction. *I never do things unless I'm* "*supposed to*," I realized with surprise. I tended to do what was "expected" of me because I wanted to please or be considered "good," not because I wanted to do the right thing.

Glancing over at Emily, I watched her scrawny little body bent over, intent on her patch of ground. She had no agenda, she never felt put-upon when asked to help. Instead, she would set herself to the task, her whole attention taken by what lay in front of her.

With some chagrin, I saw myself in comparison with Emily. I couldn't keep my attention so focused. In fact, unless I was doing something for myself, I just tried to get it done so I could get back to what I wanted to do. And if the chore took a long time, I would spend it thinking about other things that interested me more. This was the reality of myself when I wasn't under the scrutiny of someone like Mrs. Popoff or taking part in a "work" effort.

Barbara June was humming to herself, plunging her hands into the dirt, dropping weeds onto a pile at her side. She sat back on her heels, cocking her dark curly head, listening to a bird chirping. A smile brightened her angular face and she looked up at the garden wall, exclaiming in a delighted tone, "Oh, there you are! Hello." She bent diligently back to the weeds, humming.

Even though the sun was shining, the air was crisp with a damp scent of moist earth and fallen leaves. I dug and pulled, wishing I had a basket to put the weeds in instead of leaving them in messy piles on the ground as I moved forward. It was nice out here, although the thought that I could have been inside, writing in my journal or washing my socks, irked me.

I started thinking about not looking for things to do unless they were assigned, not offering help on my own initiative, my laziness in getting to work sites on time. I saw with a shock that these were habits, the results of ingrained attitudes. Attitudes towards my own inner work. *So, do I really want to work? Do I really want to change?* If not, why had I traveled all this way to be here?

This was the first taste of what I was up against here—myself!

PART THREE

THE SECOND BASIC COURSE

> Progress in self-perfecting is not automatic; it requires use of the right methods and the determination to persevere against all discouragement. Very few people can achieve it alone; and, for this reason, 'Schools of Wisdom' have existed from time immemorial to provide instruction and to create environments in which all can contribute to the common aim.
> —J.G. BENNETT

CHAPTER TWENTY
Entering the Stream

The few students from the First Basic Course who had been invited to stay to help prepare for the Second Basic Course had departed. Jack and I, along with others arriving early to lend a hand, were now assimilated into a much larger group of approximately one hundred. This was the morning of the start of our Course and of things being different—I could feel the shift. Not only was the morning exercise going to be forty-five rather than thirty minutes long, but there was a gravitas in the air that I had not felt in all the preceding days since we'd arrived.

Mr. Bennett strode the long aisle between two silent masses of sitting figures on the floor of the ballroom. Impossible as it was to see another face in the black velvet of early morning, I could feel the crackle of excitement and hear the thrum of expectant silence.

At the far end of the room he turned, a gray shape looming tall and straight above us. "Please stand," he said, his voice floating down the length of the still ballroom in his clear, precise British accent.

After a pause to allow for energetic rustlings to cease, he said, "I would like it if those who can, would sit on their heels rather than cross-legged on the floor. I have been practicing this myself and find it most helpful in keeping the spine straight, which is a great benefit for us in this work with Morning Exercise."

Mr. Bennett's figure, seeming to float mist-like above us at the end of the room, suddenly plummeted downward in one motion and disappeared amidst the sea of dim figures. I rearranged myself into this unfamiliar position together with the women around me, moving my cushion so that I knelt on the bare floor with the bolster between my calves and behind. I noticed the small of my back felt relaxed and straight. This was an improvement from sitting cross-legged and struggling with drooping shoulders and collapsing spine.

After leading us through a relaxation and sensing exercise, Mr. Bennett rose upright in one swift movement. We had been sitting on our heels for forty-five minutes. I could barely feel my legs; they were so full of pins and needles it was hard to tell which were the moveable parts. At last I stood, little black spots dancing in front of my eyes, blood rushing to fill my legs. I heard a loud thud. A shadow on the men's side of the room had toppled out across the aisle separating us. Someone had fainted.

Mr. Bennett's disembodied voice rang out, "As we stand here, we acknowledge the higher part of ourselves, our own real 'I,' the first *ruku*."[1] He bowed, his back a straight parallel to the floor, hands on his knees.

We followed suit in the pale cream light of the newborn day. He stood, abruptly. Presence radiated from his posture.

"To that which is the same in all of us," he said. Announcing, "the second ruku."

In unison, we bowed with Mr. Bennett, rising together when he said, "And up."

"To that which we do not understand, but from which Great Source we ask for help with our Work today, the third ruku," he said, and bowed the third time.

In deep silence we bowed and rose and stood unmoving as Mr. Bennett's long legs took him out of the room, never breaking stride as he stepped over the fallen student.

It felt like a gong had sounded, heralding a journey that this group of students, the Second Basic Course, had embarked upon together. A year that would be unique to us as a group and to me personally. A year that would not be a carbon copy of the First Basic Course, in which the students had to cook in an ill-equipped kitchen and deal with unreliable plumbing but had not been asked to sit on their heels.

---

[1] Ruku: Islamic ritual bow, an essential pillar of prayer

Mr. Bennett's teacher, G. I. Gurdjieff, was a master of the unexpected, skillful at stripping away a student's expectations and assumptions in order to "dig deeper," as Mr. Bennett would call it. Pop psychology and political correctness had yet to take hold of society. A student was lucky to find a true teacher and when he did, it was understood that he or she placed themselves under the direction of the teacher, even if it involved hard knocks. A true teacher helped their student go beyond personality rather than inflating their own. One could discriminate between the two only with experience.

Rather than rush to the side of the student who had fainted, Mr. Bennett knew it would be better for the student and for all of us not to be drawn into unnecessary drama. The student would recover his circulation and the rest of us would not invest the results of our morning sitting on becoming identified with needless expressions of concern. We were here to work in ways we were not accustomed to.

CHAPTER TWENTY-ONE
Inaugural Address

October 15, 1972—"This way," I said to Jack as I wrapped my hand around his and pulled him to sit up front on a floor cushion. I knew he would have hidden on a chair in the back of the room, but I wanted to be able to see and hear Mr. Bennett give his talk. Rows of chairs had been set up facing the bay windows in the ballroom behind the array of cushions.

Mr. Bennett sat in his signature straight-backed wooden chair with faded red velvet upholstery, his hands draped over the scrolled, wooden arm-ends. Eyes closed in thought, lips pursed, his expansive brow was bent as we filled the room. Students and staff alike gathered to hear Bennett's Inaugural Address for the Second Basic Course.[1]

Two days ago, the last few experienced people remaining from the First Basic Course had left as the new student body poured in. We were truly on our own now. One hundred bright and expectant countenances faced the front of the room. I looked around for the seven familiar faces who had come with us from Mrs. Popoff's group in Long Island. They were scattered among the multitude of strangers.

Scraping chairs, rustling fabric, hushed whispers all came to a halt as Mr. Bennett picked up his head and opened his beacon eyes, scanning the room with a toothy grin that set off his white hair, bushy brows, and mustache. Satisfied, he closed his eyes again, the atmosphere in the room growing still with him.

"Why have we come together, and what do we hope to do in the year we

---

[1] Adapted excerpts from John G. Bennett, "Inaugural Address: Second Basic Course," *Systematics* 10, no. 4 (March 1973) Estate of J. G. Bennett, 2009.

shall spend together?" he said, raising his head to look up at us. "There are two questions to be answered: What kind of person do I want to be, and what kind of world do I want to live in?

"Each one of you knows that there is something you have to find out about yourself, about how to become what you ought to be. And yet a veil hides a great part of what we most need to know."

Mr. Bennett paused, looking carefully around the room. His gaze enfolded me. I knew these deep and unformed questions, this feeling of helplessness at not knowing who I was or how I could become a better person.

He continued, "One thing we shall try to do in this course is to face this question together and see for ourselves something which cannot be conveyed by words, but only by an inner vision of the emptiness in us and how we are to pass through it and find the Reality that is beyond it."

Bodies stirred like fledglings ruffling up their feathers anticipating the glories of flight, perched together on a limb, their feet still clasping tight to the branch. In a matter-of-fact tone Bennett went on, "The work is traditionally divided into three phases, which we call the exoteric, mesoteric and esoteric. By exoteric, we mean coming to terms with the outward problems of our own nature, coming to know ourselves, to know how our bodies and our feelings and our minds work, to learn how to control ourselves."

Closing his eyes, he fell silent for a long moment, as if looking inward, remembering his own experience, saying, "We come to the mesoteric phase, when we seek to penetrate more deeply into our own nature and understand for ourselves how it is that we are not in touch with our own reality. The divine seeing in us has to be awakened." Sucking in a long breath, he continued in a deliberate voice, "Then we begin to face the real problem and see that it is this blindness which is the cause of fear and lack of confidence in ourselves. This is what produces all the foolish manifestations in the world—vanity, pride, greed. Facing this is our gateway to reality. Far from fearing it, it is through that gate we have to go."

His demeanor resonated with a familiarity so conversational and so sure that it seemed all this was quite straight forward, just a matter of fact. Obvious, of course, to be speaking of divine seeing and the gateway to reality. I had no way of knowing that I would indeed experience everything he spoke of within the next ten months.

I looked at his broad brow, creased with the concentration of choosing the right words, his rumpled pants and old houndstooth jacket, wrists sticking out of the sleeves, and felt the sincerity of his wish to impart what he understood so well, the difference between seeking reality versus living in a world of appearances.

"Those who can, will come to the point where they will enter the world of Reality. This is called the esoteric phase. Whether it takes ten months or a whole lifetime, that is a successful life in the objective sense, in the cosmic sense."

Jack was sitting next to me, radiating like a sonar picking up a long-lost signal, his domed forehead smooth, taking it all in. I looked around the room and spotted Aisha sitting not far away, her face upturned, lips slightly parted, paying close attention. I saw Pierre Elliot, the Frenchman with the close-cropped beard lining his jaw. He was sitting on a chair towards the back of the room, smiling slightly to himself in what looked like recognition of Bennett's meaning.

My attention went back to Bennett as he was saying, "What kind of world is it that we want to live in, for our children and our children's children? The people who live in the world now are not facing reality. We stumble from crisis to crisis, the larger the organization the worse is this tendency to avoid the big issues. If only we were prepared to discipline ourselves and not grasp at everything. But nobody is willing to give because they fear to lose something, they have become attached to quantity." He shook his head with pressed lips.

Then he looked right at us, light shining from his eyes. "Value is not in 'how much' but in 'how real.'"

I hung my head, afraid he might be looking at me, realizing I had never gone hungry, that I had a closet full of clothes at home. I glanced over at Jack, remembering how he never drank the last sip from a bottle being passed around, or took the last cracker from the box, because he might need to offer it to someone else. I'd grown up with admonishments of, "Finish it up, make room on the shelf for more."

I looked up at Mr. Bennett and was surprised to see no sign of accusation. Instead, he was smiling kindly at us and saying, "You have all come here thoroughly conditioned by this grasping world. If you are not willing to struggle with this and to get free from it, how can we have anything which would appear to show what the world could be?

"In accepting you, I tried to arrange it so that we had people as varied as possible, with varied ages and varied types, varied positions in the world."

I swiveled around on my cushion, peering at the room full of strangers, the majority of which looked young, many looking liked hippies, like me and Jack (although I didn't really consider myself to be a hippie, just a lover of hippies). I knew there were a lot of people here from different countries, and I had no idea from what walks of life, even if the majority looked college age.

I twisted back as I heard Bennett say, "In this little world that we have here..." He was posing the question whether we could live at Sherborne in a way that would teach us to be satisfied with having just enough, so that there would always be enough for everyone. But then he added, "That will be possible only if we deny ourselves."

I caught sight of Mick Sutton, who had accosted almost everyone as they arrived, demanding to know if they were vegetarian, and if so, giving them notice on the spot not to expect to be catered to. He was standing at the edge of the room leaning nonchalantly against the eggshell blue wall, arms crossed over his chest with a bemused look.

Mr. Bennett was taking another turn on the path he had started. I recognized what he was saying next as a fundamental principal of the Gurdjieff work. "One cannot be a satisfactory human being so long as one is dominated by likes and dislikes, by attraction and aversion. If there are people here to whom you feel attracted and other people to whom you do not feel attracted, then we would ask you to turn your attention to these latter. If there are jobs to be done that you would prefer to avoid and jobs that you would like to do and that fascinate you in some way, then give special attention to the jobs you dislike and try to do them very well."

Bennett turned a stern eye on us. "If you are not prepared to do this and do not remember it constantly, you will be wasting your time here. Let us say some food is put out to be taken which everyone wants to eat and enjoy. But if those who come first take more than their fair share and those who come last do not get any at all, then you are repeating the characteristic behavior of the whole world. If we wish for a just world, then our own actions must be just."

There were nods of agreement from heads here and there around me, everyone looking earnest and sincere. We were all ready to do our part to make the world a better place. Beginning right here, right now.

Scanning the room again as if to inventory us all, Mr. Bennett said, "I look around and see a lot of nice faces. I think it would be very much easier if there were a few real monsters here." With a conspiratorial grin he added, "We have all of us got a monster hidden somewhere, so that maybe we can manage without any imported monsters."

He paused a long moment, eyes closed. Then, "The work has to come from within. It has to come from our own need, our own decision."

J.G. Bennett. Photo courtesy of J.G. Bennett Foundation, taken by Avis Rappaport.

The day's fading red and gold rays filtered through the tall windows behind Mr. Bennett's chair. By diffusing my gaze, I could see a nimbus shining through his white hair.

Popping his eyes open he continued, "Some of the people from last year's course said they felt sorry for you because you wouldn't arrive in a stone-cold house with the kitchen ceiling collapsed and only one broken-down stove to cook for a hundred people. They feared that you wouldn't know what the life here was like." He shook his leonine head. "I don't think that is necessary every time.

"We have got the Stable Block in front of us as a challenge and we have a lot of work to do both inside and in the garden. Every one of these jobs provides an opportunity for acquiring skills, improving attention, learning to work with other people, learning to work on all your functions.

"We will do a good deal of work with Gurdjieff's Movements. These are beautifully designed for developing not only the bodily powers, but complete balance of mind, body, feelings, and will.

"You will also have history and psychology classes with Dick Holland."

I glanced around and saw a small man sitting stiff and straight as a rod on a chair along the side of the room. He looked quite elderly and frail. Also quite military, almost as if he were wearing jodhpurs and carrying a switch to slap against his leg. I wondered what kind of teacher he would be. Then I turned my attention back to Mr. Bennett, who was finishing up.

"If we can't come to the point where we have no barriers between us and different kinds of people; between us and different kinds of activity, where it's all the same thing to be a dustman or a prince, unless we attain that, we are not free."

"Sounds like the stuff we've been doing here for the past month," I whispered to Jack, leaning towards him, my hair falling over his shoulder.

Mr. Bennett rose from his chair, beaming what I later came to think of as his Cheshire Cat grin. He concluded the inaugural address with, "Shall we get on with it, then?"

CHAPTER TWENTY-TWO
Now It Begins

Jack and I walked out of the ballroom, found our shoes, and went to look at the bulletin board. There was already a number of curious people crowded in front of it. Luckily, I was wearing my wire-rims so didn't have to stand six inches away to read what was tacked on the board. Jack stood behind me, a head taller. He pointed out our names under Group C. The first week's schedule ran like this:

Monday

First Bell:	6:00 a.m.
Second Bell:	6:15 a.m.
Morning Ex:	6:45 a.m.
Breakfast:	7:30 a.m.
Period I:	8:30 a.m.—Theme meeting, all groups
Period II:	10:00 a.m.—House Duties-Group C
Period III:	11:30 a.m. House Duties continue
Lunch:	1:00 p.m.
Period IV:	2:30 p.m.—House Duties
Tea:	4:00 p.m.
Period V:	4:30-6:00 p.m.—House Duties
Reading:	7:00 p.m.—Beelzebub's Tales reading, all groups
Dinner:	7:45 p.m.
Free:	8:45 p.m.

Breakfast, lunch, tea, and dinner were always at the same time, just as the Beelzebub reading was always at 7:00 p.m. Throughout the ten months, on every Monday, Period I was devoted to the presentation of a weekly Theme that Mr. Bennett presented. After dinner every Friday, at 8:45 p.m., a follow-up Theme meeting was held. That was when we shared a personal experience that we might have had related to the Theme, or asked a question. Every third day, each group took a turn being on House Duty. On the days we were not on House Duty, Periods I and II were scheduled as Garden or Practical Work, with various "classes" scheduled for the other periods of the day.

Tuesday

Period III:	Movements
Period IV:	Art
Period V:	JGB Talk
8:45 p.m.:	Movements

Wednesday

Period III:	Movements
Period IV:	Psychology
Period V:	JGB Talk
8:45 p.m.:	Movements

Thursday

House Duties—same schedule as Monday

Friday

Period III:	Art
Period IV:	Movements
Period V:	JGB Talk
8:45 p.m.:	Theme meeting- all

Saturday

Periods I and II:	Free
Period III:	History

Period IV:	Movements
Period V:	Free
8:45 p.m.:	Free

Sunday
House Duties-Group C

The day before a group was to be on House Duty, someone was quietly informed that they would be the House Supervisor. It was their job to assign all the duties and then troubleshoot any problems that arose. They would post the assignments after dinner.

We'd just finished eating, and I was leading Jack by the hand down the long hallway to see if our house duties had been posted. The evening was free, and I was looking forward to having time together, provided he wasn't on breakfast. "Don't you want to know what you're doing tomorrow?" I asked, when he didn't look at the board with me.

"Why do you worry so much about what I'm doing?"

"Because I know you too well," I said.

"You don't know me," Jack said. He pulled away, ignoring the lists and notes pinned all over the huge board. He headed down the hall to his room.

Damn! Why does he get so moody?

I stuck my tongue out at his back and peered at the newly posted House Duties list. There it was—*shit!* My name was next to the assignation, Breakfast Chief Cook. Another name, one I didn't recognize, which was most of them, was also assigned for breakfast.

Thank God I just did this the other day with Martin, at least I know what needs to be done. Chief Cook! My stomach tightened a bit at that thought, but I figured I'd better start asking around and find out who I was working with. We'd have to do the prep work tonight.

I scanned down the list to see what Jack's assignment was, hoping he'd be cleaning the second floor. All those sinks and tubs, not to mention toilets—that would serve him right! But then I saw it—he was House Supervisor. No wonder he didn't need to look at the board to know what he was doing tomorrow. *He could have told me. What's wrong with him?*

I went looking for my cooking partner. Sure enough, the person I was cooking with was brand new, I couldn't remember his name, but we set everything up like I had with Martin and things went smoothly.

CHAPTER TWENTY-THREE
Burnt Toast

The next morning the kitchen clock told me we had ten minutes to go before ringing the bell for breakfast. Then, Mr. Bennett and Elizabeth showed up.

"Bobby Jo, is there a problem? Morning exercise is over and everyone is lined up outside the Servery waiting," said Elizabeth, concerned. Mr. Bennett stood towering behind her and did not look happy.

"Oh, man. The oatmeal is done, we just need to get it upstairs," I stammered.

By the time I pulled the last pot of tea up on the dumbwaiter, all the toast was gone and there were still people coming through the line. Sweet Mary Cornelius, Mick's counterpart and alter-ego came to the rescue. She caught me running back down to the kitchen and came with me suggesting, "Let's just cut more bread, my dear, and serve it untoasted."

"Gosh, you're a lifesaver, Mary, thanks!" I was grateful, relieved that she had come up with a solution. I watched her expertly cut uniform slices and realized I had cut mine too thick, afraid they'd fall apart.

My sneakers made little sound on the wood floor of the dining room as I walked from one table to the next, offering the bread. I reached Mr. Bennett's table and leaned in, extending the plate. Looking up from his oatmeal, Mr. Bennett's eyes grew large, glaring at me. In a loud voice he bellowed,

"That's just what I told you not to do!"

I froze.

Sherborne Dining Room. First Course. Photo courtesy of J.G. Bennett Foundation.

Then several things happened at once. My pounding heart sent blood rushing into my face, my stomach took up residence in my feet, and my thoughts jumped in to the rescue.

Of course! Oh, thank you Mrs. Popoff! Mr. Bennett is "hitting me on the head" just like I experienced with you, just like Mr. Gurdjieff did with his students. He's not really mad at me.

All these thoughts wiggled through my head, hanging on tight as a kite string to my self-esteem. I knew what Mr. Bennett meant. He'd just talked about this last night. If the first students in line hadn't helped themselves to two slices of toast, there would have been enough to go around. What looked like abundance turned out to be finite. Now the lesson of taking less so there's enough for all was lost, because no one ended up going without.

Face aflame, I slunk away from the table, my heart thumping inside my head. Back down in the kitchen I buried myself inside the oatmeal pot, scrubbing with industrious zeal.

Sometime later Mick swung in, rummaging around, pulling out a bag of onions, a box of potatoes, getting things ready for the lunch cooks. I raised up from the sink, stretching my back. Eyes bright, he folded his arms, cocked his head to one side, and said, "Well luv, you certainly went down in flames. You aren't the first and shan't be the last, neither."

CHAPTER TWENTY-FOUR
Theme Talk

"Bobby Jo, you'll be late if you don't stop now," said Jack as he waited outside the Servery. Reaching up on tiptoe, I slid one more plate onto the shelf with a clink and closed the glass paneled cabinet, the door giving a little sigh and squeak as it wedged shut. We hurried downstairs to the Horse Parlor, Jack in the lead. Everyone was filing-in for the first Monday morning Theme of the course.

Mr. Bennett's straight-backed wooden chair was still empty. We settled ourselves, sinking down cross-legged onto a thin Persian carpet together with other course participants, everyone crowding onto the floor. Older staff used the few chairs lining dark wood-paneled walls. Just off the Great Hall, the Horse Parlor looked like a private library or study.

Mr. Bennett arrived. Folding himself into his chair, he took note of who was there. "Pierre, where is Mick?"

Just then Michael Sutton slipped through the door at the back of the room. "Here, sir," he called, a bit out of breath, having hurried over from the kitchen.

"Ah yes, then." Mr. Bennett closed his eyes for several long moments, then began to speak. "Every Monday morning, I will put before you one Theme with which you should, as far as possible, occupy your attention during the week when it is not required for the activities in which you are engaged. The main purpose is to have a direct perception of the real world to which the Theme belongs.

Meeting in the Horse Parlor, First Course. Photo courtesy of J.G. Bennett Foundation.

"The really important objective in the thematic technique is that it should give us the power to move in depth. For this, we have to accept and be convinced that there is more in simple things than meets the eye.

"You have to set the Theme before yourself in this way—that from Monday until Friday night is the time you have to penetrate into the Theme that I shall give you. I advise you to picture it to yourself in this way: that what you are looking for is really a world that you are not, in your ordinary state, in contact with.

"In our ordinary state we can see and touch things, we can think about them, we can reason with ourselves about them, we can compare our memories. This is not enough. It is a hard thing to accept, but it is really like that.

"This is impossible for people to grasp until they have experienced looking at it from another world and seeing how it is.

"Do you remember what Gurdjieff said about the two streams? There is the stream which flows automatically and is emptied into the nether parts of the earth. There is another stream which flows actively and merges into the boundless ocean. One is the stream of evolution. The stream of evolution is the stream of life, the stream of transformation. Our aim and hope is that we should belong to the stream of life, the stream of transformation. It is not enough 'just to wish and you cross.' For as Gurdjieff said, a long preparation and a great deal of hard work is required. This is what we have set ourselves to undertake here."[1]

Mr. Bennett stopped, looking carefully around the room at us. He had not been speaking from notes, and at times his eyes were closed as if he were reaching into a bank of vast knowledge. As he carefully chose his words, his hands worked the curved ends of the wooden armchair in which he sat.

Looking up out of his fathomless depths, Mr. Bennett said, "Right. This week we need to consider the world of Material Objects. When one comes in contact with a material object, what is one's relationship with that object? What does one know about it? What can one discern? How does it affect you personally? How do you affect it? Have you ever really considered this particular object before? Its Life; its Reality? This object which consists of living atoms, as we do? Can I come into contact with this object's reality?

"What is my relationship to Material Objects?

"This is the Theme I want you all to carry with you internally this week. Don't *think* about it but carry the question inside yourselves as you go about your daily tasks. The rest—the classes, the practical work, the household duties—these are merely the trappings of ordinary life. You can do those things anywhere. What is important here at Sherborne, is that you come to new understandings by getting out of the way of your ordinary habits of thinking."

I sat there, stunned. Here we were, a thousand miles away from home, living a cold, monastic-like life, and we were not here to give up material objects but to *understand* them? I listened intently, my assumptions shaken. How many revelations would come in the course of washing a hundred dishes and cleaning muddy garden tools. There was something here I hadn't quite grasped, but I felt was immensely important.

As we filed out the front and back doors of the Horse Parlor, I had that

---

[1] Excerpted dialogue: J. G. Bennett, "Material Objects: The Sherborne Theme Talks Series (London: Coombe Springs Press, 1977).

expectant feeling of a new horizon dawning in my understanding. It was just out there—behind the clouds, waiting to reveal itself.

We were trudging up the narrow staircase that would bring us to the main hallway and Jack's dorm room. It might be easier to understand my relationship with material objects than with Jack, I was thinking. It had been days since we'd had time together. He was silent, and I was irritated because he seemed preoccupied.

"So why are you angry with me?" I demanded as we reached the landing.

"Who said I was angry with you?" Jack's face was blank, but I could feel an uncomfortable distance between us.

"Well, you are, I can tell. And it's rubbing off on me, and now I'm getting mad and I wish you'd just cut it out!"

"I'm not mad at you," Jack said.

"If you're not mad, why am I? You started it the other night when you wouldn't look at the bulletin board." I could feel my heart thumping, the muscles in my shoulders tensing.

"What does that have to do with anything? You're the one who's mad, not me," he replied.

"That's not fair. I didn't start out mad, you're the one being distant and making me react."

"I'm not making you do anything."

"So, if there's something negative between us, you have nothing to do with it?" I turned in disgust and stomped the rest of the way upstairs past his floor to my dorm room.

CHAPTER TWENTY-FIVE
Dark Horse

I'd decided Todd was the most handsome guy on the course. He was tall, well-built, had dark hair and a chiseled jaw. He struck me as the outdoor type. He was older too, perhaps late twenties. We spoke at teatime. He told me he had a master's degree from the University of Pennsylvania.

Well-put-together physique, advanced degree—just the sort of guy my parents would approve of. Even though we'd only chatted once or twice, he was another student who seemed immediately familiar to me, like Aisha. In fact, he set off vibrations in me. What was that about? It made me feel like I had to be sneaky when I looked at him, let alone spoke to him, like I was betraying Jack. Was I? Jack didn't fit the silhouette of the future husband I had dreamed about as a kid; he wasn't exactly tall, dark, or handsome. Todd was all of that.

Wow, what if Todd is the man I'm supposed to meet? Maybe that's what's goin' on. I've never been drawn to good-looking guys before. Never felt like I could trust 'em. Like they'd be empty spiritually, like blondes are supposedly empty headed. So why is Todd different? I don't know, but it sure feels different. I'm getting goose bumps just thinking about him!

One day, passing in the hall, he looked at me. I was a lot smaller than he, so I looked up and chirped, "Hi."

Todd stopped, smiled down at me and said hi, like we knew each other.

I felt a little thrill go through me, something I wasn't used to. *Jeez, is he checking me out?* I wasn't used to that, either.

"Hey, man, you know, you just seem so familiar to me. It's like we've known each other from before or something." I looked up at him with my open face, my heart doing a little pitty-pat tattoo under my heavy flannel lumberjack shirt. People were passing us in the hall on their way to the next class session. For that moment we were a little island.

"Well, Bobby Jo? That's your name?"

"Yup."

"I expect that familiar feeling is just type recognition, it's normal in a big group like this," he said and moved on.

I blinked and walked down the hall, trying to remember where I was going. *What did he mean, type recognition? That we're compatible? Whoa.*

I remembered a very vivid dream from a few nights before. I'd written it down in my journal. I was riding a large muscular black stallion with flowing mane and tail. His broad back was as comfortable as an easy chair, secure and safe. There was no saddle or bridle, my fingers entwined in his mane, my legs gripping his sleek back. Our communication was nonverbal, he knew what I wanted and where we needed to go. Was this metaphor of a strong, dark horse a premonition about meeting Todd?

I shook myself out of the daydream and remembered I was on my way outside for Practical Work in the garden. I was not fond of working in the garden, had never liked doing yard work at home, raking leaves into piles on our suburban lot. Daddy loved to work outside, never coming in right away when Mom called at dinnertime. I'd rather do homework than drudge around outside.

In the kitchen garden the earth was damp from a recent rain, the air smelling of chicken shit and rotted greens, which were mounded in composting piles. The deep-rooted dock weeds were easy to pull. I was getting a lot done. I picked up a stray potato lying in the path and pitched it into the thistles growing alongside the stone wall. As it left my fingers, the Theme jumped to mind. My relationship with material objects. I realized, too late, that there was nothing wrong with that potato, it wasn't rotten or anything. Someone may have left it there to take back to the kitchen.

A small wave of sadness washed through me. Poor potato. I remembered Mrs. Popoff telling us last summer that the life of the food we eat consciously can be transformed in us for its own evolution. Now the energy of that potato will be "food for the moon" as she called it. Instead of being part of a greater transformation in one of us, it will decompose. Dust to dust. Compost.

On Wednesday morning, our group was working in the Stable Block during Practical Work. I hadn't been out there since before the course started. We were sanding the spackled walls in preparation for painting. It was tedious work. My mind wandered, thinking of handsome Todd, wondering what it was about my "type" that recognized his type? When it came down to it, my physical type was much more like Jack's, short and slight. I always felt comfortable being around Jack. Maybe that was it, we were too much alike—did that mean my type recognized that Todd was the "opposite type"? Because opposites attract? Was he the dark horse of my dream, or was it a part of myself? It hadn't occurred to me that the horse could be an aspect of myself.

I concentrated my attention into my hands to stay present. Stroking the plastered drywall seam with the flat of one hand, I was aware of the contrast between the heat of my palm, its sensitive skin, and the cold sharpness of the bumpy plaster. My other hand held a small rectangle of wood with fine-grade sandpaper wrapped around it. Sanding an area with one hand I could feel the change with the other hand, guiding my strokes until the seam was smooth and even. Too little sanding and the painted wall would look raised, too much and the wall would have depressions. I sensed my hands and became aware of the action of the sandpaper on the spackled drywall, feeling the rough spots smoothing away.

Suddenly there was a relationship between me, the sandpaper, and the wall. For a brief moment, I *knew* these material objects—like they'd come alive. I felt the presence of the wall, the interaction of the sandpaper guided by my hands. The rough sandpaper block, the smooth wall, my sensitive hands. Each its own entity, each alive; all of us communicating back and forth.

CHAPTER TWENTY-SIX
Material Objects

On Friday evening I stuck my head into Jack's dorm room. "Hey Jack, you ready?"

Jack was standing in the middle of the room, juggling lacrosse balls. One of his roommates, a balding cerebral German concert violinist, was looking at a pile of assorted two-by-fours he'd collected next to his bed to make a desk, he said. Another was standing by the fireplace, gazing at it. Van was lying on his bed, reading a book.

"What time is it?" Jack asked as a ball sailed over his shoulder and into his long fingers.

"It's time to go. The Theme meeting starts in ten minutes."

"Okay." Jack caught two balls in one hand and the third in the other.

We stepped into the broad corridor and streamed along with everyone downstairs to the Horse Parlor.

Mr. Bennett's chair—with its curved arms, red cushioned seat, and straight wooden back—faced us at the head of the room. It took a while for all ninety-plus of us to squeeze in and get situated. We quieted down, expectant.

Mr. Bennett swung open the door behind his chair and in two strides was seated. For several hushed moments he sat quietly, then raised up as if from a reverie, looking deliberately around the room. Leaning back, he smiled his Cheshire grin.

"Well then, who has something to say?"

A strapping eighteen-year-old with red hair spoke up. "I was on p.m. service Wednesday night, washing the dishes. Carrying a stack over to the sink one of the cups fell off and smashed on the floor. All of a sudden, I remembered the Theme. As I was sweeping it up it came to me that someone had made this cup, it had been 'born' so to speak, with a mission to serve as a vehicle for sustenance. I felt like I had killed it. Now, when I wash the dishes, I handle them with more attention. Almost reverence."[1]

Bennett nodded slightly and looked about the room. "Who else?"

Someone raised his hand and launched into a preamble leading up to their observation. Mr. Bennett interrupted, "No, one just needs to describe the experience. Who else?"

One of the British students raised his hand. "I had some pretty unpleasant revelations this week. I always thought that I was not attached to material objects, but I found quite to my dismay that I am very attached. It was 'my' pitchfork. If I were using a particular towel to dry dishes, it was 'my' towel. I found a fierce possessiveness which I did not know existed in relation to objects. It was astounding!"[2]

Mr. Bennett answered, "We use this word 'my' and never stop to ask ourselves what it could possibly mean. In what sense is this 'my' chair? What kind of relationship have I got to a chair? Really there is something about our relationship with material objects which ought not to have this word 'my' in it. Yet we are so accustomed to it that it is difficult to picture ourselves in a world where we do not have 'my.'

"It is partly connected with our emptiness. We cannot say that we own ourselves. We do not want to admit that. Therefore, we must say we own something."

Another hand went up, "I have this feeling that we are inextricably bound in this problem of having to pay for the way we are in relation to the world. Today I had to go to Northleach and I went by automobile. I realized that the world is becoming such that even though we know the automobile is harmful, we seem to be fully dependent on it. Even if we do not own one ourselves, we use buses and trains, or planes, or use a lot of

---

[1] Note: unless referenced, dialogue is created for illustration or from approximate memory.
[2] This quote and the following dialogue is excerpted from "Material Objects: The Sherborne Theme Talks Series," 17–28.

electricity. We are caught up in this, and as a result, who is to pay for it and how?"

"Do you remember in *Beelzebub's Tales* where Beelzebub's grandson, Hassein, speaks of this in the chapter on becoming aware of duty? 'What has been involved in our being able to live in the way that we do and what debt have we incurred as a result of this?'" Mr. Bennett paused, closing his eyes and exhaling a slow, whistling breath out through his teeth.

"Eight or ten thousand years ago people discovered that it was possible out of seeds of grasses to obtain the seeds of primitive wheat. From this, one could get nourishing flour. A whole process was discovered. Try to think of a state of affairs in which people did not know about this. Then they discover that not only can they take the grains and chew them, but they can dry them, grind them, and cook them. This provides man with something exceptional for his whole existence, his body and his psyche also. What do we owe to the people who found all this out? How do we pay for all the things that Hassein expresses in a few sentences? Did you connect what you were saying just now with that reading?"

"Yes" was the simple reply.

Mr. Bennett continued, "It is an important thing when we connect one thing with another. This is the way that it begins to turn into understanding. Here I am. I am able to go to London and come back in the same day. I was able to be with you at the exercise this morning and come back to have three meetings with you in the afternoon. For this to be possible mankind has become involved in a terrible tangle of all the consequences of this rapid locomotion: the destruction of the land, the pollution, and the waste of resources. There are also extraordinary advantages in rapid locomotion and communication. What have we incurred by being in that situation?"

Someone I recognized from my group raised her hand, and Mr. Bennett nodded at her, "After we left the Theme meeting last Monday, I went up to the second floor to mop. As I was mopping, I was aware of how worn with human hands the mop handle felt. I wondered how many people had used this mop before me, and I felt a bond with all of them. It then came to me that this mop handle had been a tree, and this phrase that we say at meals; 'All life is one,' suddenly seemed to make a good deal of sense. I had a different kind of respect for this mop than I had had a few minutes before, I thought about it a lot at the time, and since then, this feeling has come back to me occasionally."

Mr. Bennett nodded in recognition. "I said before that it is very useful, even necessary, to have these insights. They come just by a combination which allows us to come into a different kind of awareness. One minute it is just a mop, and the next minute you see it. You see its history. You see how man and nature have combined to give this to you. The great thing is to see and to let this moment of seeing remain unspoiled.

"This is a good example of seeing. It is more penetrating than thought, because thought can only do one thing at a time, but insight can see the whole. If you have this moment when you see it in a piece of wood, the tree from which it came and the life which made this possible, then this is a true insight. If it came back to you a number of times, that is also good. But the great thing is not to spoil it by adding something to it."

I listened to the observations as they resonated with my own. I didn't know many of the students by name, yet we had something out of the ordinary in common. The term, "Material Object," would never again simply signify a "thing."

Around 10:00 p.m., looking at his watch, Mr. Bennett beamed at us and announced, "That will be enough for today. We meet for morning exercise at 6:45 a.m., is it? Good night, then."

CHAPTER TWENTY-SEVEN
Stepping Out

After Mr. Bennett left the room, it felt vaguely vacant, even with all our bodies packed together on the old Persian carpet. We began to slowly file out, Jack walking beside me. If this had been New Jersey on a Friday night, we'd be thinking about who to get together with, no matter how late the hour. This wasn't New Jersey. We were in the Cotswolds, in the middle of the English countryside. No cars, no cities, no friends to party with. We weren't ready to go to bed; there was too much energy in the air.

Instead of climbing the winding stairs to our rooms, Jack took my hand, which he didn't often do, and led me through the darkened ground floor to the kitchen service door. He pushed it open, pulled me outside and looked up at the moon. It was full and bright and familiar. Gazing at it, I imagined everyone at home looking at this same sphere from their side of the world. It was my first pang of homesickness.

The moon was so bright it illuminated everything around us, the fifty-gallon trash bins by the kitchen door, the empty stable yard and the brick octagonal shed in the middle. Thick gray Cotswold-stone walls enclosed the area, running out beyond to the kitchen gardens. Shining down on it all—glinting off stones, bins, and metal—the moon smiled in autumnal glow. We started walking down the driveway, our feet crunching on pea pebbles. Our hands exchanged warmth and energy. As we wandered down the lane toward Sherborne Village, I looked up at the moon and imagined my mom and dad looking up through the night sky at this same bright moon. It made me feel close to them, as if we could touch each other.

"Jack, do you miss your family?" The moon peeked in and out through boughs of shedding trees that overhung the road.

"Yeah, I guess I do," he replied, voice soft. "When I was in high school my mom used to lock me out of the house. I'd have to break in through my bedroom window to sleep at night. She thought I was a bad influence on my little brothers 'cause I got stoned. But yeah, I do miss her." The frayed hem of his striped bellbottoms picked up dry leaves and made a pleasant rustling as he shuffled along.

"You know, out of all four of your brothers, I think you're the most like your mother. At least, you have her nose, that's for sure," I said.

"Prominent people have prominent noses, as Sherlock Holmes notably said," Jack rejoined, smiling.

We crunched on in silence. I thought about my mom, coming all the way to New York to see me off at the airport, and how surprised I was to see Jack's mom there. She didn't drive and besides, she worked.

"Were you surprised that your mom got your friends to bring her to the airport to see us off?" I asked.

"Yeah, I never expected that! I guess she got over all the stuff about me being a bad influence."

"Well sure, I think she figures you're doing okay. Look, you got to England and all." I squeezed his hand, feeling close to him again after our tiff from the other day.

"Yup!"

"Whadaya think, should we go check out Harry's Pub?" I wondered aloud, as we neared the village.

"They call it the Social Club," Jack reminded me.

"Do you think we'll get in trouble?" I asked. The assumption that we were breaking the "rules" by leaving the property made me feel uncomfortable, yet reckless.

"We'll just stick our heads in and check it out," Jack replied.

"Okay." It almost felt like we were back in West New York looking for action on a weekend night. He used to take me to the On Tap, a local bar where his friends liked to hang out and play pool.

It took about five minutes more to walk to the Social Club along the narrow, deeply set road. The post office was the first house in town and the Social Club was next to it. Both were single-storied, low-slung, and had slate roofs. There was light and noise seeping out through the windows of the Social Club.

We stood in the doorway looking into a single rectangular room with plain wooden chairs and tables. Half the clientele had just been at the Theme meeting. Surprised, we walked into the noise and haze. There was no bar, not even a counter. Chairs lined the walls with a few crowded tables in the middle. People sat alone or in groups, most holding large pint mugs of dark beer. Cigarette smoke hung in clouds. A well-used dart board dangled on the wall, feathered darts sticking out of it and the wall.

We stood aside as a table was vacated and then sat down. It was hard to talk, since everyone was already doing that, pretty loud.

"What will it be, then?" A matronly woman asked, raising her voice in a business-like tone above the clamor.

"Do you have any mixed drinks?" I asked.

"What do you mean, mixed drink?"

"Uh, d'ya know what a Brandy Alexander is?" That had been my first experience of a mixed drink.

After some consideration she said, "Well, we could make you an egg cream. And you, sir?" She smiled at Jack.

"What kind of beer do you have?" he asked.

"Newcastle Brown and Guinness," she replied.

"I'll have the Newcastle," Jack said without deliberation. She nodded approvingly and was called over to another table.

"Eric Burdon's from Newcastle," Jack explained. "So that was an easy choice. You know, he sang with the Animals, and they did 'House of the Rising Sun.'"

"Oh, okay. I remember 'House of the Rising Sun.' That was one of the songs the guys I met up at Fish House used to sing when we had campfires on the beach."

I looked around the room recognizing fellow students but also noting older men and women, some with their children. Everyone was laughing and talking. One group huddled around the dart board, plucking feathered missiles out. I'd always thought darts was a kid's game, but these were serious players divided into teams, concentration furrowing their brows.

The only source of heat in the room came from warm bodies wearing worn tweed jackets and caps or woolen skirts and sweaters; cigarette smoke curled throughout, trapping exhaled molecules of illusory warmth. No one seemed to mind.

Jack's pint of Newcastle came, and he offered me a taste. It was room temperature, which meant it was cool but not icy. Golden brown in color, it slid down light and smooth. My egg cream, made of eggs, sugar and brandy, was thick and yellow, sweet and rich. I savored it slowly, taking little sips as my father had taught me to do during cocktail hours at home.

The walk back was quiet, our heightened state from the Theme meeting dissipated by alcohol. We held hands and spoke little. I left Jack at the door of his room with a light kiss and made my way down the now familiar corridors and up the stairs to my dorm room. My roommates were all asleep as I crawled into bed. I was happy to have had this stolen evening with Jack, but sorry the special energy generated from the Theme meeting had been squandered instead of internalized. It was like something precious had been spent on a night out instead of saved up for a larger reward. It made me feel a little uneasy, afraid I might be wasting the opportunity to find what I was looking for—which was the energy to transform myself into a balanced person instead of what felt like a bundle of false personalities.

Just what did I think would happen when I transformed—which I knew I wanted. That sex and fun would not matter? That those parts of myself would disappear? Or could my higher and lower parts all coexist? Could this be what Gurdjieff meant by, "the wolf and the sheep are both assigned to our care?"

CHAPTER TWENTY-EIGHT
Work On Oneself

"Yes?"

I half opened the door to Dick Holland's large room which he shared with his young daughter, tucked away in a corner of the house.

"Come in," Mr. Holland encouraged me.

"Hi, Dick, can I talk to you?" I asked, stepping inside.

He didn't correct my calling him by his first name but replied in his clipped crisp manner, "Of course. Here. Have a seat." He indicated a chair next to where he was sitting by a wave of his hand, a Capstan full-strength cigarette glued to his fingers, smoke curling around his head. He had a book on his lap and was sitting in a comfy-looking, old, wing-backed chair.

I pulled my chair up a little closer to his, squeaking along the old wood floor and perched. "Well, I'm having trouble with the morning exercises," I began, plowing right in. "It seems like the more we're given, the less I can do. I mean, every morning exercise gets more complicated, and instead of building something up, it seems to be breaking down. Like, you know, I used to think I knew what sensation was, but now I realize not only am I kidding myself about sensing, but the more I even work on relaxation, the more tense I become. Or at least the more I realize how tense I really am." I paused, catching my breath, looking at my hands clenched in my lap.

Dick nodded, a slight smile on his thin, sharp-featured face. "What you thought you knew when you arrived, you are not as confident about now, perhaps?"

"Yeah, I thought I knew how to sense. I thought I knew how to relax.

I thought I was prepared to do a morning exercise," my voice sounded squeaky, exposed, despairing.

"How do you intend to work with this, then," he inquired, not unkindly.

"Well," I stopped, surprised by the question. Dick sat still, pulling on his cigarette, allowing me time to look inside myself. What, indeed, could I do?

"I think all I can do is go back to working on relaxation and not worry about trying to do the exercise Mr. Bennett is giving us this week, even though I'd love to be able to open myself to Lord Have Mercy," I said. Relief trickled through me like a sip of hot chocolate now that I'd made a plan.

"Quite right. This is a big step for you, Bobby Jo. You must find your own beginning and start there."

I sat for a moment, a flood of sensation tingling in my hands as the tension ebbed. "Thank you, Dick," I said.

I left the room looking forward for the first time in weeks to the next morning's exercise. I was ready to let go of everything else and simply open myself to relaxation, working at my own pace, not worrying about whether or not I could "do" the exercise Mr. Bennett was teaching us.

Getting up with the first tolling bell at 6:00 a.m. was no chore. But scurrying down the cold hallway on bare wooden boards into an equally cold sink room was not my favorite thing. On my way back I passed Emily sitting on top of the hallway radiator, pulling her green sweater tight around her.

Since Mrs. Popoff had made a point about starting the day with ablutions, I did not mind splashing cold water ritualistically three times on each part of my body in the sink room. Starting with hands, then the eyes, snorting and blowing out from each nostril, rinsing each ear, gargling, splashing onto the throat, the base of the neck, rinsing from elbows down to hands, splashing onto my privates (which was messy at a sink), then the backside and tailbone, from knees to ankles and finally, feet. It didn't take long to get over being shy about nakedness, there wasn't time for that, but I was surprised other women just washed their faces and didn't perform ablutions like they were supposed to.

In the chilly air of the ballroom the cold water from ablutions made my skin feel alive and warm, tingling with the cold trapped in old stone walls. I sat inside my layers—long johns, wool skirt, cotton turtleneck, wool sweater, the white angora shawl I'd been knitting draped around me like a tent with its blue tassels. I understood for the first time in my life the English infatuation with real wool and my mother's exhortations to "dress in layers."

Concentrating, I felt the top of my head, becoming aware of my scalp, then scanned down over my forehead, noticing little tensions. It was the noticing that was important. Rustlings in the room from scores of people settling themselves was quieting down. For the first time, I let go of what I was "supposed" to do and feeling inadequate when the tensions I noticed got worse instead of "relaxing." Dick's words had released me, allowing me to move on, focusing attention from forehead to nose, around the eyes, down over cheek bones, to mouth, tongue, jaw; *whoa, lots of tensions there.*

This big cavernous room is so cold no wonder my shoulders are tense. Okay. It's just cold air. My jaw and shoulder released, little movements moving down my throat, letting go. I wasn't sure if the back of my neck was letting go, but awareness moved down from there over my shoulders, noting left shoulder tight, higher than the right. It dropped. Little prickly sensations moved down both arms. I followed them—a warmth down my upper arms, through the elbows, down the lower arms, inside my wrists; hands becoming alive, fingers tingling. Someone near me coughed, jarring my concentration.

I moved my attention back to the top of my head and concentrated, then swooshed down again more quickly over my face and scalp, down my neck and shoulders, coursing through arms; tensions melting, draining, flowing out warm through my fingertips. Back to my neck and down my torso, aware of chest and abdomen, then my back. Upper back, middle back, lower back. All kinds of little tight places. *Don't dwell on them.* Directing my attention, scanning downwards, moving the energy down and out of the body. Releasing or at least intending release of tight, tense muscles each time I noticed them and moving on . . .

Something twitched. *My hand, wow.*

I became aware of an itch on my scalp but was able to feel it without moving. The afferent-efferent (action/reaction) nerve pathway that Mrs. Popoff had taught us about, which normally we have no control over, hadn't followed its normal course. My hand hadn't automatically reached up to scratch my head where it itched. Something deeper, stronger, had called the shot. *So that's what it means, mastery over one's body. Not feats of strength but intention and the ability to be in charge of intention. If I intend to sit still and am Master of my body, it will be still.*

When I had read the book Jack lent me, *The Master Game*, by Robert de Ropp, the first crumb on my path had been gobbled up. That enticement eventually led to Mrs. Popoff, Mr. Bennett, and the course at Sherborne.

So, what did I want to be Master of? Easy to say, "Master of myself."

Now I was beginning to experience the difference between thinking and doing. This had the taste of something real.

CHAPTER TWENTY-NINE
Gratitude

It was Mrs. Popoff's birthday and I thought of her, pushing the heavy string mop from side to side on smooth cold flagstones, but then my mind wandered. *Why did they have to have metal buckets instead of plastic? They're so heavy, and jeeze, I'm going to have to lug this thing all the way to the back door each time to dump and refill. Who's supposed to be on the ground floor with me? Larry? Gary? Ron? John? That tall thin British guy—which one, aren't there two of them? They look kind of alike, short dark hair, short name, is it Ron or Don? No, Don's the hunky blond from Alaska. Oh, whoops, too much water, better wring this thing out more. God this mop is heavy! I wonder if Mrs. Popoff got the tape we made in time for her birthday. I hope they listen to it in the group meeting, I can picture them all sitting in the meeting room listening to our observations about this place. Cool—except for my voice, I sound so squeaky and artificial, yuk.*

"Oh, hi," I said looking up with a smile. *Damn, what is his name? I'll have to ask Jack. He'll know.* "Are you supposed to be cleaning with me?" *And where the heck have you been?*

"Hi Bobby Jo, yes, I'm on ground floor with you, but the House Super asked me to go help upstairs before joining you. Sorry I am late, how are you getting on?"

Man, I just love those British accents.

Clanging pots and muffled voices escaped the kitchen door near us. My stomach twitched as aromas of baking yeasted bread mingled with dirty ammonia water.

"Can I empty that for you?" Peter, as his name turned out to be, picked up the bucket and returned soon with fresh water. He set it down and watched me push the mop in narrow pathways here and there.

Blisters battling with my grip on the handle had simmered their way to the surface of my red hands, numb from cold mop water and ambient air. Any sensation in my feet had been lost in the chill of hard flagstones, my nose was sore from blowing, my shoulders ached from pushing.

"Excuse me, but may I?" He reached for the handle. "Here, try this."

He turned facing me and started moving slowly backwards, swinging the mop in wide arcs from side to side. "See, if you use your hips, you can take the burden off your shoulders and arms. Let the mop do the work." He was halfway down the hall; I had to run a little to catch up. "The secret in mopping is to use very little water." He stopped and dunked the mop up and down, then rung it out thoroughly, in sections rather than all at once.

"I'll go get another mop and we'll finish here in a trice!" Handing the mop back to me, he walked off down the corridor.

Prickles of sensation flooded into my hands as they relaxed their hold and began communicating with the mop handle. A vision of Mrs. Popoff came to me. In her checkered bib apron, sleeves rolled up, leaning slightly forward, she looked at me with deep brown eyes. I became present.

I became present, sensing my hands, raw against the stalwart wood; the mop and I both—here. We could work together. My lower back leaned in as my hips began to dance, swishing back and forth with the mop, shoulders untangling. Blood tingled inside my skin, my body enjoying the rhythm. I moved down the corridor, the heft of the mop an advantage as it swung back and forth of its own momentum, the breadth of thick strings covering wide arcs of floor. Here was the flow of mop, the dank smell of basement, the baking bread, roasting buttery carrots, and my attention returning over and over again to letting shoulders drop, grip loosen, the NOW replacing my self-pity.

A roaring appreciation filled me. *Thank you—thank you—thank you, Mrs. Popoff!* With tasks and tools, she had taught me to focus attention so I could see my mind wandering, hear the complaining, feel the expense of energy. Practicing sensation, I embraced the present moment and inhabited my body.

How could I begin repaying Mrs. Popoff for all she had taught me before coming here? What gift could I possibly give?

We did indeed finish our a.m. cleaning early, and so it was that I found myself upstairs turning by the ballroom, going down a quiet corridor to the Bennetts' flat.

Knock, knock. I waited outside the wood-paneled door, which looked like all the other doors. The only indication that this was the Bennetts' living quarters was the fact that there were no other doors nearby.

"Yes, come in!" I could hear Mr. Bennett's distinct British accent coming from a distance on the other side.

Surprised, I found myself stepping into a cute little apartment, complete with kitchenette and a living room where Mr. Bennett was sitting at a small table surrounded by piles of books and papers. He was working on a manuscript.

"Come in, come in." He looked up from his writing and smiled that toothy grin. The one where he looked at you, right into you, only you felt like he was looking through you because there was nothing solid in you for him to see, and you saw it too. And that was scary because he was always fully there, all of him—a presence emanating from everything about him. I began to worry that I'd better have a good reason for being there.

"Hi, Mr. Bennett, I—just wanted to ask you something."

"Yes, yes, what is it?"

"Well, it's Mrs. Popoff's birthday, and I was thinking about her and remembering all she's done to prepare us for the Work and feeling all this gratitude and I just want to do something to repay her—like take the emotion I'm feeling and redirect it somehow," I grabbed a breath, "and I'm just not sure how," I blurted out, realizing too late that maybe one didn't just barge in on Mr. Bennett.

Mr. Bennett's grin softened. He turned towards me in his chair, "Madam Popoff, a wonderful woman. Come, sit down."

I found a spot to sit and he looked at me intently and then gazed off into the past, "Madam Popoff is a Compassionate Idiot, you know."

"Well, she told us that Mr. Gurdjieff toasted her as a Compassionate Idiot when she was at one of his famous meals and they were doing the

'Toasts to the Idiots,' I acknowledged, filling in the silence. Without allowing Mr. Bennett time to speak I rushed on to say, "My problem is, I know I'm supposed to use my emotional energy for the Work. I'm just not sure how."

I waited. I was sitting on the edge of a rather old fashioned, tightly upholstered, uncomfortable couch. The room seemed messy, with books piled up on the floor and side table. Manuscript pages were sitting about here and there. I noted that Mr. Bennett seemed to own one old houndstooth jacket. The one with brown leather elbow patches, the one he had worn at the talk over a year ago in New York City at the Gotham Book Mart. The talk where I had turned to Jack and said, "We're going!"

"First, you must have Intention," Mr. Bennett was saying to me, giving me his full attention as he put his pen down gently. "And you must understand and recognize the difference between subjective emotions and objective feeling. We will work much more on that later."

He was looking intently at me, as if assessing what he might convey that I could take in. "For now, whenever you think of Madam Popoff and a feeling of gratitude arises in you, allow a Wish to arise in you also." He was watching me with a soft expression about his eyes, looking into me and yet at the same time within himself. The atmosphere around us seemed to vibrate a little. "Take this feeling of gratitude and *Wish* that the debt you owe her can be paid for with your Work."

Mr. Bennett's presence was larger than his six-foot-plus frame. The intensity of it imbued everything around him, including me, with immediacy. I was suddenly aware of my body sitting on his couch, of my hands resting in my lap, of my heart thrumming ba-bum, ba-bum, ba-bum in my ears and yes, of my breath threading into a little warm spot in my chest and out again into the electric air around us.

As I sat on Mr. Bennett's couch, love and gratitude towards Mrs. Popoff flooded into me, as if some pure form of Mr. Bennett's appreciation for her acted to magnify my own feelings. The warmth in my chest expanded and I felt something. Yes, I felt a *Wish* stir. A wish that, if spoken, would ask that my honest efforts at work on myself might go towards repaying the debt I owed her for all she had taught me.

A memory flooded back. The day Mrs. Popoff had taken me aside during a seminar. We were outside working. Everyone was busy with their practical chores for the morning.

She had said, "Bobby Jo, most people need to learn to bring their heart to their head. You need to learn to bring your dear little head to your heart." Smiling kindly, she added, "You have a big heart, you know."

I didn't know. And I didn't get what she was saying.

"I want you to stop whatever you are involved with this morning and go down for a walk along the beach. Come back at lunch and see me," she concluded.

I had been shocked. Profoundly touched. Mrs. Popoff really cared about me personally? What she was telling me wasn't making sense, but I knew it was important. I couldn't believe she was telling me to walk away from all the work that needed to be done and take time for myself. *Why me? Why did I need to go for a walk?* But she was my teacher, so there must be something to learn by doing this. I had never heard her tell anyone else to go for a walk in the middle of a practical work session.

I hoped no one saw me walking down the steep narrow lane to the water, gravel crunching under my feet. *What would they think? That I was special? No. That I was playing hooky? Yes.* I ducked my head, hoping no one was looking over the porch railings as they painted. At the bottom of the tree-draped lane I picked my way along the uneven stretch of beach, feeling unobstructed sunshine warming the top of my head. I cast about in my mind, confused about what I was supposed to do with this gratuitous time.

The acrid smell of the Sound left a vague salty taste on my tongue. I was feeling special and weird at the same time. Gulls screeched, gliding over the water. My mind darted about. *What does it mean to bring my head to my heart?* A gull landed near my feet, strutting. *Think! Think! What is she trying to tell me? Is this like, think before you speak?* Waves lapped at the narrow rocky shore. I gave up trying to figure it out. I lifted my face to the sun. I listened to the gulls. I watched the freighters plowing through the channel.

Mrs. Popoff was giving me permission to pay attention to my heart and my feelings. Something I never gave time to. Maybe she was telling me that rushing about, ticking off the 'to do' lists in my head and blurting out whatever floated foremost in my thoughts was short-circuiting my heart.

Like when I told my dad about boys I had one-night stands with because I wanted to clear my conscience. I guess he hadn't appreciated my confession. Mom took me aside and explained, "You know, your dad doesn't want to know *everything*."

I could see the problem, but I couldn't see the solution. I had always been this way. Maybe it had to do with my Scorpio sun sign, like Jack had said when he was first getting to know me. One day we were talking in the student lounge and I must have said something that stung because he'd stopped talking for a long moment and then said, "You know you say stuff like that but I don't think you mean to hurt people. I think you don't know you're doing it. Maybe it's to do with your sun sign." His face brightened a little as he looked out through the curtain of golden-brown locks framing his face and concluded, "So I've decided to like you anyway."

The better I liked someone, the more I wanted to be truthful with them. I couldn't help it.

I pondered, watching the sun fleck off the white caps as the gulls complained. It felt good to be doing nothing, with permission. I breathed in salt and sun and spray, something unhooking inside.

Mrs. Popoff had been behind what she called the Russian Kitchen when I returned just before lunch. She was sweeping the walkway with her old babushka tied around her head. Wisps of white curls still escaped to halo her face. I wasn't sure what to say. Resting her short, stout body on the broom, she observed my expression with her own liquid-brown eyes. She could see something had been working on me. There was still confusion, but there was something else too. Perhaps she saw a softness in me that had not been there before.

"You see Bobby Jo, the work we are doing here is to give you the tools you need to do the real Work with. We work along three lines. Work on Myself, Work with Others, and Work for the Work. You are beginning to see that you have your own individual work to do." She straightened up, her short-waisted back holding her presence, grounding her. "We all do," she had said adding, "You need to bring emotional intelligence into your speaking."

Capturing me with the presence her back radiated, she told me pointedly, "There is a saying, 'stupid sincerity; intelligent insincerity.' Think with compassion before you speak."

No resistance met her words. She was giving me truth and I was glad. This was what I was thirsting for. I wanted to discover the real me, good and bad. The leaves on the cement walkway had rustled, kicked up by a cool breeze as the enticing aromas of lunch wafted up from the kitchen.

I had drunk in her words and felt her empathy as she concluded, "For you, this will not be easy. It will be part of your own personal work of transformation."

Sitting now with Mr. Bennett in his flat, I sensed him sharing this long moment with his own memories of Mrs. Popoff. The silence was warm. She had trusted that Mr. Bennett's Basic Course would deepen our work.

The room was quiet, the sounds of other activity in the building muffled with distance. I could hear the clock ticking on the mantle. No one else seemed to be in the flat.

I sat still. Something like longing crept into my chest. I focused on it and it grew. Somehow pure, it didn't make my heart race or my throat swell with emotion. It subsumed the gratitude, blending it into this feeling alive in my breast. It was as if *Wish* spilled out, watering a seed Mrs. Popoff had planted and a tender green shoot was poking through.

In years to come, I came to understand how this sort of energetic alchemy could indeed pay back my debt to Mrs. Popoff within the cosmic world of energies. It could also feed something greater, an action alive in the world referred to as "the Great Work," an energy fundamental to the direction of Life on Earth.

Through Gurdjieff's teaching, I had the possibility of being an active participant. The Work would either utilize energy I created intentionally, now, through efforts at self-transformation, or "willy-nilly" with energy released at the time of my death.

The work we were embarking on at Sherborne was to gain the knowledge to transform our own automatic behaviors, to support each other as a group and to create finer energies for higher purposes. Work for Myself, Work with Others, Work for the Work. We could participate consciously and strive to be Real Human Beings or we could remain unconscious, automatic participants, jerked on strings pulled by invisible forces.

This school, the Basic Course, was an experiment Mr. Bennett had undertaken to share in ten concentrated months what had taken him a lifetime to obtain, which would take me the rest of my life to unpack. Mr. Bennett was helping me taste what was possible. My emotion had been transformed into something pure, a feeling, a *Wish*.

Faintly, brassily, the lunch bell was ringing. Feet clumped towards the dining room out in the hallway. I could sense the house marshaling for lunch.

"Thank you, Mr. Bennett," was all I could muster.

He looked deeply into my eyes, which must have been shining because they were full of tears. I guess I hadn't subsumed all the emotion after all.

He simply said, "Good. You may go."

CHAPTER THIRTY
Noticing

"Hey Bobby Jo, it's time to go to the Theme meeting. You better go ahead. I still have to change my costume."

"Okay, see you there." I was always amused by this one roommate's constant re-dressing for every event, which she always referred to as "changing her costume."

When I arrived at the Horse Parlor, I found Jack and settled on the floor next to him. Mr. Bennett came striding into the room and sat down in his chair. He looked around at us, then dropped his gaze, going inside somewhere we could not follow. His hands worked the curl at the end of the chair's wooden arms. I noticed Todd across the room.

Mr. Bennett looked up, smiling. He scanned the room, his gaze seeming to linger on me. Did he know about my feelings for Todd?

He spoke, "Noticing—who noticed this week?"

A few hands went up. Mr. Bennett nodded at one of Jack's roommates, a nice-looking young Brit with thick, curly, sand-colored hair who had the wholesome air of someone who'd grown up in the country. His father was a stone mason.

He began, "Well, I have been working on a project in my room, building a stone fireplace. I have to be very attentive in choosing stones that will fit together and look right. I noticed that when I am sensing my hands my attention is more active. This one stone did not seem to fit, and I had set it aside. However, as I worked with my sensation, I suddenly noticed the perfect placement for it."

Mr. Bennett smiled at the stone mason's son, a bit too broadly. "And this project in your room, of whom did you ask permission to build it?"

"Oh, no one, sir. I simply thought it would be a nice enhancement for our dorm room."

"No, no, my boy. This is self-will. You must dismantle it, immediately!"

The poor guy, he looked crestfallen. He had been laboring over his fireplace for weeks, in every spare minute, proud to show off his skill as a mason.

Mr. Bennett had allotted himself ten months to bring us to see ourselves as we were and beyond that, to taste what we could become without our habitual notions separating us from what was real in ourselves. A hard pill, but what we were there for.

Mr. Bennett gazed out across our faces again, "Now who here has worked with noticing this week?"

My hand went up. He nodded at me.

"I notice in my morning exercise that I've just been fooling myself, thinking I am doing it. But if I just let go of trying and go back to—"

"No, no," Mr. Bennett interrupted, his gaze including everyone. "You must come to me privately to talk about your morning exercise. Who else?"

The stone mason's sister, Jane, raised her hand.

"Yes," Mr. Bennett nodded, encouraging her.

Jane usually kept quiet. She was a pretty girl with an open face and an abundance of reddish-blond curls.

"I was on p.m. service yesterday. We were setting out the cups for tea and I noticed that several had not been properly washed and some were chipped. I also noticed that no one else had noticed and that my inclination was to carry on. But instead, I stopped, took back the dirty ones, washed them properly and replaced the chipped ones. No one noticed what I had done, but that did not matter to me. I saw what mattered was that I had noticed and then acted on it."

"Yes, Jane. Very good. 'Tis just so. When we notice, truly notice, it puts us in a different relationship, a different world, as it were, and we find we have a choice to act from a different place in ourselves. It is a kind of responsibility. The more we respond in this way, the more we are given to respond to."[1] Mr. Bennett smiled kindly at Jane and looked about the room again, asking, "Who else, then?"

As we were filing out of the Horse Parlor, feet shuffling, clothes rustling, politely waiting for this one and that one to pass through the door, Jack pulled me aside from the flow and said, "Wait."

I looked at him in surprise. We stood in the hall until everyone else had left and then went back into the room. It felt larger and colder without all the bodies. Jack closed the door. The few chairs pushed back against the wall were hard and straight, so we sat down again on the worn carpet. I brushed my hand over its red and gold colors, muted with time. Old leather books on the recessed shelves in the paneled back wall leant musty scents of dust and print. I sat cross-legged, curious, facing Jack.

From under a chair, he pulled out a roll of sketching paper and a small box of black charcoal sticks which he laid out on the floor. Stretching out next to them, fair hair hanging, he started working on a drawing without saying anything. I watched for a while, wondering why we were there.

Finally, he sat up and said, "There's something going on. You're drifting away."

Silence between us. The air cold and still, my hands numb.

We both felt it, a distance between us that was new. We'd had our squabbles in the past, but never a sense of disconnect.

I assessed the long nose that his face hadn't caught up with yet, the set of thumb and forefinger lightly holding a stick of charcoal. I thought of Todd; strong, handsome, masculine.

I sighed, "I don't know Jack, I'm kind of feeling attracted to Todd. I just keep noticing him. I think he's been noticing me. I don't know."

Jack didn't move. He didn't storm out of the room, he didn't react. He bent his head back over his work, hair screening his face.

"I was afraid something like this might happen." He put down the stick of charcoal and held up his hands, looking at them. "I can only juggle four balls."

---

[1] Jane's observation from Theme Meetings.

He counted off on his fingers, "Working on my Independent Studies for Livingston College, studying Bennett's Communication Tetrads, reading *Beelzebub's Tales to His Grandson*, practicing my juggling, spending time with you. That's five—but I only know how to juggle four balls. I put you down, and now you're rolling away."

After a pause he asked, "Do you think you love Todd?"

"Of course not!" I retorted. "We've only spoken a couple of times. I hardly know him." *But I bet my parents would think Todd a good catch, better than my usual hippie choices.*

"Let me tell you a story," Jack said, his tall brow creased. He sat up hugging his knees. "Remember I told you about Kathy?"

I nodded. I'd never met her, but I remembered Jack had mentioned her at times.

"I really loved Kathy. But then she started to drift away. And she waited too long to tell me what was going on. She thought she was falling in love with my best friend!"

Oh my God, really? Those two were like soul brothers.

"But she waited too long to tell me, and something in me choked off."

I was surprised to feel a sense of relief prickle up inside me. It evaporated as Jack continued. "By the time she realized she'd made a mistake, it was too late. I couldn't be with her anymore." With a strong look and in a quiet, flat voice he said, "If you go with Todd, you can't come back."

The house was graveyard quiet, and my hands were so cold I was clenching them in tight fists, my head bowed. I'd always known Kathy had been special for Jack. I never knew what had ended it. As I sat there thinking of Todd, something happened in the room. I looked up. Jack did too.

An energy field, a soft fluorescent pipeline, looped across the room shimmering as we watched, fascinated. I could feel it pulsing. It undulated like a floating snake and attached between our two navels. The energy felt thick, blood-like but held translucent colors sparking red, green, blue and gold—as if composed of aerial gems. Thoughts about Todd were still in my head, my feelings unsure. Suddenly the cord began to constrict as if it were a baby's umbilicus being tied off. The pulsing, vibrant colors, so alive with glittering lights a moment before began to dim in the middle—and it hurt! This living presence, our etheric connection, was being choked off. I felt the constriction as a pain outside my body but just as real.

Time had stopped or disappeared. Time was meaningless. Everything was *Now*, in the energy flowing between us, held in the hands of my thoughts and feelings. The pipeline responded by glowing or going cold and dim, depending on whether I was thinking about Todd or my feelings for Jack.

I couldn't stand the physical or mental pain of losing this tangible, ethereal connection with Jack. As soon as I knew this with every fiber of my being, the cord grew strong and vibrant again in response. And then we were sitting on the old carpet in the Horse Parlor in silence. No words were spoken. I had made my choice and our connection was restored.

Jack picked up his paper and charcoal sticks, and we walked back through the quiet night halls to our rooms and never mentioned what we had seen and felt, because everything had changed. Todd was no longer a contender.

How does one speak of a phenomenon that is not of the world you live in? Gurdjieff speaks of Higher Worlds with fewer "laws." Bennett speaks of other Dimensions and Time. Jack and I understood that we had experienced an event that was outside our ordinary frame of reference. Something had transpired between us that was real. The reality could only be cheapened by words, since we had no words with which to explain what had happened. Many years later, Jack confirmed that on that day he, too, had perceived the etheric umbilicus connecting us.

CHAPTER THIRTY-ONE
Mayvor

Sitting ramrod straight in Mr. Bennett's chair in the Horse Parlor, looking very thin and small on the high-backed throne, Dick Holland sat reading from Mr. Bennett's *Dramatic Universe* for our History class. Thirty people were sprawled out on the carpet in front of him.

Suddenly, a slurred and accented voice interrupted from the back of the room, near the door.

"Why you do this? Why all this read, read, read! Words, all words! Just *teory*—just talk! When we start doing something? When something *real* happen?!"

Dick looked up and replied sympathetically, "You must be patient, Mayvor." Unruffled, he bent his head, one finger tracing the lines back to his place in the text. He continued reading in his soft monotone.

Mayvor stormed out of the room, letting the door swing shut with a wooden thud.

She was thirty-three years old, compared to most of us twenty-somethings. Swedish born, Mayvor's muddy-red hennaed hair belied her past ten years of living in India. She gave the impression of someone barely surviving throughout most of her life.

Mick had met her in India. She was living on the street, telling fortunes to tourists. She must have heard him talking about Sherborne and Mr. Bennett, because she showed up on the doorstep after the course had started, insisting on admission, though she had little money.

What Mayvor did have was gangrene, malnutrition, alcoholism, and drug addiction. With no money and few possessions, she would often make home-made candy at night in the kitchen, helping herself to supplies and then disappearing for a few days. People thought she was going to London to sell her candy and get a fix.

The class carried on, but ten minutes later she was back, bursting into the room, her tough, ruddy face streaked with tears. We'd never seen this world-traveled gypsy upset before.

She was yelling, "Stop it, Dick—*Dick!?*"

The room went still.

Between the sobs and her accent, it was hard to make out what she was saying. Something about being trapped, about going in circles, about Sherborne being her last chance, and she had to start doing something about it—now!

Dick was looking from *The Dramatic Universe* to her and replied in an even, patient voice, "This is so for me also, as it is for you, Mayvor. But man cannot 'do.'"

I could barely make out her words, but the atmosphere was electric. There was a kind of horror in the air, her angst resonating, infusing me. I understood her urgency and was surprised to acknowledge a feeling of appreciation for Mayvor, a sort of backwards happiness for her.

She's the only one who gets it, who's truly ready for Sherborne, for Mr. Bennett.

Through her I was feeling the "Terror of the Situation," as stated in *All and Everything*. Tears drizzled down my cheeks as I felt the desperation of Mayvor's wish, a Wish to Be. To be something other than what she was. She no longer wanted to read about it, talk about it. She wanted to *Do* something about it. So did I, but she seemed ready to work for it. Was I?

It seemed something was shifting, as if a spaceship was gearing up for liftoff.

Dick Holland closed the book and stood up.

"Class dismissed."

He walked in his measured, stiff way up to Mayvor and guided her out of the room.

Our group sat still for several moments and then began to rise and leave. I rubbed my hands over my eyes, drying them before blowing my nose on a used handkerchief from my jeans pocket, then left the room with the others.

Our art instructor was in the hall making his way upstream to the door leading outside. He always wore colorful psychedelic patterned pants and wasn't much older than we were. With a large black portfolio under his arm, he was heading for the Orangery on the other side of the walled kitchen gardens, an old greenhouse utilized as the art studio.

"What do you do when you can't do anything?" I asked as we passed. It just came out like that; I don't think he even heard me.

I went to my Period II practical work session, but my heart wasn't in it. Something in me was blank. When Period III started and it was time to go to Art, I found myself wandering down the driveway in the opposite direction from the Orangery. I looked around at the brown leafless trees. Everything was brown, but the sun was still shining on the fields through the bare branches, throwing patterns on the gravel.

What was I feeling? Nothing. Just tight—dammed up inside. I wasn't doing what I was supposed to be doing, inwardly or outwardly. What was I supposed to be doing? Where could I go? I didn't know. I heard my feet crunching the gravel as I moved, aimless, down the drive. A sensation, layers of myself, started unraveling and falling away like the layers of an onion. When the last layer fell away, there was empty space at the core.

Oh God, I'm just, nothing!

Tears, wet and cold, slid down my cheeks. Overhead, the sky was bright blue, the autumn sun nearing its peak. It cast late morning shadows down at my feet. I looked and saw a little shadow. My shadow. There I was—substantial enough to create a shadow. So, there is something. If I was truly nothing there'd be no shadow. Gathering up hope together with my emptiness, I walked back to the house to hide in my room.

CHAPTER THIRTY-TWO
Gerald

I couldn't bear the thought of going to tea with everyone that afternoon, so decided to visit Gerald Wilde. He was the crazy, wild-looking old man I had glimpsed around the laundry room. I needed to talk to someone who could understand me. I couldn't understand myself right now but had a feeling Gerald could.

Gerald was a famous artist who had some kind of non-verbal connection with Bennett's ideas. He expressed them in tapestry-sized, brightly painted, expressionist works. Some of them hung on the walls in the halls of Sherborne.

I walked out the back kitchen door, past the garbage bins lined up along a ten-foot-wide stretch of ancient stone wall. The wall continued all the way out to the kitchen gardens, dividing the formal expanse of back lawn from the service entrance at the side of the manor. A wooden door set into the gray stone wall had a hand scrawled sign on it that read: DO NOT KNOCK OR ENTER.

I knew others had visited with him. Standing there, I stared at the sign. Finally, I just yelled out, *"Gerald!"*

The door opened. His eyes were a bit weepy and bloodshot but alert. His gray hair was thin, longish, and combed back off a balding forehead. He was short and stocky but not fat. His clothes were rumpled, of course.

"Hellu."

"Hi, Gerald. I'm sorry, but I didn't know what to do."

"You did all right."

"Oh, okay."

"Here, come in, then."

He led the way, shuffling with quick little steps into his shed-like home in the wall. I followed.

A little pot-bellied stove kept some warmth in the old stone walls and there was a wooden table and a couple of chairs, but mostly it seemed cluttered yet sparse. He had what he needed—a solitary space to create his art.

He sat down in a straight-backed chair and I sat down in the other. The wood stove put off a comfortable heat, which felt good in the cold air of the room. There were large drawings on the table, sketches of crazy ladders or maybe the backs of chairs. I couldn't tell and it didn't matter. I just liked being there with someone I didn't have to make sense to.

"I saw you in the laundry room once," I ventured.

"Yes." He sort-of looked at me with one eye, the other looking in another direction.

"I'm kind of confused," I continued. "I just needed to visit you."

"Well, here, let me show you this." He rose and shuffled over to the table. Too bad, my back had just gotten nice and warm. I stood up and looked over his shoulder. The sketch had bold lines; it felt a bit wild but connected with lots of movement, direction too. It affected me in some way I couldn't explain, something about lines that weren't straight.

"So, there is something here, right Gerald? Something'll actually come of all this?" I fluttered my hand at the Cotswold stone, indicating Sherborne House and the course. I had come here to be transformed, to become a good person, a Real Human Being. Wasn't that what all this striving was about? "I don't want to, you know, just end up like this—the same old Bobby Jo."

"How do I know?" He was looking out of those cockeyed eyes.

Of course—how could he know how I'd end up? He was far from being a Realized Being. He was an alcoholic and half-crazy and all.

We bonded right then. There was room for me in his otherness that conventional standards did not allow for. Gerald knew something about the "unconditioned world of potentiality" Bennett talked about, and I was just starting to find out things weren't always as they seemed.

"Would you like some tea? I was just about to make some."

"Oh, thank you! It is teatime, isn't it?" Sitting back down, I looked around. There was a bed in the corner, and wooden boards lined the wall behind the stove for shelves. Paint cans, brushes, pencils, paper, all seemingly strewn about—it looked like a workshop that he slept in.

"Gerald, do you like it here?" I asked.

"Oh yes, it's so nice and quiet, no one disturbs me. Of course, you students come by on occasion. That's all right."

He took the kettle off the wood stove, poured hot water into the teapot, swished it around and dumped it back into the kettle. Spooning measured black tea leaves into the teapot, he poured the boiling water back into it.

We sat in silence while the tea steeped. He got up again and poured the pungent smelling tea into two thick cups.

"Do you take milk and sugar?" he asked.

"Oh yes, please. One lump is fine."

"There, then," he said as he dropped a lump of sugar into the steaming cup and poured the milk. He handed me my cup and saucer with a spoon.

"Thank you, Gerald," I said feeling welcome and warmed, stirring the sugar and watching the white milk swirl. We sat in silence and I sipped from the rounded lip of the sturdy white porcelain cup. Something in me shifted, settling. Here was someone I didn't have to explain myself to, with whom I could just *Be*.

I looked into the bottom of my teacup and asked, "Gerald, can I come visit you again?" And looking up added, "When I need to?"

"Oh yes, anytime. Except not when I'm working, you know."

Somehow, I knew I would know.

"Thanks. I think I'd better be going now."

Stepping outside into the late afternoon of the English fall, I realized that Gerald's door was framed within a larger opening. The original doors swung back against the stone wall like wings. This must have once been a carriage house.

Gerald stood, half in-half out of the threshold, watching as I walked back to the kitchen entrance.

"Bye, Gerald," I called out and waved a farewell.

Gerald in his doorway. Photo by Judy Goldhill.

"Goodbye," he returned.

"I'll look for you!" I promised.

He'd already stepped back inside, pulling the wooden door shut with a bang. Gerald was gone. But the sign remained: DO NOT KNOCK OR ENTER.

I smiled to myself as I reentered the house.

By the end of the week, my newfound equilibrium from my tea with Gerald had evaporated. As I left the Horse Parlor after the Friday night Theme meeting, I passed Dick Holland at the doorway. I stopped and whispered, "Dick, I need to talk to you."

He regarded me with his kind eyes, "Come with me, then."

We walked the back hallway to his room. He settled into his wing-backed chair, and I perched on the little couch next to him.

"Now then, what is it?" he asked curiously.

Pent-up emotions welling up, I babbled on about everything. "No matter what I do, I just can't seem to bring real feeling into anything.

When I cook, I mess up all the time. Art class? I can't even face Roy, or get myself to go to his classes, which isn't his fault. I had a bad experience with art in junior high school and just can't do it." I sucked in a shaky breath. "Nothing happens when I try to work with the morning exercise. When I speak at Theme meetings, I feel stupid afterwards, like there's nothing real in my words. I keep feeling like I'm just layers and layers of personality and there's nothing underneath. Nothing I can reach or recognize. I know Mr. Gurdjieff said, 'Man cannot Do'.[1] But I can't just *not* Do.

"Dick, I can't just keep crying all the time!" I blubbered. "And Mr. Bennett is always 'hitting me on the head.' All he has to do is look at me, and I realize there's nothing real in me at all. I just feel so empty!"

"And who is this *I* that can't feel, can't speak, can't Do?" Dick asked.

I was familiar with the idea of the "little i's" as opposed to having one real "I."

We had read about this in *In Search of the Miraculous*.[2]

"Oh," I said.

With a thin-lipped smile that turned up at one end, Dick replied, "Who is this Bobby Jo? It appears you are beginning to experience and understand that Bobby Jo, at present, is composed of a myriad of little i's. One cannot feel, one cannot speak, one cannot Do. You see? You are identified with all these little i's. Remember 'it' is i, i, i. There is no one, single, real 'I' in you yet. 'It' cannot do, 'it' cannot feel, 'it' cannot speak. All these little i's can only pretend to be you."

His words eased into me.

Quietly he added, "You must be wary of too much introspection. Spending energy on introspection can be dangerous."

Man, I've spent a lot of my life on introspection.

"Dick," I said, "I think that could be a real part of my problem."

"It's good that you can recognize this, Bobby Jo. Have you heard of 'reverse effort?'"

"No, what do you mean?"

"When one sees oneself engaged in an undesirable pattern of behavior,

---

[1] Ouspensky, *In Search*, 21–22.
[2] Ouspensky, 59–60.

rather than trying to stop it, simply continue doing and observing more of it. Chances are, it will stop of its own accord. When one tries to subdue a negative behavior, instead of going away, it often reemerges in another form. You have to be smarter than 'it' is."

Dick stood up. It was time to go.

Walking upstairs to my dorm, I mulled over what Dick had said, curious and hopeful again. Here was another tool in my belt.

Saturday morning, as we concluded the morning exercise with the three rukus, I felt for the first time that there was something inside of me that I was bowing to. I was bowing to an empty space. It still felt raw, but it was not being torn at anymore. At least for now.

CHAPTER THIRTY-THREE
Surprise!

As Jack later related, he had gone to the door of the Bennett's flat and knocked. It seemed cool to have this apartment within the larger building. Larger than a simple suite of rooms, it had an interior stairway leading to a second floor with bedrooms, enough for the Bennetts to live privately with their two young daughters, Hero and Tessa. Their two boys were old enough to be off on their own and weren't often seen at Sherborne.

Elizabeth opened the door. Her ruddy cheeks, flyaway brown hair, and smiling eyes belied her businesslike, brusque countenance.

"Yes?" she inquired.

Jack paused, collected himself, then put forward his case. "Elizabeth, Bobby Jo's birthday is today, and I would like to make her a cake. Would it be okay if I used your kitchen?"

"To make her a cake?" Elizabeth asked in surprise.

"Yeah."

"Is this what Americans would normally do at home?"

"Sure," Jack replied.

"And you have nothing else to do this afternoon?"

"Not until p.m. service. Mick thought you wouldn't mind," Jack persisted.

Elizabeth hesitated, "Did he now? Well."

There was a look in her eye Jack couldn't quite interpret.

"Well. I suppose if Mick thought it would be all right. Let me show you." She led the way to her galley-like kitchen, "Here then."

"Thanks," Jack said, as he lay down the bundle of ingredients he'd been carrying and looked around.

The kitchen was small but complete. Elizabeth had disappeared. He found a bowl, spread out the directions he'd copied out of a cookbook, and started measuring and mixing. He'd never made a cake before. But this was special. It was my twenty-second birthday, and he had nothing else to give me but the drawing he'd been working on and this. Having no idea what he was doing, he figured if he did exactly what the directions said, a cake would result.

As the tins went into the oven, Mr. Bennett strolled in. He looked up from the letter in his hand and stopped in surprise.

"Hallu! What's this, then?" Mr. Bennett took in the eggshells on the counter, the dusting of flour on the floor, the mixing bowls and utensils smeared with batter piled in the sink. He fixed his gaze on Jack.

Jack looked up at him, "It's Bobby Jo's birthday and I'm making her a cake." Feeling like a small mammal about to be pounced on by an eagle, he added, "Mick said we couldn't do personal cooking in the kitchen and I should come here."

"Did he now?" A momentary shadow crossed Mr. Bennett's brow, then his face lit up. With his long-toothed grin, eyes wide, he exclaimed, "So Americans make cakes for grownup children? Well, then! Carry on," and strode out of the kitchen.

Jack convened a surprise birthday party for me in one of the gabled attic bedrooms. Our friends from Mrs. Popoff's group came. Trudy supplied a bottle of wine—Vicky, peanuts. Jack brought the cake. One of my dorm-mates, Susan, squeezed in. People sat on the mattress or the floor along the edges of the room. This party, our first since arriving in England, signaled the beginnings of feeling at home in Sherborne's cold, drafty, eighteenth-century manor house.

"Thanks for coming, you guys, this is great!" I looked around, taken aback.

Seeing Jack, a warmth of happiness flowed through me. I was certain that the extraordinary experience we had shared in silence the other evening in the Horse Parlor had created an irrevocable bond between us.

"Bobby Jo, this is for you," replied Jack, unfurling an eighteen by twenty-four- inch charcoal sketch of Van Gogh's "The Sower."

Bobby Jo, Dick Holland, Irmgard's Pigeon, Barbara McLoughlin.

Oh Man! I couldn't believe it. I'd been watching and critiquing this piece the whole time I'd been struggling with how to tell Jack I might have feelings for Todd, and he'd kept working on it.

"This too." He handed over Ouspensky's *Talks with a Devil*, the edition introduced and edited by J. G. Bennett. Jack had used the opportunity of making my birthday cake to ask Mr. B to sign the book.

I was speechless.

I produced my sister's gift, a cassette tape wrapped in brown paper and international stamps, along with family birthday cards. What I hadn't expected was the fruit from Van, the small cross carved out of boxwood with a beautiful grain to it from Vicky and Kip, and Trudy's gift of a leather string necklace with the interchangeable decorations of a polished chestnut and a small ceramic tile. As I opened my sister's package, a bright array of party balloons spilled onto my lap.

Birthdays had always been special family occasions. I would come downstairs to find gaily wrapped presents at the breakfast table, which would set the tone for feeling celebrated all day. After dinner in the evening, "Happy Birthday" would be sung as Mom presented my candlelit birthday cake. Passing out cake and ice cream was the "cherry on top" for the day.

Tonight, I felt celebrated by tokens of caring created from what was at hand, from people who were getting to know me in a way my relatives did not. I still felt special, but part of that feeling was based in a growing sense that everyone at Sherborne shared that specialness.

CHAPTER THIRTY-FOUR
Exeat

The tack board declared Exeat—a free day for groups B and C, our first since the course began one month ago and since arriving two eon-like months ago.

Looking out the bus window, Jack and I barreled down the A-40. Stone houses with compact flower gardens put to bed for the winter clustered in hamlets. The road ran straight on a high grade while hills, rills, miles of low stone walls and hedgerows curved up, then down, dipping out of sight amidst cultivated fields as we scooted past. Narrow, winding lanes ran off at right angles from the highway, so old they looked like trenches cut into the hills. I imagined cars having head-on collisions at every blind curve.

I gazed at fellow passengers, struck by how old-fashioned the country folk looked. Like World War II times. Women in woolen skirts, knee-high wool socks, white button-down blouses with cardigan sweaters, scarves tied under their chins. Men wore wool trousers topped with high rubber Wellington boots nicknamed "wellies" or heavy thick leather work shoes. Many wore woolen vests but no ties. Wool caps sat atop jauntier heads. We picked up a Scotsman at a stop along the way and he swung on board, kilt swaying, knees showing above plaid knee-high socks. People suppressed low titters behind their hands. I thought that was mean, although I couldn't help sneaking peeks, myself.

Finally, our coach, the British name for bus, rolled into Cheltenham, which smelled of exhaust fumes, fish and chips, cigarettes, and perfume. A big city with big city streets and big city buildings. People walked briskly, no time to lose, shoppers and businessmen alike. The ladies in pairs or singly, skirts swishing, gloved hands holding paper shopping bags crinkling at their sides—men in suits and ties, brown or gray felt fedoras jammed or perched on their heads, grasping briefcases. I had an eye appointment to keep.

The exam showed my eyesight had improved, which explained why my glasses had been giving me headaches. The Bates eye exercises were working. We walked out of the office with a new prescription to fill and hope for my future in sight.

Strolling down the street, business accomplished, Jack and I decided to revisit Marks and Spencer, the department store we had shopped at before the course started. We pushed through the heavy doors at 173 High Street. A wall of heat from the central heating smacked me in the face. That was not the familiar nor welcome experience I had been looking forward to.

We wandered. There were so many things to look at. I walked around one table loaded with hard wax sticks of burgundy, black, gold, and silver—like thick rectangular crayons. Rolls of white, black, and blue linen rag paper stood on end, displayed like wrapping paper. These were for making rubbings of the brass grave plates we'd seen embedded in stone floors of old churches.

Family birthday money weighed heavy in my pocket. I looked at the choices, finally settling on a deep bright blue paper. The roll was two feet wide. The wax sticks were stamped with a kind of seal or design. I chose silver. I'd later come home from England with brass rubbings from the graves of a wool merchant and his wife in a Northleach church.

Even though I enjoyed looking around, I was sweating and felt my inner thermostat spinning in circles from the central heating.

Jack had been poking around too. He came over to the table and started looking at the brass rubbing stuff. He had no spending money, so was content examining the materials with his artist's eye.

"Hey Jack, I need to go find a wool skirt, so I don't have to borrow Amy's anymore. I'll catch up with you later, okay?"

"Sure."

It was a relief to take my clothes off in the dressing room. Peeling off my thermals, I left them in a pile and put my outer clothes back on to go shop.

I finally found a full-cut wool skirt that reached down to my ankles. This would do nicely. I could dress up in the cold evening hours after mucking about all day. It even had the desired "swish" when I twirled, accentuating my waist. Next, a turtleneck sweater with a snug fit to show I did have breasts after all. Both items were made of real wool in earthy tones of brown. The skirt had flecks of color—blues, greens, red.

Now for the boots.

I found just the right thing. Purple knee-highs of synthetic leather, with a small heel. These would go great with the polyester outfit Mom had made me for my birthday, a long straight bright pink patterned skirt with matching vest. My hot pink turtleneck would work just fine, and the fabric design had purple in it, which would match the boots and tie it all together. Just the thing for feast nights.

The shawl I'd knitted looked rather like a Jewish prayer shawl, with its bands of blue and green color on either end. Of soft fluffy white angora wool, it was finished with blue and white fringe. On top of my new wool skirt and brown sweater, I'd be quite comfortable and just as swishy as everyone else. Making use of the dressing room mirrors, I noticed how long my hair was growing. Thick and slightly wavy, it reached midway down my back.

When I was done, I looked around, wondering where Jack was. But he found me.

"Are you ready?"

"Sure. I'm getting hungry, isn't it about teatime?"

What a relief to get away from the stuffy confines of the store and back out into the cool, crisp English air! I had put my long johns back on in the dressing room. I bet Jack had just suffered silently, as usual. Over the years I began to notice he never threw open a window if it was too hot or shut one if it was cold. Was that a guy thing? Lack of initiative? Or was he simply "working on himself" against his likes and dislikes as we had been encouraged to do? I could never tell.

Two ladies chatting happily in front of us crossed the street and we followed. They were heading for a public looking building, sort of like a large rambling house, with wide double stairs fronted by grillwork leading up from the gray stone-tiled sidewalk. We saw it was a restaurant and followed them in.

The place was bustling with activity. A maze of rooms accommodated diners sitting in groups of two, three, or four. A lone man sat with his paper at a corner table. Conversation and the chink of silver on china created a happy cacophony.

"Table for two?" asked the maître d'.

"Yeah, thanks."

A waiter came up, "This way, if you please." He threaded his way through the tables, and we followed him out to a sunny room overlooking the street. He pulled out my chair and waited a moment as we settled. A cart rolled by, showcasing a tiered array of puffy creamy pastries. The waiter held menus and waited expectantly.

"Tea, is it?"

"Oh yes, thank you."

"Will you be having the cream tea, or would you prefer a high tea?"

I thought of the pastry cart and how much money I had left.

"I'd like to see the menu for the high tea, please."

"Oh no, madam. The menu is for meals only."

"Oh. Well, how much is the high tea?"

"Eight pounds, mum."

"Okay. So how much is just a cream tea?"

"Two pounds, fifty."

"Could we get the cream tea and one of the fancy pastries from the cart?"

"Oh no, mum, I'm afraid we can't do that."

I could hear him groaning to himself, "Oh, these Americans!"

"Thanks," I replied. "Then we'll just have the cream tea."

He waited for the "please," but I'd forgotten to tack it on this time. By then we were feeling a bit out of place anyway.

Most of the other diners were either ladies out with their friends, gloved and hatted, or businessmen with their suits and ties, speaking earnestly with associates. The ladies chatted lightly, the late afternoon sun filtering in warmth through the windows. China clinked, waiters strolled by pushing pastry carts or carrying away empty plates. It was four o'clock and life had come to a pleasant halt in whatever kind of day anyone was having.

I sat, realizing we were misfits looking in from the outside, taking it all in. Yet we were here, in a British town we'd never heard of before coming to England, with two solid plump scones, a mound of deep yellow clotted cream, and a dish of strawberry jam in front of us.

The waiter appeared again, balancing a silver tray with a flowered cloth-covered teapot, small silver pitcher and two round silver bowls, one with white sugar cubes the other with brown.

"Would you like your tea with milk?"

"Yes, please," I said, looking demure from behind my granny glasses.

He poured the steaming black tea into my cup and then a little milk.

"Thank you," I remembered to say.

"And you, sir?"

"Yeah, sure. Great," Jack said.

The waiter didn't quite roll his eyes, but he didn't need to. Even though we were feeling out of place, we were enjoying it just the same.

My hand started tingling with sensation as I lifted the delicate china. My awareness opened, and I noticed the slight weight of the cup, the sharp scent of tea, the frothy milky bubbles. In silence, sipping tea, we shared this expanded moment of experience. Two young American hippies—long hair, loose clothes, with little money or manners, surrounded by proper British citizens having a proper English tea. Yet we were living in a manor house in a small village with new British friends and beginning to feel at home here too.

The scones were still warm. I broke off a piece and spread it with a dab of jelly and then topped that with the cold clotted cream. I washed the crumbling jam and cream-covered scones down with hot tea. I still coveted those flaky cream-puffed pastries rolling by our table, but this would do just fine.

It was getting late, and we needed to find the bus stop and get back. We paid our bill and stepped out onto the street. I felt like I had been transported to a movie set, through a surreal space/time warp. It was as if we were aliens moving within this foreign culture. Walking back the way we'd come, we found the stop, and the coach pulled up a few minutes later.

Cheltenham's city glow quickly melted away in the fading dusk as we headed into the countryside. I pressed my face against the window and watched twinkling lights in distant villages as they appeared and disappeared amidst the rolling hills. It was nothing like the crisscross network of blacktop in America, with its endless suburban sprawl, billboards plastering the highway. In fact, there were few road signs at all and the ones that we could see were small and inconspicuous. I started noticing the leafless trees stripped of their camouflage. Black silhouettes against a dusk-gold glow, arms akimbo. I had never before noticed the beauty of barren trees.

I gazed out the window, drifting until the coach stopped and we disembarked with our shopping bags at the top of the road leading down to Sherborne Village. We walked the long road in silence, tired but happy. Turning onto the graveled drive leading up to the house, I no longer felt like an alien. I was coming home.

CHAPTER THIRTY-FIVE
Hermeneutics

Bennett had launched his International Academy for Continuous Education at an Institute for the Comparative Study of History, Philosophy and the Sciences conference in London. When one of the speakers dropped out, he approached a young student of phenomenology, Henri Bortoft, to ask if he would give a talk. The following was Bortoft's initial response, according to his notes:

> I was taken aback and told Bennett that I had no idea what to talk about. He went silent, as was his custom, and after a while he said, in the ex-cathedra manner which was also his custom, "You should give a talk on 'The Whole: Counterfeit and Authentic.'"
>
> Looking back, I am astonished at how this encapsulated the struggle that had been going on in me at the time—and which Bennett had himself put up with at times with remarkable patience. In the event, the talk was well received. I later wrote an extended version which was published in the journal Systematics, September 1971.
>
> It was against this background that Bennett asked me to give a series of workshops at his new residential adult education center. The aim was not to fill the students' heads and notebooks with intellectual material of what this or that philosopher said, but to bring them to the point where, some of them at least, could begin to get a taste of this way of seeing for themselves. It seemed like an excellent opportunity. However, there were a number of drawbacks,

not the least of which was the fact that I hadn't the faintest idea how to do it. My anxiety level began to rise—especially when I learned that I would be expected to take three different groups of students, each for two sessions a week, for a total of twelve weeks.

The day before I was due to begin, I went for a walk in the countryside in the hope that this might at least have the effect of reducing the level of anxiety I was now experiencing. I made my way to the bottom of the valley through which a small, clear river ran. I stood on a bridge, looking downstream at the river flowing away from me. For some reason this made me feel uneasy, and I crossed to the other side to look at the river flowing towards me. This felt better, and I spent some time there, looking upstream. I began to be drawn into the experience of looking, plunging with my eyes into the water flowing towards me. When I closed my eyes, I sensed the river streaming through me, and when I opened them again, I found that I was experiencing the river flowing towards me outwardly and through me inwardly at the same time. The more I did this, the more relaxed and free from anxiety I began to feel. But of course, the moment came for the first workshop to begin.

I remember walking down the long corridor toward the room where the class was to take place, feeling I was about to be extinguished. The door at the end was closed, the students were already waiting inside, and as I turned the doorknob to go in, I expected to fall into an abyss on the other side. Instead, as I walked into the room, I heard myself say,

"Our problem is that where we begin is already downstream, and in our attempt to understand where we are, we only go further downstream. What we have to do instead is learn how to go back upstream and flow down to where we are already, so that we can recognize this as not the beginning but the end. That's phenomenology!"[1]

---

[1] Henri Bortoft, *Taking Appearance Seriously: The Dynamic Way of Seeing in Goethe and European Thought* (Edinburgh, UK: Floris Books, 2012).

Phenomenology, the study of direct experience, had led Henri Bortoft to a new concept of what theologians call hermeneutics, the science of interpretation.

Other than his wild, curly, red hair and beard, Henri did not look extraordinary. He was easygoing and engaging as an instructor, funny and serious by turns. Gently, he steered us into a strange new world he called hermeneutics.

"Write this down," he began, as if we were in a normal classroom.

Our group had already met with him a few times and was now gathered in the Horse Parlor. Gray November daylight lit the room through tall unadorned windows. I hardly noticed the Cotswold cold numbing my hands as I began to write.

"The grass is green."

"The length of the table is five feet."

"His fist was clenched."

"At the bottom of the hill there was a swamp."

Henri stopped suddenly and asked, "Is grass green? Is that what grass is?" Henri looked at us with excitement sparking his eyes, "How are these sentences disclosing worlds?" He waved a freckled hand saying, "Look at this table. The length of the table is five feet. What does that tell us about this table? Do we know this table? Is that what this table is? Look."

We looked at the table, which was quite ordinary.

"This table is made of wood, a living material. The wood of this table is composed of atoms. It has a life of its own. But do we see or even say any of that? What do the words we use to describe this table disclose to us? By describing the table by a length of five feet, our words disclose that we do not know this table. The words in all these sentences do not disclose, which is the disclosure!"

Henri paused, then pronounced, "Language only has to do with words when words disclose."

We looked at him, clueless.

Henri encouraged us, "Go ahead, describe this table to me."

"It's five feet long and three feet high," said Kip.

"It's made of wood," offered Vicky.

"The wood is mahogany and a deep brown," chimed in Jane.

"And what is the experience of this table? What is it to be this table? What is this table—really? How did this table come to be?" Henri asked this in earnest, looking at us and then at the table.

Suddenly, I started seeing the leg of the table. It wasn't solid wood at all. It was, in fact, made up of zillions of atoms, all floating and moving around each other in a dance of shapes and space. How could this be holding up the tabletop?

I raised my hand, "Henri, I don't understand. If our ordinary way of describing things doesn't work, then what?"

Henri's face lit up, "Ah, what then, indeed?

"Goethe made the distinction between the kind of thinking that begins with the finished product (the Object) and dynamical thinking, which looks instead at the Coming-into-Being of that object.

"We tend to break everything down into a macrocosmic and a microcosmic level. The macrocosmic level means that you look at the measurement. Everything comes down to a measurement. But what is before the measurement? Before the measurement is the Coming-into-Being of entities."[2]

Sitting on the edge of the table, Henri smiled. "So yes, you are correct. Our ordinary way of describing things does not work, does not disclose the reality. Instead, we refer to everything in abstractions. The table is five feet long, as if that is the reality. Yet, this is the language that is used to construct objects of technology, like telephones, radios, and airplanes. So now we have reality constructed by abstractions. We can define this with a simple diagram. Picking up a black marker, he drew two circles on a piece of paper hanging on an easel next to the table. One had the word "inside" in the circle, and the other, the word "outside" in the circle.

---

[2] Conversation with Henri Bortoft, London England, 7/14/1999 Claus Otto Scharmer, https://www.presencing.org/assets/images/aboutus/theory-u/leadership-interview/doc_bortoft-1999.pdf.

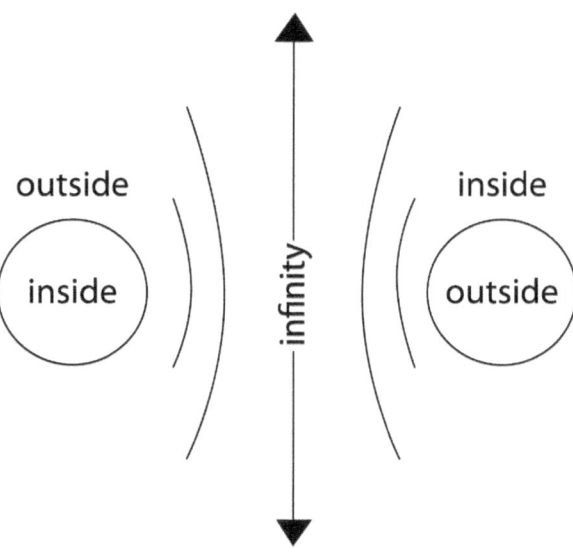

"Let's imagine that our knowing about a thing is a string and the string can become straight and then re-form so that the outside of the string is now on the inside. So that what was inside the circle is now outside and what was outside is now inside.

"Hermeneutically: We think that we know, not knowing that we don't know. Knowing that you don't know equals knowing. True language only has to do with words when words disclose."

I felt a sense in the room that we were on the verge of understanding something, something big. But it was just out of reach.

"What I would like for all of you to do," Henri said waving the uncapped marker. "Is to try practicing hermeneutics. Listen to your talking. Then listen to your listening. Drop a written line when you're having an insight so you can work your way back to it. Like in Uncle Tom's Cabin—jump from ice flow to ice flow to get to the other shore."

Carefully replacing the black cap on the marker, Henri looked up with a furrow on his brow, "Just be careful you don't fall into the river. Practice writing experiences as they are, without writing about them. Keep little notes in the moment to ground them and see what begins to happen."

One day I decided to go for a walk after lunch mulling over what Henri had said about being downstream from perceptions. The air was autumn crisp, the trees outlining the river across the field were almost barren, still clinging to their last brown-gold leaves.

I saw different shades in brown—shades of light and dark bark on tree trunks, brown-gray branches lacing a muted November skyline. I heard a faint gurgle of running water, I shuffled through tall golden field grass. Dead leaves rattled, swirling, mooring into small piles along Sherborne's tree-lined brook. The browns took on definition and interest, they painted the scene in a patch-work cloak of tints. I opened myself and allowed the impressions to seep into me without carrying on my usual inner chatter.

Back in my room getting ready for class, I picked up a dull sepia-colored postcard of Sherborne Brook running beside a field with trees along its bank, much like where I had just been. Barbara June had painted a small fried egg, white with a bright yellow yolk, floating above the water like a little spaceship. I sat on the edge of the bed gazing into the photo.

In the same way I'd opened myself to experiencing brownness without automatic associations, I felt myself drifting. I gazed at the surreal scene in muted tones with the realistic egg floating above it all. Like the egg, I entered into the postcard. Was I "upstream?" Was this hermeneutics?

Flying-Egg Over Sherborne Brooke postcard.

Lazily, I wondered if I would be able to get back out of the photo again. It was so peaceful here, the stream gurgling, the soothing sepia light, the field of gold grass undulating. This was really cool, maybe I'll just stay ...

Thoughts percolated into my head, "What if I can't get out when I want to? What if I become trapped inside this postcard?" Fear rippled through me.

Pop!

I was sitting on the side of my bed staring at the postcard. Pitching it back onto Barbara June's bed, I hurried downstairs to class.

At the next Friday Theme meeting I launched into trying to describe my experience of hermeneutics:

"And so, I went for a walk outside, you know, thinking about hermeneutics and the color brown. And everything was so, you know, brown. The trees, the grass, that November brown thing."

My words tumbled over each other as I stumbled and groped for what I was trying to describe. "And I kind of got into it; just getting into the brown-ness of everything ... Well, and so, I think I was kind of having a hermeneutic experience ..." My voice trailed off, sounding flat.

Looking thoughtful, Mr. Bennett said, "Bobby Jo, you speak of having an experience, perhaps a hermeneutic experience. Yet when you speak, I hear your words, but I do not feel their connection with reality."

It was true, I knew. It seemed lately that whenever I spoke up in a meeting I was left with a cold, empty feeling. As if I'd been talking with nothing but air coming out.

What I had wanted to convey, was that on my walk I was thinking about hermeneutics and trying to perceive nature in an open, unfiltered way. And that back in the room, still in this unfiltered state, I had almost been trapped inside a postcard.

CHAPTER THIRTY-SIX
Lataif

Just like waking at six o'clock each morning to the brass tones of a hand-rung bell passing down the hall on its way from the kitchen, morning exercise had become a familiar part of our day. In later years, those of us who kept up the practice noticed that the quality of our exercise informed the rest of our day.

Relaxation follows a path now. After careful attention to the features of my face, it moves down my neck and arms like a melting, a flow of energy that exits my palms and fingers. Sure, pockets of tension remain in my neck or shoulders or wherever, but I note them as places to revisit, not to get stuck in.

Focus. I became aware of my upper back and chest muscles opening, softening, a sense of movement, a kind of liquid energy, a draining. Here and there a little pop, as held tension releases, surprising me. A deeper breath expands my abdomen, exhales in a long sigh. My state shifts into a softer quality, almost dreamlike, but my eyes are open. My attention goes from torso into hips, a sense of the pelvic girdle, of buttocks; a flowing down from upper legs through knees, lower legs, ankles; energy exiting out my feet. I turn my attention quickly to the top of my head and one more whoosh through my body, noting how my muscles are softer, more open, attended.

I concentrate on the bottoms of my feet and they tingle, become warm. The warmth grows, filling both feet. I can easily recognize sensation now as it rises up through my lower legs, filling them with prickles of nerve endings, the flow of blood. I become aware of life in my knees, sensation pulsing up through my upper legs, hips, throughout my abdomen and chest, up my back like liquid electricity. I move my attention to my fingers. They light up inside. Tingling, pulsing sensation fills my hands, wrists, lower arms—and moves through the elbows to my upper arms, shoulders and neck. Right up over my face, up my scalp to the top of my head. I'm like a lit lava lamp.

In the dark predawn, Mr. Bennett's voice floats disembodied in the ballroom. It's Monday and he is introducing a new exercise. "There are five sacred impulses associated with, but not part of, certain areas of the body. Wish, Hope, Belief, Acceptance, and Love. These objective feelings are not to be confused with our ordinary emotions.

"Objective feelings, *lataif*,[1] as they are called in Arabic, can be experienced in us with practice. We must learn to activate and use these objective feelings in order for our inner work to progress."

He instructs us where to concentrate our sensation.

"Here we can contact the first latifa: Wish. Hold your attention there. Allow a feeling of longing to arise—longing desire. We are not quite sure for what—for reality, for enlightenment—a kind of spiritual hunger. Concentrate this longing into the power of Wish. If it does not come at first, simply wish to Wish. Work with this now, in the time that is remaining."

As Bennett's voice fills the room so, too, does the energy of his presence—his *baraka*,[2] a vibration in the atmosphere more intense than the usual quiet concentration.

Did I just feel something stir? *Wish, wish*, I repeat to myself like a mantra. But they are words, just words. What happened to that feeling I had in the flat with Mr. Bennett?

Everyone is so still, such rich silence. Adjusting my spine, I refocus. A tickle licks the specified area, different from sensation. At least I can feel that. Just sit with it. And I do.

---

[1] "*Lataif-e-sitta* are special organs of perception in Sufi spiritual psychology, subtle human capacities for experience and action." (Wikipedia.)
[2] Baraka, in various Eastern traditions, denotes a spiritual power believed to be possessed by certain persons, objects, or places. A blessing; an indwelling spiritual force; an energetic transmission of knowledge.

"Bring the exercise to a close." Mr. Bennett's voice reels me back from wherever I've drifted off to.

"And stand," he says.

In one fluid motion Bennett's massive frame comes erect, facing us at the far end of the room. Men rise up to his right, women to his left. Later in the course I would learn to appreciate the difference between male and female energy. Right now, it is enough to see each other as dawn creeps into the room, and I come into an awareness of my presence as part of our collective energy.

"To our own higher self. The first ruku." Bennett's voice is clear and sure.

Bennett bows from the waist, hands on knees, back straight. A hundred bodies follow. I bow, searching for this higher self that is hidden from view.

"And up," Bennett says.

We raise up.

"To that which is the same in all of us. The second ruku."

We bow again and I wonder what it is that's the same, all the time aware of our energy thrumming, filling the room.

"And up," a crisp movement. This time we stand upright in unison with Mr. Bennett.

"We bow to a higher power outside ourselves that we do not understand but from which source, help comes. The third ruku."

With the third bow I feel more on familiar ground, acknowledging what I have no trouble calling God. In fact, we are old buddies. I've been chatting it up with Him since I was a kid. The best part is He always knows what I mean even when I don't.

"And up."

Mr. Bennett strides down the center aisle and out of the room as all one hundred remain standing in silence.

After he passes, I pull my shawl tight across my chest against the fall chill, which seemed to have receded during the exercise. I pick up my cushions and shuffle out of the ballroom with the crowd, depositing them onto the colorful pile by the door. I locate my shoes in the sea with all the others and look for Jack. Together, we walk down the corridor to queue up for breakfast—a soft shush, shush, of feet echoing the quiet of my inner space.

We inch our way up in line as I anticipate slathering a thick piece of toast with butter and jam, washing it down with hot black tea. Mr. Bennett stands inside the narrow Servery behind the island, serving ladle in hand. Nutty steel-cut oat steam curls into the air alongside white porcelain bowls and metal trays of wheat toast, fresh baked.

Pink golden beams bounce in through the windows above the sinks as I pick up my toast. Mr. Bennett ladles oatmeal into my bowl. His gaze pierces the smile on my lips, exposing the facade that I address the world with—a smile that says, "Like me." Not "I am here," not "What can I do for you?"

Bennett is Here. Where am I? I've wasted his invitation to participate in a real moment by daydreaming about toast. Searching for real people has led me to the course. It's why I came. But it isn't another's presence I need to find. It's my own.

I take my bowl and hurry out into the crowd in the familiar dining room.

We continue to work with the lataif during morning exercises. Mr. B (as Mick Sutton refers to Bennett, so of course now we all do) suggests we use sensation to locate the position of each latifa. The problem is getting a specific feeling to arise, feelings the quality of which we have never experienced before.

This morning we concentrate on Hope combined with a breathing exercise.

I sense my left breast and control my exhalation—a pause, then a long inhalation invoking hope. Breathing and sensing, I add a very slight swaying to the rhythm of my beating heart—tick, tick, tick, tick, tick, tick. No room for thoughts—only breath, heartbeat, sensation of left breast and—Hope awakens. It blooms in my left breast like yellow daffodils holding the promise of sunshine, of fragrant breezes, of growth and change. An intense feeling that has no "for" attached to it. It's alive, it's tangible, it is Hope. Amongst all the lataif, I have this, I have Hope. This is real.

Gray light dissipates the shadows as Mr. B's voice floats out, "And bring your exercise to an end."

Like a flower pulling in its petals at day's end, Hope folds back on itself and melts out of sight, sinking into the hidden recesses, safe from usurpation by personality.

CHAPTER THIRTY-SEVEN
Decision Exercise

We had been hearing lectures from Mr. Bennett on will and learning the distinction between will and self-will, essence and personality—the former coming from an objective place in us and the latter from what I thought of as an "I want" place. I was familiar with Gurdjieff referencing man as an automaton, going through life asleep even in his normal waking state, so it was no surprise to hear Bennett say we have no sense of real will.

In the book he was writing,[1] Bennett quotes Mr. Gurdjieff from notes taken during a lecture: "What you call 'will' in yourself is only from personality. It has no connection with real will. Something touches personality and it says, 'I want' or 'I do not want' 'I like' or 'I do not like' and thinks it is will. Will can only be in essence. As you are now, your essence has no will, only automatic impulses."

If I thought about it, I could see plenty of my own examples. For instance, who's in charge of my body? I'm happy to run to the end of the dock in New Hampshire and dive into cold lake water, but don't ask me to walk around in the rain and get my head wet. Who's in control of my emotions? I watch a frightening scene on TV and my heart races out of control, but as I walk into the next room to get ice cream, I'm suddenly full of anticipation. Who's setting my New Year's resolution? We all know how long those last. Yet I still think decisions are mine to make, that I'm in charge of my own volition.

---

[1] J. G. Bennett, *Gurdjieff: Making a New World* (New York: Harper & Row, 1973), 134.

DECISION EXERCISE

It was fairly early in the course during a special talk that Mr. Bennett presented the Decision Exercise. Afterwards, he began to leave time at the end of morning exercise so we could prepare our decision, following the steps he'd laid out. Morning exercises came and went, but the Decision Exercise was a daily practice that many of us continued even after the course ended. There was nothing exotic or hard about it, but without saying so, we understood this was the way to forge a connection between our thinking, emotional, and moving centers that was directed by conscience, or what we hoped would become our real 'I.'

It's the end of morning exercise, my core is quiet, still. Sitting in familial comfort amongst the women, I prepare my decision. Three chores scroll through my head from ones I contemplated before going to bed last night. It's important to choose simple physical tasks that don't involve other people but may not get done otherwise, like writing a letter or sweeping the walkway. This morning, darning my sock seems least likely to happen on its own, so I choose that.

I ask myself, what is my decision? I will darn my sock.

Why am I doing this? Because it needs to be done.

How is it to be done? I visualize myself sitting on the side of my narrow bed. I sense my hand threading the narrow eye of my needle and poking it in and out of my blue sock.

Will I do this? I wait. There's a gravity here. The answer cannot be taken lightly. I listen to my body for the answer. A firm "Yes, I will do this," reverberates through me from the reflecting pool of my morning exercise.

That night, before sleep, I play back the scene of myself darning the sock. It hadn't happened before teatime as I had imagined but after dinner before Movements class.

I see myself sitting on my bed in dim light sending the needle in and out across the hole where my toe had poked through. The hole is getting smaller, pulling together, and then, in my mind's eye I remember looking over at Barbara June's empty bunk and her flying egg drawings taped to the wall. I remember bringing sensation into my hands as I saw myself sitting in the ballroom during morning exercise, picturing the darning and how I had pulled that picture forward, my hands growing warm with sensation as I imagined moving the needle. It was as if I was both inside and outside myself, seeing the needle move and feeling sensation in my fingers.

If I'd forgotten to do my chosen decision before midnight, I would have had to skip a meal the next day or hold my arms out to remind myself that I was serious about doing what I had decided to do. That was how Mr. B suggested we communicate to our body that our conscious will was in charge. Sounds easy, holding out your arms for ten minutes, but just try it. It only took a couple of times. It was interesting how much my body did not want to go there and would even remind me to get my decision done. All of a sudden, the task I'd chosen would pop into my head or a limb would start sensing. It was as if something was forming a command center in me that had nothing to do with whims or likes and dislikes.

Not every decision ended in a *yes*. Sometimes there was a strong *no*. In that case Mr. B had told us not to try to do a decision that day. Often it turned out that some unforeseen circumstance occurred that would have made the decision impossible to carry out—a sudden illness, a change of schedule. It was as if we were hooking-in to the Universe and it was talking to us. Jack remembers Mr. B saying, "This [the Decision Exercise] is the lifeline I throw you."

CHAPTER THIRTY-EIGHT
Thanksgiving

November 1972—George Cornelius, full of beef and bluster, in charge of practical work with Pierre, was overheard boasting about pulling strings to get salmon flown in from Alaska to be served on crackers as hors d'oeuvres with fruit punch. Crab meat salad, mashed potatoes, two kinds of stuffing, giblet gravy, and two thirty-pound turkeys were on the menu as well as pumpkin, apple, and mincemeat pies.

An undercurrent of excitement and expectation was stirring the house like bees intuiting a change. For two days now the focus of everyone's efforts was preparing for the feast. Only American moms were allowed to cook; only American guys were to serve the meal. Hard to tell if Mr. B was teasing the Americans—encouraging us to "go the whole hog, including the postage," as Gurdjieff would say.

Standing in the dining room, I scanned our p.m. service handiwork. The large dining tables were set end-to-end in long rows, mimicking the traditional American image of the first Thanksgiving feast. Nuts and fruits laid out on pine boughs decorated the tables. Taking in a long breath, I tasted pine trees and summers in New Hampshire, penny-store candy and maple sugar.

The big room was still dark with paneling and had the familiar chill of the house, but the red berries, spiked cones, and yellow and orange fruits made it less austere. Excitement rippled through me at the prospect of a festive evening.

Later, Jack was hanging with the guys in his dorm when I arrived. He looked good in his turtleneck and doeskin-colored overshirt.

Jack and Bobby Jo dressed for Thanksgiving.

"Hey Van, can you take a picture?"

"Sure."

I gave him my Kodak.

I was wearing my birthday finery—the almost spongy synthetic ankle-length skirt and matching vest Mom had made me, the hot pink turtleneck that matched the pink in the skirt pattern, the purple knee-high boots I'd bought with birthday money.

If Mr. B was trying to make a point, then yes, I saw myself in all my American-ness as I pictured my dad watching football, my mom cooking in the kitchen, my high-school-age brother puttering around the house, my sister and her boyfriend visiting from New York.

The halls echoed with chatter as students made their way down the corridors, everyone dressed up: long wool skirts rustling, fringed shawls and bright scarves, button-down shirts tucked into regular pants instead of blue jeans. Even a jacket here and there (mostly the Brits).

Oohs and *aaahs* drifted on the air as we entered, slam-dunked by the bounty of food, the reflection of candlelight dancing off silver and paneling. Logs popped and hissed in the hearth. Chairs clunked and scraped as bodies settled shoulder-to-shoulder at the long tables. A warm camaraderie filled the room.

Were we students becoming a family?

I'd always had a hard time remembering other people's names, but I'd never let that bother me much. Now I was beginning to know people from their observations at Theme meetings, their questions and Mr. B's responses. I could feel them, not things about them, but them. I wanted to remember these names. For the first time in my life, it mattered.

Rachel, for one. She intrigued me with her graceful way of moving. I was becoming more attuned to the energy of women, a new concept for me, having been a tomboy growing up. Rachel favored loose clothing and draped shawls, making me think of the Middle East. I was surprised to find out that she and her boyfriend, Larry (they had their own room!), were both from the Midwest. Larry was adroit and funny, tuned in to people. Then there was Lynne and Fish. Lynne was pretty, bright; I could easily imagine her a cheerleader. Fish, despite his nickname and long hair, had a clean-cut, thoughtful appeal. They seemed to go together like the sun and the moon. Jack and I were beginning to gravitate towards both couples.

Before the plates emerged from the Servery, Mr. B stood and we all invoked the prayer that Bennett had created, imprinting in us one of Gurdjieff's primary principles, the Law of Reciprocal Maintenance.

> All life is one, and everything that lives is Holy.
> Plants, Animals and Man—
> all must eat to live and nourish one another.
> We bless the lives that have died to give us this food.
> Let us eat consciously, resolving by our Work
> to pay the debt of our existence.

Lunch and dinner were usually eaten in silence, but not tonight. I saved a chair for Jack, who was serving, as were Fish and Larry. When they could, the guys sat down with heaping plates. Next to me, Jack sat, hair screening his face as he lifted his fork.

Remembering past Thanksgivings, I turned and asked, "Hey Jack, you missing your family?"

"No. I'm eating mashed potatoes."

"Oh, come on!" I gave him a shove. "Really."

Jack looked up from his plate, fork in hand and admitted, "Yeah, I miss them."

The moment passed and we fell back into our conversations. Animated voices rose, hands gestured, elbows propped chins, wine was poured. I was having a great time dusting off my social personality for the first time since arriving at Sherborne House.

Above the growing din, Mick Sutton stood, looking dapper in his jacket, tapping a wine glass until the chatter and clatter of eating grew quiet. Mr. Bennett looked up from his plate, encompassing the room with his Cheshire grin and announced in his distinct British accent, "Let us all meet in the ballroom for Movements in fifteen minutes. Our honored guests," he nodded to Harry the Postmaster and his wife, Mavis, "are invited to observe. I would like everyone to help clean up so the kitchen crew can participate also."

Shock—an inaudible groan floated around the room. Movements? How are we going to do Movements stuffed with food and saturated with wine? He's got to be kidding!

The silent answer resonated within me: Super Effort.

I thought of Mrs. Popoff and the maxim, "Do what It doesn't want to do." How else can we become our own Master?

Voices started up, subdued. People began rising from the tables, scraping and stacking plates, carrying them to the Servery. Thoughts of a wine-hazed, lazy evening evaporated. Everyone pitched in to help. The student body had fifteen minutes to do what the usual cleanup crew did in one and a half hours.

Efficiently, dishes moved from dining room to Servery, where practiced hands scraped, stacked, washed, and rinsed hundreds of plates, glasses, and silverware. Others wiped down the large wooden tables, rearranged and set them up for breakfast, while still others swept the floor. The kitchen downstairs clanged with the washing of huge metal pots, mixing bowls, serving utensils, and cutlery. Food was wrapped, labeled, and stored—counter tops cleaned, the floor swept and mopped. Everyone knew what to do and did it.

Fifteen minutes later, we filed into the ballroom—all of us.

Harry and Mavis, always polite and curious, sat with Elizabeth, Dick Holland, and other staff members. What were our guests thinking, I wondered, as they faced us in our feast-day finery and bare feet? We filled the ballroom, standing row behind row. It was pitch black outside.

I was nervous, my head a stick of cotton candy. I definitely did not want to be performing in front of an audience. What if I didn't know the

Movement and messed up? How was this going to work anyway, with so many of us in the room?

Mick faced us as we arranged ourselves in multiple rows of six files. He moved off to the side, and it was Mr. Bennett who stood tall and straight in front, commanding our attention with his own. He did not address our visitors.

Later, when we had official Movements demonstrations, Mr. B would address the audience and say something akin to what he was writing in *Making a New World*. "Gurdjieff told us that his system develops all sides of a man's nature and that these exercises were not only to acquire control of the body and its movements and postures but had complicated patterns that called for a powerful effort of mental attention. That a very severe training of body, mind, and feelings is required to enable the movements to be carried out correctly.

"This is quite different from ballet training in which the basic elements are automatized, leaving the dancer to interpret the theme through his mind and feelings. In Gurdjieff's exercises, the body must be itself in a high state of consciousness which unites the three functions of thought, feeling, and bodily sensations into a single integral act of expression."

But now, still facing us, Mr. B only trumpeted, "Number 17."

The first gesture for my file swam into focus in my mind's eye, calming me. I settled, became still, aware of the sensation of my body.

DUM—dum, dum, dum. DUM—dum, dum, dum. Piano strings ring, rhythm pounds; ninety bodies jump into action. Arms go up, hands vibrate, legs step, tap, jump, or circle in an arc as each file takes its own gesture for eight measures then moves to new positions on the floor. Heads turn sharp right, sharp left every other measure.

Mr. Bennett walks over to stand by Mick in the corner of the room, his gimlet gaze upon us.

My gestures are the same as those in front and behind me in file five. But I move on the floor within the context of the students to my right and left who comprise my row.

RIGHT, left toe, heel; RIGHT—I take a step forward at a diagonal. My row has split apart. Files one and two move in rhythm behind and to the left. On the eighth measure my row connects again, but now I am in the third file instead of the fifth. The music does not falter DUM—dum, dum, dum, and I take the arm gestures and foot pattern of the third file. The rows begin to move backwards diagonally. Fifteen rows split and reconnect. The ballroom shakes, hands vibrate, heads turn in unison.

My body assumes its gestures as flesh and bone, muscle and tendon, move across the floor. Stillness enters me, there's room to focus, to connect with my row as we multiply:

142857 x 2 becoming 285714;

142857 x 3 becoming 428571;

142857 x 4 becoming 571428;

On the fourth multiplication, 571428, file five leads the split. I move forward behind Rachel, towards file one's place within this moving mass of bodies, leading my row to take our new positions and gestures symbolizing the initiating number, 142857.

The music does not wait. My arms, legs and head need no coaching, they know their gestures and take them representing position one. Counting the measures, listening for cues in the music, I begin the slow diagonal move back home and resume the head, arm, and foot pattern for file five.

Sweat beads under my arms, runs down my back, exhilaration expands my heart, keeping the wine-induced fuzz in my head at bay. We rock the room, filling it with attuned attention zinging between us, connecting us; we form and re-form, completing the multiplication to the sixth place. We are a moving representation of multiplying an esoteric number that holds more secrets than we know.

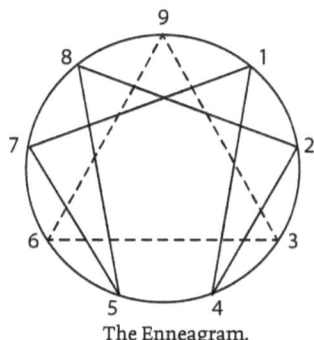

The Enneagram.

According to Mr. Bennett, Gurdjieff brought the Enneagram to the West. He attributed this circular symbol, embodying the secrets of the numbers we were multiplying, to an ancient brotherhood in central Asia. In the book he was writing, *Making a New World*, Mr. Bennett said that the Enneagram is the symbol of self-sustained evolution or transformation: a triple symbol of a triangle and hexagon inscribed in a circle.

"Enough!" Mr. Bennett's voice rings out.

We may not know all the secrets of the Enneagram, but something has just happened. As a group we have made an effort. Instead of blowing our energy on a party, we have created energy that feels finer, rarer. That is what I know and that is enough for now.

CHAPTER THIRTY-NINE
Movements Practice

After Thanksgiving, new groups were assigned. Jack and I were in Group D with most of the other couples. We dubbed ourselves the Demonstration Group as we prepared for the first Movements demonstration to be given by the Second Basic Course.

Slipping into the ballroom, I stood in front of the mirror to practice the First March before going outside for practical work. I wondered, as I gazed at this girl reflecting back at me, what were my faults? What were my strengths? Sometimes people just laughed and said, "Oh Bobby Jo, you're so funny!" But I hadn't made a joke. What did they see?

I looked at the reflection of a girl with a slight frame, a long neck and too much hair for the small oval face. But did I look relaxed, balanced? Did my straight back and lifted head make me look elongated and weightless, or rigid?

I assumed the first position of the First March. Looking in the mirror, I saw a bent wrist as my fingers touched my waist. The importance of precise gestures was stressed in our Movements classes. We were told Movements was a "language" that conveyed esoteric truths to the audience and within ourselves. Straightening and rotating my wrist brought my elbow away from my body. It felt weird but made the line from elbow through fingertips straight. Closing my eyes, I aroused sensation in my arms and shoulders, feeling the discomfort of them being pushed back, pulling down, and lengthening my neck. I relaxed into the discomfort, using sensation to communicate with my body that this was correct. Each posture became cemented in my body through sensation until arriving there felt familiar, like I was filling a mold.

It was time to leave for Period I, which was practical work. For the first time I looked forward to the Movements class that would follow during Period III.

As director of practical work, Pierre often ran with a wheelbarrow or sawed huge logs of wood, always pushing his physical limits and setting an example for us to do the same. I can't remember ever seeing him standing still outdoors. As a Movements teacher, he was a different person.

My bare feet padded onto the cold wood floor of the ballroom. We arranged ourselves according to height into the usual six files, five rows deep. I found myself in file five behind Rachel and next to Lynne and Robin.

Pierre's wife Vivien waited poised at the grand piano in a bright purple theatrical silk tunic with silver trim, hair swept up and held in place by a thin gold fillet across her brow.

Pierre stood in front of our class, socks pulled up over his dark pant legs, white ballet-style slippers on his feet. Everything about him was contained, still.

He started marching in place, throwing his legs out and pulling them back briskly, bobbing slightly, hips loose, hands relaxed at his sides. I watched until I caught the idea of the rhythm, then began imitating him as he faced us.

Vivien started playing, creating a beat with the piano. I let my body feel the music, relaxing into my legs and hips as I marched, watching Pierre for the inevitable changes in the pattern that would come. This was a warming up exercise and we never knew what to expect, but falling into a rhythm was my strong suit and my body rejoiced.

As soon as Pierre saw that most of us had the rhythm established, he began to move his left arm at right angles to his body in a series of four precise gestures. After repeating the pattern a few times, he added a different set of gestures for the right arm.

"Rest," Pierre called loudly, and Vivien stopped playing.

Starting to march again he added a foot pattern, moving forward and back. Vivien played, adjusting the rhythm to match. We watched. The front row picked up the new pattern and began to move as the rest followed.

Standing behind Rachel's mane of dark curls, I admired her fluid way of moving. Lovely Lynne was to my right, sure of herself, athletic. To my left was Robin, shorter but like me in body-type, unassuming.

With the rhythm as my anchor, I copied Rachel until I knew the gestures and foot pattern. I took smaller steps moving forward and larger moving back, feeling connected to Rachel and Lynne. The music was key. My body began to know where to go and what to do in response. Just as I got it, Pierre stopped.

Standing with still arms at my sides, I resisted the urge to tuck in my shirt. I was down with discipline but wasn't inclined to like all this geometry because I loved the fluid grace of ballet, the freedom of modern dance. But now, in this moment, here I was—fingers closed. I opened them. Inside myself I noticed my tense stomach, my locked knees. I flexed my knees, breathed into my abdomen; it occurred to me these still moments were as much a part of Movements as were precise gestures.

During his own search for truth Mr. Gurdjieff explored Asia, collecting temple dances, rituals, and folk dances. Over the years he added exercises, dances, and music he created to a growing repertoire that became known as the Movements. Gurdjieff used Movements as a direct way of teaching and transmitting universal truths.

My truth is that one day a moment of grace comes and "a Movement does you." When that day happens, it is a taste of all your parts working together without interference. It makes you want the whole meal.

PART FOUR

JOURNALING:

DOWN THE RABBIT HOLE

> "It's no use going back to yesterday,
> because I was a different person then."
> —ALICE, IN *ALICE IN WONDERLAND* BY LEWIS CARROLL

CHAPTER FORTY
Slip-Sliding Away

December 2, 1972—Something in me is percolating. Like air bubbling up through the muck of a river-bed. It actually tickles. At inexplicable moments I suddenly want to giggle. I don't mind at all. It feels like there's something new, what I want to call a "Ridiculous I," growing in me. An "I" that can be silly. What a relief!

There's an old Zen *koan*, something about a goose inside a bottle. I wonder—am I the goose, or am I the bottle? Either way, how does the goose get out?

December 4—The pace of the course is quickening, moving faster, as if there's something inside me like yeast in bread. It's becoming difficult to write in my journal. Hermeneutics teaches us to write the whole, disclose the experience, not *about* the experience. When I read my written words all I hear is the ring of false personality ricocheting off the page. How do I capture what is *real*? Maybe what's real is the fact that I am not.

Turkish too—whew! Sixty words and verbs and grammar: endings, sounds, constructions to learn in two days. We can speak Turkish at silent meals. "*Tuzu uzat!*" (Pass the salt.)

Mr. B says Turkish helps us change the construct of our thinking patterns because it isn't put together in the logical way we are used to.

If studying hermeneutics changes our experiencing—and Turkish, our thinking patterns—it's no wonder it feels like we are forging into uncharted territory. Inner territory, where nothing is as it seems.

Sometimes when I speak, my voice sounds hollow, like it's coming from inside an old, dead tree. It's getting hard to stand myself. I see how little I notice others. Mr. B answered my question in a meeting the other day and suddenly a bubble was around us, as if he wasn't speaking to anyone else, as if I were the only atom in the universe. I'm more and more aware of how self-centered I am, and I see that I don't see. It feels like things are shifting, heating up. As if Sherborne House is a cauldron that is starting to simmer.

December 6—Mr. B came into our Movements class today and took position one in the front row. I've never seen him do Movements before. We worked on Number 17 with him for fifty minutes. The only way not to fall over dead was to keep relaxing my tensions, stay focused in my body and out of my head. Mr. B didn't seem to tire at all and he's in his seventies. By the end, the room was charged with energy and I was winded but relaxed—interesting!

December 8—Dick Holland spoke about three-centered self-observation in class today. Each one of the three centers—moving, thinking, and feeling—can be broken down into three parts as well. Apparently, it's not enough to just think about "remembering oneself," which is a one-centered activity using only the "mechanical" part of the intellectual center. But I think that's a way to start.

He said the next step is to transfer the thought into action, like sensing your hand as you make a gesture, which uses the mechanical part of your moving center. If you sense your hand, you can bring in feeling, using the mechanical part of the feeling, or emotional, center. But something else has to take over, as in we have made an effort but cannot presume to "do." We must get out of the way to allow the energy generated to transfer to other parts of our moving, feeling, or intellectual centers. I experience that sometimes in Movements. Like the moment the other day when I raised my arms towards the ceiling while sensing them and had the feeling of being a conduit of receiving. Since I was sensing my arms and not chattering in my head, my feeling center opened to the meaning of the gesture.

Dick said real self-observation only happens with our higher centers—the feeling part of our intellectual center. The danger, of course, comes with subjective emotions and becoming self-identified. Since we live in our ordinary subjective state, it's impossible to observe ourselves with any objectivity until we separate from our egotism and begin to "self-remember," which is like seeing ourselves from the outside. Dick suggests we can start by observing our postures, gestures, and facial expressions using sensation and feeling. Mrs. Popoff said the same.

But what makes me wake up enough to see a facial expression? Or catch how it's making me feel?

December 12—Trudy and Emily and Steve and Gloria were already sitting in the Horse Parlor when Van, Jack, and I showed up. Kip and Vicky arrived a few minutes later. We had gathered to make a Christmas tape for Mrs. Popoff.

Emily seems as much a part of our Pinnacle group now as any of us. Everyone appreciates having her help in the kitchen. She's a master at chopping vegetables, tireless and happy in that role, despite her supposed mental handicap. Besides, the kitchen is the warmest room in the house, which isn't lost on her.

We sat in silence, a tight circle on the old carpet with the tape recorder and its little microphone in the middle, collecting ourselves inside so that when we spoke it would come from someplace real. Kip reached over and pushed the button to turn the machine on.

"Hello, Mrs. Popoff. This is Kip. We are sitting here in the Horse Parlor at Sherborne. It's almost the middle of December. I want to thank you for preparing me to come here. It hasn't been easy, but I am grateful you encouraged me to come. Every day I see how my self-will gets in my way. But at least now I'm seeing it."

Trudy leaned into the microphone. "Mrs. Popoff, this is Trudy. I remember you told me to watch out for laziness. At the time I reacted inwardly, denying it to myself. I couldn't understand what you meant. How could I possibly be lazy? But now I see the tendency clearly in myself. And it's not just physical laziness, but mental as well. Now I struggle against reacting when I see my laziness, so I can separate and observe it."

"Hi, Mrs. Popoff, this is Gloria. I really hate it here. I'm cold all the time, it's so dark and damp. But then there's these moments of absolute wonder. I'm homesick a lot, but I would never have come if it wasn't for you, so thank you—I am glad I came."

Steve spoke up. He was partially deaf, so he always spoke in a loud voice.

"Hello, Mrs. Popoff! This is Steve. I am learning a lot from Mr. Bennett. You were right to send us to him. I always thought I was pretty good at paying attention to details, but now I see there is much more to it. It's more like creating a kind of openness and then things come at you differently.

"Like this morning when I was on practical work. We were mitering corners for some molding around a doorway. After a while I noticed Richard was also using the miter-box. Depending on where I laid it down, he could reach it without having to step around me. Noticing that, I was able to change my habitual pattern which created a better rhythm for us to work together. I care about things like that now, whereas in the past I wouldn't have."

I looked over at Steve, surprised. He didn't usually talk that much. But I appreciated his observation, as it was the kind of experience I was having with the Theme of "Noticing," too.

Jack spoke up next. "Mrs. Popoff, I'm up to five balls with my juggling. Bobby Jo and I have been working on some routines together too. There's a guy here, Elan, who plays classical music, like Beethoven. I juggled to his playing at last Saturday's entertainment night. It went pretty well. What I noticed was that the attention of the audience seemed to be the glue that kept the balls in the air in rhythm with the music."

"Yeah," I piped in, "you could really feel it in the audience too. It was like we were all connected with Jack and Elan, keeping the balls going."

"Oh, sorry. This is Bobby Jo speaking, in case you couldn't tell," I said with a smile. "You know, Mrs. Popoff, I'm seeing more and more about myself which isn't always easy, and I'm so grateful for the preparation you gave us before coming. It's helped me appreciate and take advantage of what we're being given."

"Van here, Mrs. Popoff. Ditto what Bobby Jo said. I'm having a real hard time with the cold, like Gloria, but I'm glad to be here too. Thank you."

"Mrs. P," Vicky added in her soft voice. "I feel like I was destined to come here, and it was through you. I want to wish you a Merry Christmas. You and everyone there—the whole group. I still try to visualize everyone's faces as we sat together in that last meeting, just like you suggested we do as a task. Merry Christmas!"

"Merry Christmas, Mrs. Popoff," Emily chimed in, leaning into the microphone with a toothy smile.

We all started calling out, "Merry Christmas, Mrs. Popoff—Merry Christmas, Ruth— Merry Christmas Essie—Merry Christmas Norma—Merry Christmas—*Merry Christmas!*"

There was a lot to be grateful to Mrs. Popoff for. Our time with her before coming to England had introduced me to the rudiments of the Work: sensation, presence, effort—to the Movements. She had put the first tools in my toolbox. What she could not prepare me for, other than having tools, was the journey inward to the uncharted territory of myself. As I joined in heartily wishing Mrs. Popoff and the other Pinnacle group members a Merry Christmas, I had no idea of the rabbit hole I would soon be tumbling down, Mr. Bennett lighting the way.

CHAPTER FORTY-ONE
Reversing the Flow of Forces

December 16, 1972—Friday evening before our first Visitors' Day, I came into the Horse Parlor and found an unoccupied space near Jack on the familiar patterns of the carpet. I sat down cross-legged, enjoying a moment of stillness after completing my p.m. service duties washing dishes, wiping tables, and sweeping the dining room floor. My hands were red and cold, but the part of me that was attending did not choose to place attention on that. Instead, I focused on what would come out of this week's Theme meeting, "Reversal of the Flow of Forces." Not only had the concept been elusive but having an experience to enlighten me was elusive as well.

Victor, with his radio-announcer baritone and congenial presence, spoke up first, and as usual, at great length. Tonight, he didn't spin a tale with a humorous punch line. He talked about having felt something percolating inside for several weeks which he'd tried to ask questions about before but found himself unable to.

"It felt like something inside was trying to reset but I was blocking it with my body and my mind, afraid to trust it. But I stayed with it. Finally, during hermeneutics class, I felt something in my body was set right," Victor explained. "Then, during Movements class Pierre introduced a new movement and said it was quite difficult. I almost laughed, because it seemed so easy. My body just did it." Victor was known for his irreverent humor, not his nimble body. "This energy seems to come from behind and through me, as if 'Victor' is transparent, he continued. "It's not *mine*, it belongs to everybody."

Mr. Bennett asked gently, "And how do you tie this in with this week's Theme?"

Victor considered for a moment and replied, "It's not like I'm reversing the flow of forces—I don't turn anything around; what's needed is to get out of the way so something can come through.

Mr. B nodded, "Yes, that is it. We consent to it, we don't 'do' it—reverse the flow. It's when we open and allow something inside ourselves to flow—it needs to come from Wish."[1]

Visitors arrived early in the day on Saturday. After an introductory talk by Mr. Bennett, they joined students already outside engaged in practical work sessions in the gardens. All I knew was that the course was now going to include occasional visitor days. Presumably most of the visitors were members of Mr. B's London groups and looked older than the majority of us twenty-something students. But younger people came too, from alternative communities like the Sufi-based Beshara group we'd had pre-course interaction with. Occasionally, candidates for future courses came. In the spring, folks from the agrarian-based Findhorn community in Scotland showed up. All were curious as to what was going on at Bennett's school.

In the afternoon they came to tea, where we interacted, as had been encouraged. The House crew had been *en garde* all day—answering questions, directing visitors to the various activities, and generally acting as the hosts. Now, before dinner, it was time for our first Visitors' Day Movements Demonstration.

I snuck down the back stairs to slip into the Horse Parlor in my white pantaloons and long tunic. The room was atwitter with costumed students. Vivacious Vivien, (who claimed she'd been born on the Nicoll's kitchen table in Hempstead, England, and later noticed Pierre at work days when she was just five and he was a mischievous fifteen-year-old) passed out thin gold-threaded headbands while Sally the laundry mistress distributed carefully ironed seven-inch-wide satin sashes of bright rainbow colors.

"Here, Bobby Jo, let me help you." Penny Gibson, who apparently had

---

[1] Recreated from the "Reversal of Flow of Forces Theme Meeting" tape, December 18, 1972.

done this before, turned towards me and took the green sash into her seasoned hands. She measured the end to stop at my knee and began carefully winding the rest of the nine-foot length around my waist, stopping with enough left over to tie and drape over the knot.

"There. You see how it's done?"

"Wow, thanks Penny, I never would have figured all that out!"

Once the visitors were settled in the ballroom, we filed upstairs and took our places, barefoot, sitting cross legged on the wood floor in six straight files, five rows deep. The colors of our sashes corresponded with our files: red, orange, yellow, green, blue, purple. I was in file four with a green sash. I sat as if in morning exercise, hands on knees, gazing at the floor. I could hear the blood pounding in my ears. At least I wasn't in the front row.

Bennett stood, a towering presence, wearing his ubiquitous houndstooth jacket. Vivien was poised at the grand piano in the back of the room, shimmering in her purple and silver tunic and gold-threaded headband.

The audience sat on folding chairs facing us, their attention on Mr. B.

Bennett introduced the Movements, "George Ivanovich Gurdjieff referred to himself as a teacher of dancing. Much of his teaching was conveyed through the Movements, some of which you are about to participate in tonight. I say participate because, in order to fully appreciate what one is witnessing, that is what one must strive to do. Therefore, we do not separate ourselves from the performers, nor do we applaud their efforts. For we must all make an effort here tonight to understand this language of gesture. We must attempt to open ourselves and connect to something greater in order to receive what is being transmitted. To do so, one must play an active role as observer."

Mr. B looked out over the room, scanning the audience much as he did at Theme meetings. "Tonight's work will be to share what we have been attempting with the series of six movements, which Mr. Gurdjieff referred to as the Obligatories."

Turning to face us for the first time, Mr. Bennett called out, "Stand."

In one fluid movement all thirty of us were on our feet. My eyes gazed straight ahead, looking inward. Mr. Bennett announced, "The First Obligatory."

Vivien played three slow notes and the first resounding chord. All was stillness. As succeeding chords sounded, arms shot out, to the side, and up. The pace increased with the second round and again with the third. The music repeated the slow, medium, and fast pace as we went through the leg gestures alone, and then the head. Finally, we put the arms, legs, and head together at the three different paces.

I tried not to think, to let my body move inside the music, but there was always this edge of being watched. I concentrated on moving as the chord sounded, to land my gesture in time with the music. I sought my center of balance. Tight butt? Belly? My spine?

The First Obligatory ended, and I released my breath.

We looked down our rows and moved to realign our positions. Mr. B waited until the energy in the room felt collected. Then he announced: "The First March."

Vivien paused, sensed our readiness, and began playing strident chords. Together, we moved through the military-like gestures of the First March. All of a sudden, the music grew soft as my movements took on a fluid, gentle character, fingers tracing the contour of my body. Focused on the quality of each gesture, I began to sense a connection with those around me.

"The Third Obligatory, the March Forward," Bennett declared.

With the first three steps we aimed our arms forward and marched directly towards the audience, moving with the whole of our body mass. We froze, leaning forward with arms outstretched just in front of them and passed quickly from one arm and leg position to the next, experiencing each as a stop action. On the twenty-ninth gesture we suddenly dropped to the floor, one leg bent under me and one extended; my left arm supporting my torso as my right arm arched above and I looked up into my palm. With the next beat I was sitting cross-legged on the floor, arms raised, palms cupped. As the music continued, my arms swung down and back, rocking me forward onto my knees. On the final chord, we all rose slowly as it faded into silence.

We were breathing hard. Mr. B had us sit down in place. He faced the visitors and spoke about the Obligatories being training exercises for those new to the Movements. We were beginners, he reminded the assembly, few of us having done Movements before arriving at Sherborne for the course. Thus, what they were witnessing and what we were attempting was a demonstration of our work in progress. The struggle within ourselves to be present as we worked at each movement being more to the point than a perfect execution.

Mr. B turned to us, saying, "Stand. The Fourth Obligatory."

This was the first movement that included mental work besides separate moving patterns for head, arms, and feet. Our right arms bisected the air in front of us as we bent forward and counted in clear voices, "One, two, three, four," our palms touching the floor on "four." Then the same in reverse. My body knew the sequence of gestures as long as I didn't try to think about it. What my mind had to do was stay focused on the progressive count forwards and backwards that somehow kept everything linked together.

Finally, we dropped forward, resting both hands on the floor, right legs moving backwards in measured intervals: "Three, four, five, six—six, five, four, three." A head sequence followed. Each new sequence increased in speed up to twelve and then back again by four: "twelve, eleven, ten, nine—nine, ten, eleven, twelve.

By the end our arms were flying in all directions. Bennett suddenly called out in a thunderous voice, *"STOP!"*

We froze in place, caught in mid-gesture, hopefully capturing an impartial snapshot of ourselves in that moment. I was never sure what my snapshot really looked like. Was I supposed to examine my facial expression? My body-posture? My thoughts? My thoughts were hard to catch, because they kept thinking. But I still liked the exercise of freezing in mid-posture, even if I wasn't sure what I was seeing.

After a long moment, Mr. Bennett said, "Rest."

My arms came down to my sides with everyone else's and we stood up. I allowed my muscles to relax and visualized the first gesture of the next movement. A moment later, Mr. Bennett announced it.

"Note Values," he said.

Vivien waited until Mr. B nodded in her direction. When she felt the group was connected with each other and with her, the first chord came crisp and clear. Everyone's right arm shot out in front, palm sideways. On the second note, all palms turned downwards. We listened to four distinct rhythmic notes, then began pulsing our outstretched arms in time to the music. The tick-tock of my arm echoed the beat of my heart.

Once our feet and heads were engaged, the arm gesture changed to a circular pattern. As my arm swept down and up like a slow propeller, I became aware of the rows in front and, with my peripheral vision, aware of those in the files on either side. Our arms seemed to sync with the strength of the note as it marked the bottom of the circle. For a few moments an invisible bond linked all our arms in one manifesting circle. Unlike the other movements we had been doing, this one had a pulsing, inner quality to it.

Feeling began to flutter in my breast like butterfly wings as we worked together. I wondered if those in the audience could feel it too. At the end, we were on our knees for eight slow beats, looking into the palm of our left hand. In that moment, it almost seemed like I could see my reflection there. We dropped our arms and raised one knee. As we stood on the final chord, I felt a stillness within myself that was echoed in the atmosphere of the room.

With a grin, Mr. B announced, "The Mazurka, the Sixth Obligatory."

Vivien jumped right in with the lively introduction. As I placed my fingertips lightly on the nape of my neck and my other hand on my hip, I pictured village girls with flouncy skirts and white peasant blouses. We immediately began an energetic folk dance, skipping in time to the music, tracing a triangular pattern with the tip of one foot and then the other. With cupped palms we extended our arms and brought them back to our sides as if receiving a gift.

I loved the light-hearted music. At one point, arms and head dangling, we slowly rose, uncurling our spines as we lifted our hands. All this while taking six running steps in place. It was a simple dance and repeated through three rounds of the music. On the last resounding chord, we suddenly dropped our arms with a last hop, as if sticking a landing after coming off a balance beam.

I dared a glimpse at faces in the crowd and seeing smiles, noticed a tickle of ego. I concentrated on keeping myself present, my face relaxed and neutral. Despite the mistakes I knew I'd made I felt the warmth of accomplishment but didn't want to waste my effort on self-congratulation. I wanted that energy to go towards nourishing what was real in me.

Mr. Bennett gave us a moment to catch our breath, then nodded at Chuck to lead our retreat out of the ballroom. As we left, we heard Mr. B addressing the audience, thanking them for coming and inviting them to stay for dinner.

At our table an older visitor complimented me on the demonstration. I wondered at that, since I'd made so many mistakes. But he also spoke about how important working on sensation had been throughout his life. I remember being surprised that one practice could be considered central. Bennett was giving us so many.

The dining room was zinging with energy—visitors, excitement, relief, jobs to get done, talk. Silver clinking on plates, porcelain platters rattling wood tables, questions, answers, water pouring into glasses, chairs scraping as people sat and rose.

Yet I became aware that we, the students, were holding something in check. The thought, reversing the flow of forces, came to mind. As I was getting into the habit of carrying the notion of the week's Theme inside me, it would pop up at odd moments of perception, like now.

I said something to Jack and heard the sound of my own voice despite the din. He responded and we connected, as if the two of us were inside a tranquil sphere, the energy in the room swirling over and around us. It felt like we had reversed a flow—instead of energy leaking out of us, we were contained within its flow, even drinking it in.

Tonight, the whole house feels more present, as if it's waiting for something it has tasted before.

CHAPTER FORTY-TWO
Higher States and Changing Stations

December 18, 1972—The visitors are gone but I'm still in a heightened state of awareness. There's more to this than the buzz from the weekend. Mr. B talks about the difference between being in a higher state of awareness and raising one's level of being to a higher station, or *maqam*, as the Sufis call it. Something like that might be happening now. I think I slipped into a higher state at the Theme meeting when Victor gave his observation about Reversal of the Flow of Forces. And it isn't just me. It's like when I used to get stoned and you could tell if someone you met was stoned too. It feels like that now—we're all sharing a higher state, and the house itself is containing it. We're like a school of fish swimming in the rarefied atmosphere of Sherborne House. It's become our milieu, so it seems normal until someone from the outside steps in causing unfamiliar ripples.

After Victor's question, normally quiet Jill also asked a question. She asked about the different states women go through, just before and during a menstrual period. Mr. B spoke about the importance of recognizing a passive state and allowing oneself to fully experience it, and that this is especially so for women.

He even said women should not come to morning exercise during the first day or two of their periods. This was a surprise to me, and I think for most of us, a revelation, really.

I asked Penny about it later, since she and Robert were longtime members of his original groups at Coombe Springs, the property in London where the Bennetts lived and held meetings and seminars.

"Bobby Jo, it's true. Once you start paying attention, you find yourself being more attuned to your body's rhythm. I can tell a day or two before my period starts that my state has shifted."

Capable Penny, with her black hair and ruddy cheeks and strong square-fingered hands, always struck me as an English version of a tomboy. Somehow this gave her more credence.

"We women miss a great opportunity if we go to morning exercise on those days. Instead, we should remain in our rooms and simply allow ourselves to relax into a collected state. This is the time to align with our feelings, relax our thoughts, and open ourselves to being receptive by ceasing the active work of directing our attention in a morning exercise. As women, our bodies cyclically induce a passive state, and this can open us to higher worlds where important and positive things can happen."

I had never thought of myself as a "woman." Having a period was just something to be dealt with, and if I had cramps, I'd do sit-ups to make them go away so I could carry on with whatever I was doing. This was the first time that being different from guys appeared to have an advantage. It felt special on a spiritual level, and I wanted in.

The next time my period came on, I decided to try what Penny had suggested.

"Bobby Jo, are you coming?"

Jack hung back, waiting for me to pick up the blue and white mohair shawl I'd knitted and always took with me to morning exercise.

"No, you go on. I'm going to do morning exercise here."

"In your room?"

"Yeah," I said, settling myself on the cushion I'd borrowed from the Ballroom.

"Are you feeling all right?" Jack hesitated, not sure whether to stay or go.

"I'm fine!" I said, too loud. "I'll be down for breakfast." I watched as Jack disappeared around the edge of the door frame, forgetting to shut the door.

Rising, I closed the door and went back to start again, standing above the cushion, becoming quiet inside before sitting down in one motion, like collapsing cups, into my crossed leg position, hands palm down on my upper thighs.

Resting my eyes on the oak planks a few feet in front of me, I relaxed my sight into a soft unfocused gaze, bringing my attention inwards. I followed my breath in, becoming aware of a slight pull and tug in my belly, releasing the unpleasant sensations as I exhaled and letting go the thoughts that named them. I followed the movement of muscles relaxing, starting with my face and watching softened tensions seep down like liquid through my torso and limbs, ending with my feet. Soon my feet started tingling as sensation travelled up through my legs and into my trunk. I noted twitches and fullness in my abdomen as sensation moved through, then filled my chest and back, started in my hands and moved up my arms to my shoulders, my neck, face, scalp—the rising tingle of energy connecting at the top of my head, like a net pulled together.

Too much active direction. Let go, let go. I brought my attention back to my breath, following its path in through the nose and down into my lungs and out again; in and out, in and out.

I diffused my awareness to hold how my body felt without judging it as good or bad. It was what it was. A sense of fullness that radiated out several inches all around me—a sensation of movement, a flow, centered in my abdomen. *Relax into this,* I suggested to myself.

Once I let go of trying, it was like floating on cotton, feeding on sunbeams, filled with golden light, attuned to the universe. I was a fine humming vibration, receiving and transmitting. Me but not me. The state lasted another half hour until the ache in my crossed legs told me it was time to finish.

Jack scooted over to make room for me at the table as I arrived with my bowl of porridge and plate of toast in either hand.

"How was morning exercise?" I asked.

"Good," said Jack, after a silent moment.

"So was mine." I smiled, relaxing onto the chair.

CHAPTER FORTY-THREE
My British Christmas

December 24, 1972—It's Christmas Eve and most of the Brits and some of the Europeans have gone for the holiday. I think one of the Americans had to fly home for a family emergency. I wonder if he'll be back.

The house feels empty yet full of camaraderie, the usual schedule and staff/student roles suspended. Rumor has it, Mick's been baking with abandon for two days, helped by those who know what they're doing. And Trudy is lending Jack and me her room while she and Emily are gone for the holidays. I'm excited, anticipating a romantic Christmas Eve, with lots of good things to eat and Jack all to myself. Bonus—we can wake up late Christmas morning and lounge around as long as we want, imagine that!

Jack and I have come back from church with the Bennett family. We stand inside the Great Hall, appreciating the work others have been doing this morning, draping the room in cut greens and mistletoe, filling the fireplaces with kindling and great logs.

"Hey! Watch where you're going," I say, as three kids careen around me, laughing and screeching in pursuit of each other, leaping down the tiered stone steps of the upper landing and racing away down the length of the magnificent room. Their echos hang in the air. A tap on my shoulder brings my head around. It's Richard, another student from America. I don't know him well, but he's serious about singing, and wants to start a student choir.

"Bobby Jo, there's a group of us going caroling after lunch, would you be interested?"

"Sure, who all is going?" I ask, curious.

"Oh, anyone who wants to go. I think we have about fifteen or so. Vivien is taking us around. We'll meet out back by the kitchen door."

The group trudges down a lane I've not noticed before, dressed in wool scarves, long skirts, pants, hats and mittens, crunching on gravel. My breath hangs in the sharp air, wet with the promise of snow. Wood smoke and ginger smells curl up from stone chimneys. It feels like Christmas.

"What are we singing?" I ask as we walk, watching Vivien chatting at the front of the assemblage. Without her flowing silk piano-playing costume she looks more like a down-to-earth, middle-aged English woman in the usual wool skirt, knee-high wool socks and sweater, brown hair brushing her shoulders under a knit wool hat.

"Vivien has some hand-outs. She'll pass them around when we get there, I guess," Jill of the short blond hair volunteers.

The lane is narrow with overhanging trees. I hadn't realized there was more to Sherborne Village than the short open stretch with the post office and Social Club. I'm not even sure where we are, but that doesn't matter. I'm along for the ride, enjoying my part in a tradition that feels quintessentially British. I like to sing and everyone knows Christmas carols.

"I hope they sing the same ones we do in America."

"Right."

I fall silent, becoming aware of myself walking in a foreign country, quaint and lost in time. I'm aware of the cold and relax the muscles that have tightened in response. Suddenly a heat in my right leg draws my attention. With a shock I recognize sensation. Sensation happening of its own accord. Sensation filling every blood cell of my leg with an energy beyond my experience. My thought goes to my left leg and sensation obediently blooms, rich and pulsing, inside the leg yet also outside it. *Wow. Now I understand what it means "to sense." I thought I knew, I thought I was doing it. But this is like it's doing itself or doing me. Far out!* I hold onto what is happening in my legs for as long as I can.

This unbidden moment of the strongest sensation I had ever experienced may have been the result of months of practicing sensation, learning to bring it on at my bidding, learning to direct it around my limbs—a harbinger of a shift in my "station," a new plateau from which to continue my efforts.

Vivien stops in front of a house and opens the gate. "Come on, duckies, come through, come through." Her smile pulls us together. We troop in and cluster around the heavy wood door. She passes out mimeographed sheets of lyrics and Richard leads us as we sing, "Good King Wenceslas," "Deck the Halls," and "We Wish You a Merry Christmas." Our voices are warming up, if not our hands. The door opens a crack and then widens—a sturdy, aproned woman standing there with young children on either side. Her stout husband towers behind, head and shoulders obscuring the rest of the lintel.

Warmed by having an audience, we launch into "God Rest Ye Merry Gentlemen." Soon the family is joining in the chorus, "O-oh, tidings of comfort and joy."

The little towheaded boy on the right tugs at his mother's sleeve. She bends down and he whispers loudly to her, "Can they thing Willie?"

Looking up she asks, "Do you Know 'Pat-a-Pan?'"

Vivien rifles through her papers and looks at Richard. He nods his dark shock of hair and asks the group, "How many of us know the lyrics to 'Willie Bring Your Drum?'"

I had never heard this old English carol, but a number of hands go up among the Brits.

Richard says, "Let's give it a go for this little guy." He smiles at the child, catches the eyes of the affirmative head shakers, and begins,

> Willie, take your little drum;
> Robin, bring your fife and come;
> And be merry while you play,
>
> Tu-re-lu-re-lu,
> Pat-a-pan-a-pan,
>
> Come be merry while you play,
> Let us make our Christmas gay!

Tu-re-lu-re-lu

The children make up the words they don't know and belt out *Tu-re-lu-re-lu* and *Pat-a-pan-a-pan*. I take my cue from them. We're all smiling by the last line, "Sing and dance this Christmas day!"

Our reward is a warm welcome into the little cottage, filling the sitting room as fresh cookies (what the Brits call biscuits) and hot chocolate are passed around. And so, we proceed from house to house, caroling down the village lane.

Later we see some of these same villagers, joined by the devout and/or curious, filling our seldom-used Sherborne Chapel which rises just feet beside the manor house, composed of the same majestic gray Cotswold stone. A general invitation has been extended for afternoon tea in the Great Hall of Sherborne House, following the service.

A long table on the upper end of the Great Hall is decorated and crowded with delights. Mick has outdone himself with assorted delicate sandwiches of cucumber, cheese and egg; mince-meat pies, fruit tarts, long twists of cheesy pastry and a chocolate cream-filled cake. We have never seen such a spread at Sherborne.

Visitors fill their plates, look up at the high ceiling, find their neighbors, and stand in clusters. Those of us who did not help with the cooking or decorations are asked to serve. I weave my way, offering black tea and sugar, "one lump or two?" Some guests migrate down the room to stand by the warmth of blazing logs, which for once fill the empty void of the fireplace. The scent of evergreens draping the mantle pull like a magnet, their piney resin mixing with aromas of sausage rolls and hot tea.

After the guests leave, Jack and I retire to the attic room Trudy has kindly lent us. She and Emily have gone to London. We bring the belongings we'll need for the week from our dorm rooms. I push the single mattress against the wall to make a love nest, thinking it's a good thing we are both thin. This is our first private time alone since the course started. But Christmas Eve is not over and several people want to go to Midnight Mass, ourselves included.

At nine we return to the Great Hall to find hot mulled wine inviting us with scents of cinnamon and clove, star anise and orange. Pressed into service once more, Jack and I pass out slices of Christmas stollen which has been aging for months under Mick's watchful eye in a hidden nook of the kitchen.

Drawn by warmth and camaraderie, Jack and I gravitate down the hall. We join others gazing into the Yule Log's flames, which are poked up every now and then, to spark and blaze blue-yellow, only to die low into a blanket of glowing orange embers. I sip my wine and nibble at the rum-soaked candied cake.

Hazy conversations rise and fall around me as the hour advances and my stomach begins to feel tight, my head light. I put aside half-eaten stollen and an unfinished mug of wine, concentrating on rallying. I want to experience Midnight Mass in England.

Finally, we pile into cars, the late-night air bracing, the packed-in bodies an excuse to rest my head on Jack's shoulder. Bumping and twisting down narrow roads we come at last to Prinknash Abbey, a stone edifice rising and disappearing into the dark night.

The Mass is as grand and as Catholic as I had hoped. Robed monks, candles, wreaths, incense, chants, Latin and bells; pageantry under a soaring ceiling, ancient stone walls, and the music of British voices. I kneel and sit, stand and kneel, sit and stand. For once, Christmas comes without the overriding anticipation of unwrapping piles of presents as its focus. My heart warms, full of peace and gratitude, but my stomach is not.

An unease has turned the hot wine sour and the liquor-laced stollen heavy in my belly. The return to Sherborne House is silent and long. Hurrying upstairs to our secret hideaway, I quickly change into my pajamas and lower myself onto the mattress, wiggling under the covers. Jack crawls in and starts stroking my arm.

"Don't," I say, rolling away.

"What? ...why?"

I lie silent, swallowing bile. "Move!" Flinging back the covers I push past him and rise and run out the door.

Returning from my unpleasant trip to the bathroom, I nudge Jack over and burrow into the warm spot he has made. I drape his arm over me and snuggle into his warmth, my back against his chest.

"Feeling better," he asks?

"Let's just go to sleep," I sigh, closing my eyes and hoping my stomach will behave.

December 25,

Scrambled eggs and hot chocolate for breakfast; feeling better, back to bed 'til 2:00 p.m.. Opened presents by the hearth. Jack gave me all the things he'd been wanting me to have—little trinkets, a drawing, such beautiful touchingness.

A mid-afternoon feast—turkey with all the trimmings, including Christmas pudding aflame. The Bennetts sharing their British Christmas, all of us stuffed to bursting. By nightfall, we sit by the Yule Log in the Great Hall again, sipping coffee and eating chocolates, a few of us conversing but my stomach still messed up.

For all the wonderful impressions of these past couple of days, including Trudy's gift of lending Jack and me her room for the holidays, my expectations of a lazy, romantic time together have been spoiled by this flu. I wonder if this is what Mr. B means when he talks about the law of temptation. That for every positive action, there is a corresponding negative response. It is just at this juncture, when we have done something particularly well, that we are most vulnerable to temptation. This is when we are most likely to be caught off guard and can lose everything that we have gained.

I believe I fell prey to abandoning myself to food and drink, to anticipating "time off." You think you're rewarding yourself but you're really throwing away the benefits of your efforts, because the energy is being diverted into self-satisfaction instead of building a higher body. If I'd remained "awake" rather than losing myself in grand expectations, I bet I wouldn't have gotten sick.

CHAPTER FORTY-FOUR
Shifting into Mesoteric Gear

December 31, 1972—At the New Year's Eve feast, when everyone was back from vacation and we were really cutting loose, Mr. B suddenly called a STOP in the middle of the festivities.

Afterwards, Mick, who was sitting at our table, rubbed his hands together and said, "We're in gear now, baby!" Both he and Anna Hodgson, another student from the old Coombe Springs days, seemed quite excited.

Mr. B had suggested that we make a list of how we saw ourselves, both the positive and negative. In my journal, I noted the following:

* Neat and tidy;
* Wants to do everything herself—doesn't look for ways to include others in tasks—wants to do things her own way (self-will);
* Slave to doing what she thinks she's supposed to—schedules, rules, assignments, tasks, etc.;
* Afraid to "let go";
* Confused—doesn't see what's going on all the time;
* Doesn't trust the understanding she gains from her own experience, afraid of being "tricked" by others, by herself, by her ego;
* Wants to Love—everyone, everything;
* Understands "I" = God. We're all the same "I," the same God;
* Believes if she can let ego go and Be, experience "I" in the same place and at the same time as another, then all will return to the source and become one "I."

January 1, 1973—The course started up with the weekly Theme talk this morning. Mr. Bennett told us we were entering the mesoteric phase of the course (between exoteric and esoteric). I guess this is the part where we are starting to know something, have even experienced something, but we lack understanding. If knowledge + experience = understanding, then the next step is accumulating experience that results in understanding.

Mr. B is asking us not to talk in the evenings, particularly about the Work and our experiences or feelings. He warned us not to talk about these things as if we know something. He told us that wiseacring and the need to do so is a manifestation of ego. That we need to overcome these weaknesses of ego to become strong in the Work. He also said something about confusion providing good fertile ground for "things to happen."

January 3— I am sick. So sick. Started with the flu on Christmas Day. Jack got it too. But he's better and I am not. After the holiday we went back to our respective dorm rooms. Now I can't get out of bed. I'm shivering all the time or burning up with fever.

Elizabeth Bennett came upstairs to check on me. She reminds me of my mom, practical and matter of fact. She could tell I was sick, and I could sense her concern. I'm the only one on the course who's been ill for more than a day or two, except for someone who came back from India with the mumps. My glands are so swollen I can hardly swallow. Elizabeth thinks I have the mumps and is treating me with belladonna, a homeopathic medicine. Little white pills that I must let melt under my tongue. I think they make me hallucinate.

I stay in bed with my long johns on under my nightgown and a wool scarf around my neck. In the mornings I drag myself to the bathroom, determined to at least keep up with doing the cold-water ablutions.

Emily, in her twenties but still very much Trudy's little girl, is always there in the hall, just outside my dorm room on top of the radiator, her butt robbing what little heat the old unit manages to emit with its faint clanking noises.

She comes fully dressed, skinny legs dangling, sitting and clutching her cardigan close like green moss. We all parade past her, still dazed by sleep, shuffling to the bath and sink rooms. Peering over her protruding overbite she watches me tread down and back again, no doubt wondering why she's the one society puts a label on. One day she pronounces from her perch, "You're going to kill yourself if you keep doing this, you know."

So now I just stay in bed.

The other night I awoke in a cold sweat. I couldn't tell if I was in the clutches of a nightmare or truly sensed an evil presence in the house.

I lie still, trying not to breathe too loud, staying hidden. From my corner of the room, I watch little red lights darting about. Something isn't right. I sit up, my head throbbing, drumming, screaming with the motion, but I'm drawn out of bed. Everyone's asleep, I look over at Barbara June's bed, her flying egg drawings pinned to the wall above her sleeping form. Aziza, snoring softly, is unaware of the danger lurking, lurking, somewhere. Even Nina, in the other corner bed, lies still with deep even breaths. The house feels vulnerable, too quiet. My skin prickles. Someone needs to be on guard.

I creep out of the room and down the dark hall. Nothing up here; it must be somewhere else. I make my way softly downstairs, gripping the balustrade as I descend step by step, all my senses awake, my body singing with fever as I listen intently to the dark, to the creaks, to the cold.

I tiptoe down the long corridors to the back stairs leading to the basement kitchen. Nutty, slow roasting aromas of oatmeal waft out of the Aga. Fighting against my fear, I push open the heavy door to surprise the Evil One. But he doesn't show himself. He knows I'm on to him. Found out, he has no power.

I hear myself sigh, releasing a breath I didn't know I was holding. My shoulders and arms soften as the fear lets go. A little half-smile, a sense of achievement. I have protected the house from his intrusion this night. There's nothing more to do. I drag my fever, my thud-clumping head, my glands that won't let me swallow, all the way back upstairs to bed, bare feet numb from the cold of stone and wood. At least the house and all in it are safe from the Devil tonight. Now I can attend to myself and get well.

CHAPTER FORTY-FIVE
The Two Georges

"The photo belongs to George, but perhaps you would like to make a sketch of it?" White-haired and bird-like Mary Cornelius peered at me and offered to walk me to her flat for exercise and a change of scene. As we slowly traversed the long corridor, my legs felt like rubber and I leaned on her for support. I was alarmed at how weak I felt and surprised at Mary's strength. My perception had changed too, as if there was a bubble around me now that I was out of the safe zone of my bed.

In the presence of Mary, and in their own space, her husband George seemed almost gentle, his usual manner tamed. The two of them were an interesting couple. American bluster and swagger juxtaposed a gentle British soul.

After settling me in George's own overstuffed easy chair, which he graciously vacated, she brought out the photograph of Mr. Gurdjieff. It was the same close-up head shot as the one used on the fly leaf of *All and Everything*. Mary handed me a stick of drawing charcoal. When I protested that I couldn't draw, she just pooh-poohed my objections, "You needn't be an artist, my dear," she chirped in her soothing accent. "Just do this. Gaze at the photo, that's right. Now look away and draw what you see in your mind's eye."

I followed her instructions, since no one was expecting anything special. I didn't have my glasses on, and the photo was propped up on the mantle at a distance, yet it felt good to be moving the piece of charcoal in my hand. Since I couldn't see, I wasn't worried about the likeness. There was still a soft, comfortable, bubble-like state surrounding me.

As I drew, I thought of what it must have been like when Gurdjieff was around. He was a George too, but everyone referred to him as Mr. Gurdjieff. From stories I'd heard it sounded like he emanated an exotic mix of East and West. The East, with his cushions and carpets and inner exercises; the West, with his intellect and grasp of science as well as of music and the arts. I never admitted it, but I was glad I hadn't been around when he was alive. I was sure I would have been terrified of doing Movements with him. Not just because of the extraordinary presence he emanated, but the way he saw into people and was able to expose them to themselves, placing demands on them that stretched one in uncomfortable new ways. Then again, he seemed to be gentler with young people and especially with women. Some people just felt incredible love radiating out from him.

When I was done with my drawing it surprised me to see a misty-looking face that could be construed to be a resemblance of the photo I had looked at. Mary approved my effort and admonished me to take the drawing and keep it by my bedside.

"You can draw strength from it for your recovery," she assured me.

Forty years later, reading Allen Roth's own account of his experience on the first course at Sherborne, I came across the following passage about his last day on the course and a conversation he had at the farewell barbecue with George:

> George Cornelius and I had a glass of beer together, walking and chatting. As we sat down in the circle of benches, George turned to recounting fresh tales about Mr. Gurdjieff.
>
> Being part of Bennett's English retinue, George visited Gurdjieff several times, until he received orders for duty in eastern Turkey during World War II.
>
> While there on a mission involving a radio transmitter on Ararat's slopes, George came down with a multiple infliction of jaundice, pneumonia, and dysentery. His fever rose precipitously. The army medical staff in Ankara was doubtful of his surviving the night. In the midst of delirium he saw Gurdjieff's photograph, which he requested be hung in his room.

At that moment in the story George leaned forward and looked straight at me [Allen.] "All of a sudden I heard him speaking. His voice sounded just like wind whistling in iced-up telephone lines in the winter—you ever heard that sound?—and said: 'Not worry, American, you not die.'"

George's delirium broke during the night. All he could remember of the past days was the vivid transcontinental reception of the voice. As soon as George was able, he returned to Paris to relate his unusual tale. Packed into Gurdjieff's apartment were the customary visitors and hangers-on, making private talk impossible. But he found himself seated next to him [Gurdjieff] for supper. The first words to him from Gurdjieff came abruptly, like a little thunderclap inserted between two moments. "You believe now, don't you, American? I say not die; not die."[1]

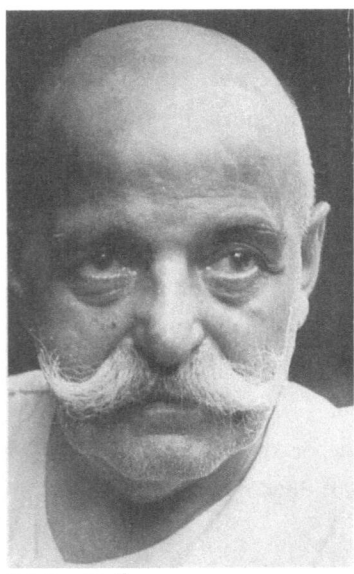 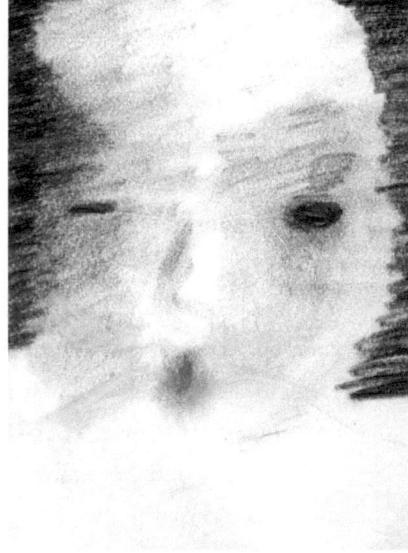

G. I. Gurdjieff   Bobby Jo's charcoal drawing.

After my visit with Mary and George that day I kept the drawing near my bed. It made me feel closer to Mr. Gurdjieff, as if I now had some kind of

---

[1] Allen Roth, *Sherborne, An Experiment in Transformation* (Santa Fe: Bennett Books, 1998).

mystical contact with him. After coming across the above story in Allen's book, I'm certain I did and that Mary had known I would.

January 13—Tonight, we celebrated Gurdjieff's birthday with a traditional Gurdjieff feast. I was well-enough to go. The plates were chained up, hand to hand, from the kitchen all the way up to the dining room. As the last person in the chain received their feast, they took their seat at one of the tables. Each course was covered by the plate above, all carefully balanced one on top of the other—dinner of savory lamb shank, roasted potatoes, and greens—then a delicate clear soup, then a small portion of Gurdjieff's special salad (tiny bits of celery, tomato, cucumber, secret herbs and whatever else) in a juicy mix that tasted slightly of licorice. But of course, the meal was really all about the Toasts to the Idiots.

We each had a small glass of brown-gold Armagnac liquor at our plates. I was sitting next to Jack, who was enjoying his soup. As the meal progressed, the ring of a spoon on a water glass hushed the room. Mr. B spoke about Gurdjieff's "Science of the Idiots" recalling the many meals he had attended just after WW II in Gurdjieff's crowded flat in Paris, at 6 rue des Colonets Renard. The first Idiot, starting at the bottom in ascending order (according to one's type), was the Ordinary Idiot. The twenty-first and final Idiot was God, the Unique Idiot. Resting my forkful of meat on the edge of the porcelain dinner plate, I listened with the hope of learning what Idiot I might be.

As the room grew quiet, Mr. Bennett spoke up, recalling one night in Paris when Mr. Gurdjieff had looked at him intently and raised his glass declaring, "To all Round Idiots." Everyone in the flat had raised their Armagnac repeating, "To all Round Idiots!" Then Gurdjieff had added, "And to you, Bennett!" Mr. B mimicked Gurdjieff slowly tracing a large circle in the air with his finger and saying, "You R-O-U-N-D Idiot. Round Idiot—always Idiot!"

Mick Sutton jumped to his feet, lifted his glass and declared, "To all Round Idiots and to you, Mr. Bennett!"

We all sang-out together, "To all Round Idiots and to you, Mr. Bennett."

There were square Idiots, zig-zag Idiots, squirming Idiots. Each level of Idiot was announced with an explanation or anecdote. Some were accompanied by, "And to you, Pierre," or "To You, Mick," when their designated Idiot was named. Mr. B even christened some of the students with a toast, naming their Idiot. We were all encouraged to discover our own Idiot, with the caveat that as we developed inwardly, our Idiot could change.

When the toast came for the Enlightened Idiot, something in me resonated. Yes, that was it! I'd found my Idiot.

January 20—

    Passing Fa
    i thought i'd learned it all
    Fourteen Days in Bed
    revelations by the score

    my Body no good
    Ego tripping to trip me up
    it goes so well, it
    keeps me right asleep

    Yet there's no time
    to rest
    to contemplate
    the rest to learn

    I learned

    All the devils in me
    are false personality

"i's"

I learned a charm
to keep me safe

I learned
it doesn't work

I couldn't write then
it's all lost now
swimming somewhere
inside my head

I'm torn apart, battered and bashed
quashed, succumbed.

Hurting Sore and Troubled
midpoint on the scale
this Enneagram circles
while I am stuck in the long dark
passage,

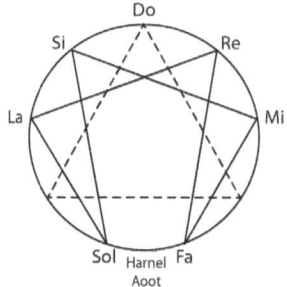

the Harnel-Aoot of the soul
with the hangnail of ego still,
just there

Rip it Out!

You think you're an Enlightened Idiot?

idiot
    Idiot
        IDIOT

fool

January 26—Last night in the bathroom, as I lay my worn toothbrush down on the edge of the sink, I looked up and froze. Gazing back at me from the rectangle of glass was a face I didn't recognize—an animal, evil thing.

I stared back, not through round, blue eyes but small, calculating ones. No cute little nose, but one that sniffed out self-interest. Not ordinary ears but those that heard only what they wanted. The grin was that of a wolf with set jaw. No heart-shaped, innocent face here but a calculating, judgmental, self-interested one.

Horrible Creature! Was this the *me* behind the mask of false personality?

A sentence comes—Ordinary man does not see himself in the glass, but the reflection of his self-love and vanity.

January 28—
So how do I get this goose out of its bottle?
— There, it's out!

Chapter Forty-Six
Fire Drill

One cold morning in late February, everyone was assembled in the Horse Parlor to listen to the local fire marshal talk about fire safety. We were to evacuate the building in case of fire and gather in the main parking lot at the front of the house to be accounted for. It seemed strange to have this local official talking to us in his earnest and somewhat pompous manor, as if we were school children.

Irmgard, a German woman who lived in one of the attic rooms with a pet pigeon she'd befriended from the roof, was sitting near me in the meeting. I didn't know her well, but I did know that she had a history of mental issues and had had to leave the course for a time.

The fire marshal said, "Now you must all go out to the parking lot and assemble there with your dorm mates when I sound the alarm." He then left the room.

When the alarm sounded, everyone dutifully began to rise and make their way out the doors at the front and back of the room. As the room emptied, Irmgard and I were left, looking at each other.

I knew she was thinking the same thing as I. That this wasn't a drill, it was real. That the fire marshal was like a Gestapo character, telling us what to do, and everyone was following his orders like sheep to the slaughter. We seemed to be the only ones who were awake to the situation, seeing it for what it was. We both knew in an instant that we each had something important to do. Looking at each other, we knew we shared the same state of awareness and would not be following the others out to the parking lot, at least not yet.

We both rose, rushing out the door to run up to our rooms. Irmgard had to save her pigeon, and I had to do something but wasn't quite sure yet what it was. I just knew I had to make it up to the room before the house was engulfed in flames.

I burst into my room and looked around. Then I knew what it was that was so all-important that I was risking my life coming up here to do. I had come here to make my bed, which I did every day without fail. That's what it boiled down to. Seven months on the course searching for enlightenment, and making my bed was the most important thing before I died. A bloodcurdling scream rose up from my inner depths and I fell backwards onto the mattress, feeling as if I were pitching off a cliff into a black void.

Irmgard stuck her head in my door. She had her pigeon in her hands and urged me to get out. We had to get to the parking lot with the others. She was already gone as I rushed out to the narrow landing and leaned over the railing, looking down. The thought came to me that I could jump over the railing and fly down the three flights of stairs. It would be faster, and time was suddenly of the essence. Wasn't I about to be engulfed in flames? I thought I could smell smoke. Something in me checked the urge to jump, and instead I started running down the stairs.

As I ran through the building, I had the experience that the fire caught up with me and I died in the conflagration. It was as if it was really happening, but in a parallel universe like a premonition of how I would one day die. I saw myself in heaven looking around for Jack, but not finding him.

"I'll wait for you," Jack had said as he filed out with the rest. Remembering his words, I knew he would find me, even if we died separately and he had to look for me in heaven. Then it came to me—everyone had gone to assemble in the graveled parking lot, so I made my way there.

I was just being missed from the roll call. I could see Mr. B standing head and shoulders over the little fire marshal. His usual wide-eyed look had been replaced by a frown.

Mr. B came up, bent down and peered at me. He looked at me disapprovingly and said loudly, "Bobby Jo, if you do not behave, we will have to send you home. I will only give you one more warning!"

Suddenly I knew we were sharing a private reality where he was playing the role of headmaster and I of the disobedient student. I was sure everyone thought Bennett's public reprimand of me was stinging, but I knew we were playing roles, and that what he had to say was for the benefit of the fire marshal. It was as if the two of us were peeking out from behind a curtain, seeing everyone on stage like marionettes unaware of the strings that controlled their movements. Bennett had lifted the veil for me, but no one else seemed aware that all of us were puppets performing for the fire marshal. That all our lives, we had just been performing—for our parents, our teachers, our bosses, each other.

My biggest concern was wondering how long I could hold on to this heightened awareness and remain "awake." I translated Mr. B's reprimand as his way of letting me know that I would have to be crafty about guarding this awareness because others wouldn't understand.

The whole experience was such a vivid and multi-layered one that I couldn't speak of it to anyone, even Mr. B, afraid the reality and meaning of it would fade or be altered. Not wanting to talk about it gave me a new understanding of "cast not ye pearls before swine lest they be trampled underfoot." I realized the danger was in the retelling and parsing of meaning which would inevitably alter my memory of the event. I stored this up inside to be pondered, like Mary had done with events surrounding Jesus.

Not long after the fire drill, I went to a Movements class that Mick Sutton was teaching. We were working on Number Ten, and the music was light and airy. It was a movement we already knew, so we were concentrating on refining it. My state was still heightened, and I began to move, sweeping my arms to one side and then the other in a flowing arc.

To my surprise, the air became infused with delicate pastel colors. As my arms swept down and up, tinkling bell tones sounded, like wind moving a chime. The pinks, blues, and greens of air molecules floated and danced in the current created by my hands. It was fascinating. The veil that clouded my vision had once again been lifted. Who knew the very air we moved through was made of exquisite color, light, and sound? Extraordinary! I watched pastel colors float and dance, listening to their etheric music.

Mick must have noticed something about my state, for he pulled me out of line and had me sit in front of the class, ostensibly to observe. It made no difference. The air still rang and danced to the currents created by everyone's movements. It was beautiful, and I wondered how long I could hold onto this expanded awareness.

As we left the ballroom and I walked back through the halls of Sherborne, the dimension of the air that I was experiencing faded. For the first time, I was unsure whether my heightened state was something to strive to maintain, or if there was a danger of getting lost in the enchanted forest of fairy-tale lessons.

CHAPTER FORTY-SEVEN
Long-Term Decisions

Mr. Bennett leaned forward in his straight-backed chair, facing us as we sat cross-legged, crowded over the old Persian carpet, our faces uplifted to catch his words. The staff ringed around the perimeter of the Horse Parlor, some in chairs, some standing, everyone waiting.

"Mick? Mick," Mr. B searched the crowd.

"Here, sir!" Mick pushed his shoulder against the wood, straightening his long back away from the door frame at the far end of the room, arms still crossed in his signature stance.

"Yes? Good." Mr. B settled back into the chair, its claret upholstery dusted with age.

Gathering the student body and staff into his awareness, Mr. Bennett began, "We will soon be entering the forty-day period known as Lent. Up to this point we have been establishing the practice of a daily decision by means of the Decision Exercise which I introduced to you earlier in the course. The period of Lent affords us the opportunity to take this work to another level, utilizing a forty-day decision.

"As you know, we have been making a distinction between individual will, linked to something higher, and self-will, a manifestation of ego. This exercise can help us strengthen real will.

"The forty-day decision would work something like this. One chooses a long-term project that can be completed within the time period but does not call attention to one's self, preferably something that benefits others. Every morning at the end of morning exercise, you visualize the completed project and then the portion that can be accomplished that day, choosing something from your preparation the night before. One then answers the questions, "What is to be done today? Why am I doing this? How do I see myself doing it? Of course, one asks the key question, 'Am I going to do this?'"

Mr. Bennett paused, weighing the import of his words on us.

A soft winter light filtered in through the wood-encased windows, shining small square patches on the lucky ones sitting in its path, bringing the promise of fresh-turned earth and new beginnings.

He continued, "Those of you who smoke and would wish to give up this habit can meet with me as a separate group. Working with an essence habit such as this is quite difficult and provides a real opportunity."

A feeling of envy stirred in my chest. I was almost sorry not to be a smoker. There was a sense in the room amongst them, almost of privilege, it seemed to me. They would get to meet and work with Mr. B privately. Those lucky smokers!

A hand went up and Mr. B responded, "Yes?"

"Mr. B, what about meat? Doesn't Gurdjieff talk about giving up meat? Would that be something we should do during Lent?"

Mr. Bennett considered his next words. "It's true that in *Beelzebub's Tales* the Kelnuanian council decided to take up Hertoonano's suggestion and fix certain times of the year to abstain from the substance Eknokh, which is the element contained in meat, milk, and eggs. But that is quite an undertaking."

Mr. Bennett asked the assembly, "This can only be done if all are in agreement. Can we come to a consensus? What are your thoughts?"

"I think we should do it," someone said, and several heads nodded.

As the discussion went back and forth, momentum began to build for the notion of giving up meat and its by-products.

Suddenly Mick Sutton was standing in the middle of the room, his lanky frame pulled up to its full height, arms decidedly crossed over his chest.

"Mr. B, there's no way I can accommodate this notion from a practical point of view. Look, there are bound to be exceptions—children, the elderly; the kitchen cannot be expected to handle all kinds of special cases. We wouldn't be able to make it work for everyone. So I say *no!*"

Mick Sutton.

Mick, who was so respectful and devoted to Mr. Bennett, stood his ground, fire flashing out of his dark eyes, South London accent bubbling up from where he usually kept it tamped down.

Mr. Bennett acknowledged Mick with a slow nod of his great head, putting an end to the discussion. Mick retreated to the back of the room.

Closing his eyes, Mr. Bennett started speaking, "In the Christian tradition, Lent is a time of fasting and looking inwards. During these forty days, there is an energy that comes, the world over, from sharing this practice of giving something up. Many religions include similar periods of time to practice some form of denial. For instance, Muslims have Ramadan, a month of holy fasting."

I watched the familiar gesture of his long fingers massaging the scrolled arm ends of his chair. Half addressing us and half looking inward, he continued, "Giving something up, denying oneself, opens one in a way that is not always accessible. Here, at Sherborne House, we also have the advantage of working together, which is a great help.

"During these forty days, besides taking on a forty-day decision I would like to propose that we fast, meaning no food or drink except water, on specified days. If anyone wants to take on something in addition, that is up to each individual."

A weight settled in the room, or at least in me as I listened, feeling rather than picturing fasting. I had experimented with fasting in college and knew I could do it. I also knew it made the day long. Yet there was something else, a gathering of resolve, a wish to Work—a recognizable "yes" coming from that place deep inside that I was learning to trust. Looking around, I felt a coalescing, the group opening to a readiness to take on a new challenge.

Mr. Bennett looked at his watch and announced, "I believe our time is up. Is there anything else?" He waited for a response, then rose in one long piece, turned sharply around his chair and exited the door behind it that led to the Great Hall.

The rest of us filed out gradually, waiting to pass through both front and back doors of the Horse Parlor. As I moved slowly towards the door, I wondered, *what can I take on as a forty-day decision? What task can take forty days to complete without calling attention to myself?* I didn't have a clue.

CHAPTER FORTY-EIGHT
Religion

Sunshine warmed the chill air of March as I sat in the back seat of the Bennetts' car, wedged in with the family. My wish to go to church had exempted me from the morning's assigned practical work. I watched fields roll by, neatly outlined in hedgerows along the deep narrow lanes that twisted and turned, taking us to Stow-on-the-Wold.

Empty streets lent a Sunday quiet as the car rolled into the village and Mr. B parked by the Catholic church. The church was small, made of buff-colored Cotswold stone, its wooden pews plain and uncomfortable. Mr. Bennett's family took up a whole row, and I ended up sitting next to him. The Mass was simple, with no choir, a single priest performing the ceremony. A wooden cross hung over the altar with the familiar figure of Christ, arms outstretched, head fallen forward, feet pinned together.

My father had grown up singing in the Episcopal choir and so had I. My mother, after growing up a strict Methodist, decided that it was more important for her family to go to church together than which church it was. So, she converted. The Roman Catholic church seemed very similar to what I was used to in the Episcopal, with readings from the Bible, hymns, a weighty sermon, communal prayers I recognized, and the sanctified bread and wine of Christ's body and blood.

I remembered back to seventh grade. The dogwoods were having a good spring. Little white clusters of petals adorned our backyard tree where I was posing, dressed in a short, white, shirt-waist dress with patent leather pumps, a lace veil draping my head and shoulders. Mom had made the dress, and I picked out the trim of little blue horses prancing around the hem, waist, and bodice. My girlfriend from Sunday School confirmation class was dressed up too. We posed to have our pictures taken next to the blooming dogwood before the long drive downtown. Parishes from all over the diocese were convening at the National Cathedral in Washington, D.C., the bishop presiding. For me this was a momentous culmination of months of preparation.

My turn finally came to kneel at the altar in that ornate and soaring space. The chamber echoed every footstep on stone, every rustle of program. Rows and rows of white-clad girls and dark-suited boys sat or stood behind me, working their way slowly towards this blessing.

The bishop placed his hands on my head. And I felt—nothing. No white dove flew down proclaiming my transformation as a confirmed Believer in the Episcopal faith. No warm flow of grace washed through me. I was devastated. I believed in God; I believed in miracles. Why hadn't anything miraculous happened upon receiving this holy sacrament?

My attention returned to the present moment in a cold and unadorned church in the Cotswolds. I rose from my kneeler as the Bennett family stood, the mass concluded. My head came up, my gaze falling on the figure of Christ elevated above me on the cross. I don't know if the expression emanating out from the carved face had been there before or if it was unveiled for me alone.

Time swallowed me into a NOW moment.

Transfixed, I saw Christ in crushing, excruciating agony, still bearing the sins of our world. A weight pierced me; my body took the blow, my mind awash in revelation.

My knees buckled as a whoosh of air and an audible *Ooooh* escaped, as if I'd been socked in the stomach. Mr. Bennett caught my arm, propelling me out of the pew and down the aisle. I had the impression that he knew full well what I was experiencing but didn't want attention called to me. It seemed clear that his capacity to take control of the situation bore testimony to the strength with which he was able to bear the import of that image for both of us.

Again, I felt that Mr. B and I had slipped into another dimension of *seeing*. Later, the thought of seeking him out in private to talk about what had happened stopped me in my tracks. What could I possibly say that wouldn't devalue what had happened, bring it into ego or personality? I knew I was not spiritually evolved enough to discuss such occurrences with the likes of Mr. Bennett. Yet I couldn't help but feel I had arrived, that I was traveling in a world of finer energies—the world of Reality.

Before this experience I had already been asking questions of myself, like today while pulling weeds during practical work. We were on the expanse of green lawn behind the Manor house. I pondered under drifting gray clouds as my group worked in silence: Was Jesus a real person? Was he really God's son? Was I a Christian?

Do you believe in Jesus? I put this question squarely in front of myself. I had to admit I had my doubts. It occurred to me that I never addressed my prayers to Jesus, only to God. I had developed a relationship with God in childhood and I was quite at ease talking with Him. I had to admit, it wasn't like that with Christ.

A memory came forward—I was falling asleep in my own room painted a pale blue, "my color," which matched my toothbrush and glass in the bathroom. My older sister's color was red and my little brother's was yellow. Mom had let us pick our colors and I was always glad I'd chosen blue. I was in ninth grade and facing my first-ever final exams. I couldn't fall asleep, my stomach was in knots, my head whirled. Had I studied hard enough? Would I freeze with pencil in hand and forget everything I thought I knew? Could I possibly remember a year's worth of—*everything? Oh, God—HELP me!*

In that pit of desperation, I reached my hand out from under the covers and in my mind's eye watched as God leaned down and held my hand. Inside myself I heard him say, *"It will be all right."*

And it was.

But this never happened with Jesus, it was always God. We were buddies.

So where did this leave me as a Christian? I dug my spoon into the spring-soft dirt to get under a dandelion root and enjoyed the little snap and give as the root popped free and I plucked it out of the grass.

My thoughts wandered to our current morning exercise, The Four

Prophets, where I was developing relationships with Mohammed, Buddha, and Lama as well as Jesus. Each of these four personages anchored a major religion. Each had millions of devout believers praying to them throughout the ages, accumulating energy which we could envision collecting above their respective holy cities of Mecca, Benares, Lhasa, and Jerusalem.

I thought about how I was able to connect to that energy and pull it back into myself to nourish my own inner growth. How each prophet could be associated with a higher emotion. Mohammed with hope, Buddha with acceptance, Lama with faith, and Jesus with love. I was learning to send a thread of sensation out into space and time and then pull it back into a sensing limb, to blend the captured energy with mine.

It seemed to me now that throughout history each of these prophets had been sent from God to bring a specific action into the world. In my mind, the prophets were equals, but love seemed the greatest gift from God, and it was brought by Christ.

"Bobby Jo, didn't you hear the bell?" Lynne nudged me with a mischievous foot.

I stood up, bringing my attention back into my body, sensing my feet. I took a breath in and became aware of the center of my chest, arousing a feeling of "I." Exhaling, I become aware of my whole body and a sense of "AM." After repeating this exercise for three breaths, I bent down and resumed my excavation of dandelions.

But was Jesus closer to God than the others? Did I, should I, worship him? What was my relationship with him?

As I dug at the weeds, the tingle of sensation drew part of my attention into my hands, the sense of "I Am" lingered in my feelings, my thoughts relaxed, and a small vision opened for me.

I saw the lineage from whom I came: my parents, my grandparents, my British and German ancestors—spooling back in time. Some had probably been Catholic, some Protestant, it didn't matter—they were Christian. I saw this thread of Christianity running through me as part of my essence, part of who I was historically, a core of essential belief. I *was* a Christian. It was my choice as to what style or church I was drawn to. I pictured myself practicing Islam or Buddhism. Sure, I could practice another religion and believe in its tenets. But underneath it all, I would essentially still be Christian. Did I have to believe that Christ was the only messenger from God and that all other religions were false in order to be a Christian? No.

Christ had presented himself. Having a relationship with him now was up to me.

I'd just had my first religious experience in a Catholic church. Between contemplating a future with Jack, who was Catholic, and experiencing a miracle in the Catholic church, I decided to convert to Catholicism. I met with the priest and he gave me a little catechism to study. I convinced myself that reading eight pages of the catechism every day could be my forty-day decision. The problem was that one hundred and twelve pages meant I'd be done in just fourteen days, almost four weeks shy of the forty days we were to work with this exercise.

I'd have to figure something out.

The now familiar mop, its wooden handle an extension of my arms, was dancing down the long corridor of the second-floor dorms, my hips swaying in time. Mr. B's secretary Zimmy was short, with pageboy-length brown hair and a pleasant round face. She found me at work and handed me a small, folded piece of paper. It was a notice indicating that I was to meet privately with Mr. Bennett. This was no surprise. Word had gone round that we were to review our forty-day decisions at these meetings.

CHAPTER FORTY-NINE
March

Feet planted firmly on the floor, sitting erect on the front edge of the straight-back chair, I waited for Mr. Bennett to speak. The knot in my stomach belied my quiet exterior, my hands sensing away like crazy in my lap. This time I didn't look around to note the bookshelf beside his desk, the glow from the table lamp, papers sitting in piles here and there. I didn't know what he would say to me. We hadn't interacted since the incident in the church, which had never been discussed.

Bennett swiveled around from his desk, the lamp shining through unruly white hair like a halo atop his high forehead and searching eyes. He greeted me with a kind smile, "Hello, Bobby Jo."

Taking a quick look at his watch, he went right to it. "And what have you been thinking of taking on as your forty-day decision?"

I told him about my visit with the priest and my intention of becoming Catholic.

He considered this. "And once the fourteen days are up and you've finished reading the catechism, what will you do then? What are you doing for a practical project to help the house? Something that is not for yourself," he added.

"That's just the problem," I complained, a sigh escaping in a long exhalation. "I can't think of anything to do that won't draw attention."

Mr. B sat back in his chair, contemplating. "How about the ground floor loo? I am quite certain that could use a coat of paint. It's rather out of the way, is it not?" He seemed to be watching me, noting my reaction to this helpful suggestion.

The knot in my stomach held, the room felt unnaturally warm. I would have squirmed if I dared. But I was so sure it was right for me to convert to the Catholic church. Shouldn't I be using my time for that rather than painting a bathroom?

I pictured the downstairs loo, a bathroom in a back hall in the basement. Rumor had it that Elizabeth had dubbed it "Richard Duffel's Loo." Richard Duffel, an elderly man with arresting indentations on either side of his balding forehead, had come on the first Basic Course and stayed for ours. Sanding and painting the dank closet-size loo in a dark corridor held no appeal. But I had to admit, no one except Richard Duffle used it much, so it wouldn't draw attention.

It wasn't just sitting in front of Mr. B that was making me uncomfortable. My forty-day decision to study the catechism didn't feel right. *But why?* Something about self-will? Nothing in me wanted to work in Richard Duffel's Loo. Yet something in me knew that was exactly what I needed to do.

"All right," I agreed, and noticed that the knot in my tummy had dissolved, even as my head said *yuk*.

Sitting cross-legged on the edge of my foam pad mattress, ankles resting on the floor, and my hands on my knees, I closed my eyes and pictured reading the next eight pages of the catechism, noting my progress through the booklet. Next, I pictured the finished loo, its walls smooth with two coats of green paint over a white primer. T o m o r r o w I would begin the project, scraping behind the toilet and sink. I sensed my hand holding a putty knife as I scraped it up and down against the flaking old paint. In these evening preparations I was getting a sense of connection with what was possible to accomplish during the day to come. My visualization and sensation guided me, seeming to know when to stop.

I came to trust that, once a decision was made, it took on a life of its own. My body would remember if my mind did not, and I would find myself carrying out the decision. It was no longer a matter of liking or wanting to do the thing.

Jack had also taken on a forty-day task that involved an inner struggle

235

with his preferences. At some point every day, he went outside with clippers and worked on trimming the hedges that defined the border at the back of the manor's lawn. Having grown up in a city, he was no gardener and was not inclined to work outside. I learned what he had taken on only after Lent was over.

Our inner work deepened with the intensity of individual and group efforts. We were learning a long and rare Movement called The Great Prayer, with lots of standing, kneeling, and prostrations—all to the weight of slow music and a count in Russian. The chosen would be asked to perform at the first visitors' weekend in spring.

The atmosphere in the house was becoming infused with a finer quality. I was not alone in having extraordinary experiences. Sherborne House had become its own vessel traveling in another dimension, and this notion did not seem odd. Towards the end of Lent, silence was added to our fast days.

For me, growing up in the Episcopal church, Lent meant giving up candy from the day after Ash Wednesday in February to Easter Sunday morning. It was a discipline I thought all children took on. My friends and I would compare notes on what, specifically, we had given up. Maybe it was chocolate bars, maybe cookies. Lent seemed interminable, tinged with the grey dregs of winter and cold March winds.

Finally, one glorious Sunday morning in April, I'd wake up with a pink, green, or blue woven basket on the floor beside my bed where I'd left a carrot for the Easter Bunny. My heart would be filled with excitement and light as I counted out my malted eggs, marshmallow peeps, and checked to see if the chocolate bunny was solid, as it nestled in fluffy strands of green synthetic grass. After breakfast I'd get to wear my new Easter outfit and go to church with my family and sing joyful Easter hymns about Jesus Christ being risen again. That was Lent capped by Easter, as I knew it, growing up.

The idea of giving up something like dairy in all its forms as well as taking on a substantial task brought a whole new meaning to my experience of Lent. It felt like a period of concentration and begged for inner examination as well as vigilance. It placed me squarely in front of the struggle between Yes and No.

CHAPTER FIFTY
Easter Break

"We look forward to seeing you at Easter, . . ." Alarm bells went off in my head as I read a new aerogram from my parents, ". . . and we've asked to tour the school and meet Mr. Bennett. Dad and I would like to take you to London for the weekend. We could pick you up on Good Friday when we come."

Our next period was about to start, and Jack was getting ready to leave for class, waiting for me to join him.

"Go ahead, I'll be down in a minute," I said, hastily folding the fragile sheet of blue aerogram paper.

He left and I looked around our little space. The shared single foam pad on the floor, carefully made up with my sheets from home, the shared four-drawer dresser next to the cute latticed window that swung out over the rooftop when I poked my head out for the weather.

Like several other couples, we'd met with Mr. B before Christmas to ask about our status as a couple. Sitting with him, he'd become quiet, going inward. Eventually he had looked up and said, "Bobby Jo, the resistance is coming from you." But then going silent again, he'd finally said, "Ah yes. I have you in my right arm. And Jack, you are in my left. There *is* something there. Although you two are not compatible in personality, you are in essence. Wait until March, we'll know by then." Apparently, he had known, because Elizabeth had arranged our move to one of the little attic rooms above the kitchen.

Was I a hypocrite, studying the catechism while "living in sin" with Jack?

What if my parents find out that Jack and I are sharing a room? My mom might not freak out so much, but Dad? He was a whole generation older than Mom, really old-school. Paying for me to go to this school and sleeping unmarried with Jack? How would that affect our relationship? I really wanted them to appreciate Sherborne and the course and Mr. Bennett. What would they think of Mr. B if they knew he was letting us live together?

What am I going to do? I started to sweat, my long hair too heavy on my neck. My eyes darted around the room, taking in the single bed, the dresser, clothes strewn about.

God, what should I do?

In desperation, the words I'd learned in childhood rose to my lips. I started praying out loud: "Our Father, who art in heaven, hallowed be Thy name. Thy kingdom come, Thy will be done, on earth as it is in heaven. Give us this day our daily bread and forgive us our trespasses as we forgive those who trespass against us. Lead us not into temptation but deliver us from evil. For Thine is the kingdom, the power, and the glory, forever and ever. Amen."

My thumping heart slowed, my frozen gut released. I took a long breath, feeling the answer come. A few days later I found Elizabeth and she agreed to arrange a temporary move back to my old dorm.

Jack took the news in stride. "If that's what you need to do."

He had only met my parents once, back when I was still going to college. They knew I liked him; they didn't know I slept with him.

On Good Friday, the day before the break, the student body was set to paint the Great Hall. With its soaring ceiling and marble floor, it would be a deep red from top to bottom, with gold and green details on the white pillars, and mantle details outlining the enormous fireplace. This was the final silent fast day and it dawned cold and gray.

Mom and Dad pulled up in their rented Austin-Morris. My dad wore a new, cream-colored, London Fog raincoat and a tweed cap perched on his balding head. As a kid I'd loved massaging that smooth pate after he sat back at the end of a meal. It surprised me now to see him walking with the wooden cane he used to dance with, side-kicking it with his foot so it twirled around his hand in an arc. Mom, the age of most my friends' mothers, also wore London Fog and carried a tan umbrella, ever the practical one. We embraced and I caught her signature Chanel No. 5 scent, reserved for special occasions.

They were ushered off for their tour and audience with Mr. Bennett. I finished packing and lent a hand in the Great Hall, knowing that everyone else had a long, silent day ahead working in that vast cold cavern of a room.

Part of me knew I was using my parents as an excuse to avoid work. Part of me reasoned that I was choosing filial duty over my own interests. Mr. Bennett had not been pleased, but I thought he was being gracious to see my parents and allow my early departure with them for Easter break.

When it was time to go, I brought them upstairs to my quiet dorm room so I could get my suitcase and they could see where I slept.

We took a tour of Sherborne Village, including a stop outside Harry's Post Office & General Store for a quick photo op. In that photo Dad looks very British in his cap and Mac, with lush green and yellow spring flowers behind the fence his hand rests upon. After pointing out the Social Club next door, my parents were keen to move on.

That first night we stayed at a bed and breakfast they had found in another village of the Cotswolds. We arrived at 4:00 p.m., in time for tea. A tea service on a low table in the living room greeted us as we were ushered in.

"Shall I be mother?" the matron asked as she fussed about, pouring tea and passing her best china around. "Help yourselves to the scones. There's jelly in the pot just there," she pointed to a little white jam pot with lid. "I'll be right round the corner," she waved in the general direction of a dining room across the hall, "and will show you your rooms when you've done."

The small living room had flower motif curtains and comfy furniture, which made me feel warm and happy. As I sipped tea and nibbled at my well buttered and jellied scone, I thought how nice it was to share this authentic bit of Britain with my parents.

The next day we drove back to Sherborne and picked up Jack. Easter break had officially started. My parents sat in the car while I found him.

They couldn't wait to get back to civilization and their American hotel in London with its well-appointed foyer, double beds, and central heating.

Sitting in the back seat as Dad drove and Mom navigated, I began to notice the sound of my voice when I spoke. This was my first extended absence from the course, and my state, used to a finer attunement, was feeling besieged.

"Jack, we stayed at a really comfy house last night," I said, aware of the lower timbre in my vocal register. As I spoke, I could feel where the words leaving my lips were coming from within me—from either depths of truth, or a higher-pitched platform of personality. Like when I tried to make conversation by saying, "Mom, Dad, I'm really glad you came and got to see Sherborne House." I could hear my insincerity and hoped they couldn't.

"It was all very interesting, but I am not that impressed with your Mr. Bennett," Dad replied, keeping his eyes on the road. I later learned Dad had been informed by a colleague that people under Mr. Bennett's influence became crazy.

Mom was more generous, "It certainly is an impressive place."

Jack remained quiet, in his reticent way.

My parents' chatter sounded empty to me. Conversing became difficult, as it was impossible to submit to idle talk, hearing the empty place it came from. My parents didn't seem to notice that neither of us had much to say.

As we drew closer to our destination, I looked at my wristwatch and offered a hopeful, "Oh, we'll be just in time for tea!"

Mom turned to look at me in the back seat with surprise. "Why would we want tea at four when we'll be having cocktails at five?"

The rest of the weekend was spent going to plays I could have seen in New York and eating in downtown restaurants that might have been anywhere. The London we inhabited was like any big city, with its rushing traffic, crowded sidewalks full of tourists and my parents' unconscious tendency to re-create their American lifestyle. American meals, American cocktails, American touristing; this was not the life-style Jack was used to nor the one I was interested in. At the end of the weekend, my parents left London to continue their travels.

Finally on our own, Jack and I moved to the recommended and economic, if spare, European hotel. Jack wanted to visit the British Museum, where we stumbled upon a wing of Egyptian art. Wandering through, we came to the mummy room, with two carved figures at the entrance.

"Whoa!" Jack came to a halt.

I stood next to him and felt it too. An inhospitable energy radiating out from the stone figures flanking the door. I felt it in my solar plexus, almost like I was being pushed away. "I don't think so," I agreed.

We hurried away from the room, hoping nothing would follow us.

The next stop was one of London's beautiful cathedrals, St. Patrick's, where the energy was radiant and calm. We spent some time there. Jack went to one of the confessional booths placed at intervals around the outer isles while I knelt in prayer, feeling a deep connection with something greater than myself.

Towards the end of our break, we stayed in a group home, a London extension of Beshara, the Sufi community not far from Sherborne. The house, which appeared to be an old storefront, was in walking distance of Hampstead Heath, an open expanse of park-like area. This was a welcome relief from the rest of London's hubbub. I was ready to get back to Sherborne, where I didn't have to make small talk, and hoped that when I did speak, my voice would emanate from that deeper place of truth. Besides, I missed dunking those dry round digestives into my afternoon tea and letting them dissolve soft and sweet in my mouth.

CHAPTER FIFTY-ONE
Mad as a Hatter

April 8, 1973—No matter what, it's always teatime in our attic room. Jack takes good care of me as I wander about hopelessly. Our little clock's hands seem stuck on 4:00 p.m.

I drift back to our room and stand in the middle, the only place to be upright. I look around, not sure what's supposed to happen next. My eyes fall on the single foam pad mattress on the floor and I note how hard that makes it to tuck sheets in. My eyes wander up to the poster on the wall, a woodland print of Mole and Mouse getting married, then over to the small wooden cross Trudy gave me for my birthday which hangs above it. Looking over at the dresser I see my travel clock in its bright blue case sitting open, showing the long hand on twelve and the shorter one on four. Oh!

The door opens and Jack walks in, faded green and white-striped bell bottoms sweeping the floor as he pulls off his heavy sweatshirt and woolen hat.

"Hey Jack, look." I point to the clock, "It's teatime."

"Uh, I don't think so. Not now."

"Sure, it is. Look at the clock!" I walk over and pick it up, holding it out to him. "Ya see?" I look at him, convinced.

"Well, okay, let's go down then."

Jack pushes his feet back into his sneakers, takes my hand, and we hurry downstairs through the labyrinth of hallways and back upstairs to the dining room as he throws his feet out expertly so as not to trip on his loose laces. He's an expert at not tripping.

We walk through the library and into the wood-paneled dining room with its array of Sherborne lords and ladies in dark oils and gilded frames adorning the yellow walls above the wainscoting. Barbara June, my old roommate, is on a.m. service and washing the last of the lunch dishes and wiping down the tables. No tea or biscuits in sight.

"Oh," I hang my head, disappointed.

"That's all right," Jack says with a soft squeeze to my hand. He guides me back upstairs to our room.

As we cross the landing and enter our room, Jack says, "You know, it's always teatime in *Alice in Wonderland*."

"You're right!" I look up, my day a little brighter. Our room in the attic is magic. It can always be teatime here. I sigh, smiling for the first time in weeks.

Jack had found a copy of *Alice in Wonderland* in the library. Leafing through the pages, Jack said, "Here, listen to this."

> "I quite agree with you," said the Duchess; "and the moral of that is—'Be what you would seem to be'—or, if you'd like it put more simply—'Never imagine yourself not to be otherwise than what it might appear to others that what you were or might have been was not otherwise than what you had been would have appeared to them to be otherwise.'"

I knew I couldn't make literal sense of it, but like my visit with Gerald last fall, I felt right at home with it.

Jack was concerned about me. It was clear to him that I was drifting in and out of altered states and not my usual self. In his LSD days back in West New York he had helped friends negotiate bad trips. He was here for me now, and as I became more and more entangled in an exotic reality, he kept me safe.

Even so, I couldn't tell him about my fire drill experience. About the fire being real, a premonition of things to come, about dying and looking for him in heaven. I was afraid I would lose the edge of the experience if I talked about it. But Jack made sure I got up and dressed each morning and followed the schedule.

"Bobby Jo, what do you want to put on?"

Jack opened the small dresser and pulled out blue jeans and the denim bib-skirt that I liked. I looked at both and shrugged. I didn't care, what did it matter? Things like getting dressed and following schedules didn't mean much. Life was too immediate for such trivia without the filter of personality guiding me. My bones, heavy from sleep, didn't want to move. Why not go with that?

"Here, Bobby Jo, let me help you. Lift your leg, that's it. Now the other one, there. Zip up your zipper. Can you do the button? Okay, good." Jack pulled my turtleneck over my head as I held my arms up and handed me a sweater. I put it on and looked at him.

"Now what?"

"Let's go downstairs for morning exercise and breakfast." Jack took my hand and led me out and down the backstairs to skirt past the kitchen by the glassed-in courtyard, down the familiar dark stone-paved corridor, and up the narrow staircase closest to the ballroom. We slipped in just in time, before the massive door clicked shut, meaning no more could enter. I settled on my cushion with the women and Jack disappeared in the predawn dark to the men's side.

Forty-five minutes later, after having worked in luxurious silence, Mr. B directed us to stand and perform the ritual bows that energetically completed every morning exercise. Then he strode down the aisle between the men's and women's sides and we followed behind in his wake out of the ballroom and into the dawn of day and the promise of a bowl of steaming oatmeal.

Jack collected me as I was locating my shoes amongst the pile outside the door. Instead of moving down the hall to queue up for breakfast, he led me to the oversized bulletin board where we looked to see the day's schedule. Our group was on House Duty, and we were both assigned cleaning.

After breakfast Jack made sure we arrived in the library in time for the House meeting. Elizabeth came in just as the House Supervisor was getting the upstairs and downstairs teams set up. She sat down quietly in a chair near the front of the room wearing her usual skirt and wool sweater, greying-brown hair pulled back in a quick ponytail, nothing about her ornamental other than her naturally rosy cheeks.

Once the assignments were doled out, Elizabeth spoke up. "Are there any questions before we start?"

Sitting towards the back of the room, I found my hand had cautiously raised itself into the air. Elizabeth followed the arm, peering into the crowd, spotting me.

"Yes, Bobby Jo, what is it?"

"I don't understand," I said.

"You don't understand what, Bobby Jo?"

"I don't understand *anything*." I replied in a small voice.

The room went suddenly quiet.

Elizabeth gazed at me for a breath, head tilted, then in a soft, thoughtful voice said, "Come with me." Taking my hand, she led me out of the library back to her flat through the empty halls.

"Now, tell me what is troubling you." We were sitting on her couch side by side, the flat to ourselves.

My voice came from a restricted place, squeaky. "I don't know, it's just that, that it doesn't make sense anymore." I sat there, limp.

"What is it that doesn't make sense to you, Bobby Jo?" Elizabeth's voice was curious, open.

"Nothing makes sense." I waved my hand vaguely at the world. "And I know now. I know, just like Gurdjieff says, 'Man cannot do.'" My hand fell into my lap. I felt completely helpless in the face of the reality that all I was composed of were bits and pieces of a false personality that had no substance. I was floating in a world of impressions with no tether.

Elizabeth nodded. She understood. I learned years later that she had fallen into a state of despair after becoming acquainted with Gurdjieff's teachings and coming face to face with her own limitations. In the end, she went to Paris and worked directly with Gurdjieff. In Paris she found an answer to her turmoil. For that reason, she was well equipped to help me with my problem. We sat together in comfortable silence.

"Bobby Jo, I am going to give you a lifeline I think will help you find your way. Come with me, dear."

She led me out of her flat and we climbed the broad staircase up to the women's floor. A cold spring sun was beaming in through the high window as we ascended the stairs. In a small closet in the hall, she found a rag and cleaning solution. We walked down the hall to the sink room with its long double row of back-to-back sinks.

"Now, Bobby Jo, here is what you can do. Sense your hands, yes? Is the sensation there?"

I nodded, the warmth of sensation filling my hands.

"Start here with this sink. Don't worry, don't think. Put all your attention on the sensation in your hands. Clean one sink at a time, then move on to the next."

She handed me the coarse white rag, a bucket and ammonia. "Come to me if you need to."

She knew from experience that the state I was in was a step towards seeing myself as I was. Without that, nothing could change.

Turning towards the sink, I focused my attention on my hand, its pulsing vibration of life, the rough wet texture of the cloth.

One porcelain sink, with its chrome faucet and porcelain cross handles, then the next. No thoughts—just focus on the sensation in my hand, the shine of the sink, the repetitive motion in my arm. My thoughts returned to bringing my attention back, again and again, to the sensation of my arm moving, the cold glint of porcelain, the twinkle of chrome, the clean smell of ammonia and water. It worked. I felt the ground beneath my feet, a restored sense of balance and purpose.

CHAPTER FIFTY-TWO
Now

Waking up to the morning bell, I take my turn in the communal attic bathroom to do my ablutions, splashing cold water over my face and body, arms and legs. Skin tingling with cold, I pull on my long johns and blue jeans, cotton turtleneck shirt and heavy cable knit sweater. I like arriving for morning exercise with time to drape myself in the shawl I've knitted with the blue and white tassels, propped on my cushion before Mr. B enters. I don't want to be the one rustling once he plummets down onto his pillow, heralding deep quiet.

I work in the familiar pattern of moving my attention down over the features of my face, allowing an awareness of relaxation to follow, feeling the warmth of energy flowing down my neck, arms, torso, hips, and legs—muscles softening along the way. Sensation—it fills my toes, my feet, moves up my legs into my torso; the vibration of life filling each cell, awakening the ethereal body within.

After allowing fifteen minutes to relax and sense, Mr. B's voice rides the still air waves. "Last week's exercise, the Nine Point exercise, was a necessary preparation for what I am presenting to you this week. One must be proficient in the Nine Point before moving on." Pausing, he allows his words to resonate with us.

"The exercise we are attempting this week is called the Four Prophets exercise. It is an exercise in conscious stealing.

"Over the ages, Divine Messengers, appearing in human form, have been sent to us. Each one had a special mission. These Messengers or

Prophets are not like us in that they come with their higher bodies already formed.

"A group of disciples, or a school composed of individuals, form around the Prophet. These people understand that their role is one of support. In so doing, they create a 'sacred image' that ordinary people can relate to and direct their prayers to. This image often includes a holy city associated with the Sacred Individual, a focus of worship and a destination for pilgrims to journey to. Through sacrifice, pilgrimage, and prayer, devotees produce an energy, used mostly for their own development. Still, a surplus of this energy collects over time above the holy city in something like a cloud. This energy cloud forms a great reservoir.

"Those who know how to transform energies in their higher, or Kesdjan, body can pass through the veil that separates the conditioned from the unconditioned worlds and tap this accumulator. However, only those who produce the same quality of energy from their own work are able to draw down from this reservoir. This is because that energy, used for one's own transformation, is in turn given to help others in their work."

Mr. B's long explanation is followed by a pause. I come back inside my body, noting and releasing a tightness underneath my left shoulder blade.

"We begin by sensing the right arm. Do this deeply," Bennett instructs.

"Now sense the area just above and between your eyes. Send out a thread from there, through time and space, connecting with Mecca. If it helps, picture the square Kaaba, draped in beautiful cloth embroidered with gold thread, with throngs of white-clad pilgrims circumambulating around its base. Now connect with the cloud of devotional energy floating above the city and with the Prophet Muhammad."

A few minutes go by as we work.

"Now pull that thread of energy back through your forehead into yourself, blending it with the sensation of the right arm. Take your time with this. When you no longer have the connection, take a few conscious breaths and turn your attention to sensing the right leg."

Sensing my right leg, I feel it pulsing with warmth. I send an out-spooling thread from my forehead towards the next destination, Benares. I picture the river Ganges, thronged with pilgrims along its banks. I'm aware of a presence, the Buddha. I sense the thread connecting with the prayer energy above the city. I spend a few minutes there. Reeling the thread back I bring it inside myself, using my right leg as a receiving station, allowing the feeling energy to blend with my sensation.

I follow a breath into my lungs, aware that some small portion of it stays within as I exhale. I focus my attention on my left leg, dialing up the sensation there. With my mind, I picture the holy city of Lhasa, envisioning a shining white edifice perched high atop a mountain. I don't picture the current Dalai Lama, but what that personage represents to the faithful. I send out my thread, allowing it time to make the connection. Then I pull it in and direct that energy into my left leg, blending it with my sensation.

Last, sensing my left arm, I send out my thread to the sprawling city of Jerusalem, with a cloud of energy floating high above. This time I connect more fully, realizing that despite my knowledge of the dark side of Christianity's history, the cloud is there, and the flavor is Love. I sense the mission that Christ was sent here for—to bring into the world the *action* of Love. A vibration set free, available to all, not just to Christians. Later we will connect Mohammad with Hope, Buddha with Faith, and Lama with Acceptance. In myself, I come to understand that all these prophets, in their turn, released corresponding higher impulses into the vibrational makeup of the world. I pull the connecting thread back into my left arm and allow the feeling of Love to blend with my sensation.

"Bring your efforts to an end, allow the exercise to settle," Mr. B instructs. A few minutes later he says, "Now turn to the decision." Bennett's voice brings me back to the room, to my cushion. I let the exercise go, turning my attention to my decision for the day.

I have chosen the task of sweeping the landing of our attic, since the house cleaners never seem to get up there. I sense holding the wooden broom handle and feel the sweeping motion, visualizing the wood floor and the stair rail of the landing. When I ask myself if I will do this, I feel the certainty of *yes*. The decision is made. As long as this one task gets done, I know the rest of the day will flow.

"And stand." Bennett brings the student body to its feet. Many have learned to mimic his rising from the cushion in one swift motion, as if pulled upright by a force above his head.

I stand for the three ritual rukus, my decision for the day secure. This is real, this is meaningful—my anchor today.

Back in our room, I write in my journal. My entries are mostly poetic scribbles, but they capture what's going on better than prose.

Now
Know each day
what is to be done.
Do what you do.
Stay on course,
see each job through.
The rest of Time
is open, free.
Embrace your own reality.

CHAPTER FIFTY-THREE
Edith Wallace

There was a new guest teacher, Edith Wallace, who was an old friend of Mr. B's. Like Henry Bortoft, she had been invited to come work with us students. She was a student of Carl Jung's and was experimenting with a way of reaching the subconscious through art. With iron-blue hair and wide streaks of white in a short bouffant style, she favored purple neck-scarves and had mischievous pixie eyes.

I walked out the front door by the Horse Parlor, shoes crunching on gravel in the parking lot. Rounding the side of the weathered gray-stone chapel, I followed a trodden path threading old gravestones to the Stable Block, where Edith was holding her classes in one of the unfinished rooms. It was a gray, chill day, but I noticed a few crocuses poking up their purple heads on delicate green stalks.

Inside the door, before I could sit at the long table, I was handed a piece of paper, about twelve by sixteen inches in size.

"Good afternoon," Edith cheerily greeted me. "Before you sit down, please take your paper over to that basin." She pointed with a ringed finger, "and dunk it in the water, then crumple it into a ball, please."

"You can sit anywhere." She smiled and turned to address the next student arriving.

I sat down near Lynne, who was wearing a white shirt with hands folded primly on the table, looking every bit the good student.

"What are we supposed to be doing?" I asked.

"Darned if I know."

Edith then explained that we were going to participate in an experiment she was developing to help access the subconscious.

"If you haven't already, go ahead and spread out your paper on the mat in front of you." She demonstrated—the crinkled, cream-colored paper in a rectangle before her. "I have paint, brushes, and cups of rinse water that you can all use," she gestured towards the center of the table as she stood. "I'll put them out, and once we start, please share."

"I want you to simply paint, in any way that is pleasing to you. Try not to think too much or plan what you are doing. We're creating images, not works of art. Don't be concerned with how it looks. That is why we crumpled the paper beforehand."

Walking over to a cabinet, she brought out watercolors and paint brushes.

Everyone was fully engaged when Jack arrived. I helped him set up his paper. Edith came over and explained. Without a word, he chose a brush with his left hand and went to work. I was having fun watching my blue and yellow swim into each other on the wrinkled paper, so didn't pay him any more attention.

At the end of the session, Edith had the table pushed back out of the way. Everyone sat on the floor with their finished pieces laid out before them. From a chair at the edge of the group, Edith said, "Who can tell us something about what they've done here? In particular, what was going through your mind as you worked? Who wants to start?"

Lynne went first. After she explained her choices of color and what she had been thinking as the colors ran and merged, she looked up, brushing a long strand of dark hair out of her face.

Edith pointed to an image that looked to her like a willowy figure. Someone else spoke up, "I see a mountain range off in the background." Another added, "Hey, doesn't that look like a road leading towards those mountains?"

When it came time for Jack to present his picture, it was obvious that his was different.

Jack's picture looked like a human figure with a bird's head and a huge curved beak. The beak was aiming at its own breast. The colors, for the most part, were washed out orange, brown, grayish-green, and some yellow. In the center of the creature's breast, protected by a golden glow, was a white dove. Everyone was quiet as Jack explained that the image came from a dream.

Edith was quite attentive. "Can anyone say something about what Jack has created here?"

"It looks like some sort of self-portrait. The way the figure seems to be moving and the style of clothing reminds me of Jack," Lynne ventured, cocking her head.

Barbara June, reticent to speak in other settings but feeling at home in an art class, offered, "The colors in his painting remind me of the interior of Sherborne House, kind of cold and dark."

"Yes, the whole tone of the image is forbidding," added Kip in his slow southern cadence.

"And yet the dove seems serene and protected," said Vicki, her own thin frame conveying vulnerability.

I raised my hand, "See how the beak is striking at its chest? It's kind of like our struggle with false personality. Every time we glimpse what is real in ourselves, our false personality tries to find and destroy it."

Gazing at his painting Edith addressed Jack, "I think this is an important piece for you to contemplate."

Speaking to us all she said, "I recommend you take your work and place it somewhere near your bed, so you see it upon opening your eyes first thing in the morning. New impressions can come in those moments before our active mind takes over."

Jack told me later that he had walked into the class fresh with a vivid dream from the night before. The dream had felt prophetic, and he was glad for the chance to capture it.

Later, Mr. B encouraged students to meet individually with Edith on an as-needed basis. Others were doing it, so I set up an appointment, not sure exactly why I was going.

Entering the meeting room, I took a seat, appreciating the sense of confidentiality and support that Edith's presence elicited. She sat perched on her chair, looking like an exotic bird—head cocked, inquisitive. I just knew she could understand exactly where I was coming from. I started telling her my experiences and how they led to higher states of reality but that I was afraid of losing my place in that magic world.

"I'm just not sure how to hold onto it. Mr. Bennett knows where I'm at, but somehow, I can't bring myself to go talk to him. If I do, I think he'll lay some kind of trip on me or something." I leaned forward, remembering the exchange with him in the parking lot during the fire drill, when he pretended to be mad and said he'd send me home if I "didn't behave."

It was a relief to be able to talk with someone I could confide in besides Mr. B about the altered states I'd experienced at the fire drill, the Movements class, and other moments. Edith's quick eye sparked with humor and understanding. She listened, interested in all I had to say. A sense of trust enveloped me.

"Bobby Jo, here's the thing." She looked into my eyes. "What we are striving to do here is to be able to traverse back and forth between both worlds."

I shifted, surprised.

"We want to build a bridge between the reality we need to function in on a day-to-day basis and the one that holds spiritual truths and higher states."

No imp-look here; her bright eyes were warm, sincere. "The goal is to not get stuck in either the one world or the other!"

Relief flooded through me. Finally, someone had said something that made sense. Of course! I was getting lost in the enchanted forest because I was afraid that if I left it, I could never get back again. I thought I had arrived, found my destination, and had no need to re-enter the ordinary world where people operated from false personality. I could sense that Edith understood about alternate worlds, the Unconditioned World, as Bennett called it. The world where magic happened. But hearing her, I knew Edith was right about living in the ordinary world of personality too. What I needed to do was to be able to go back and forth between these two realities so I could share the knowledge I'd gained.

I pictured an arched bridge of cream-colored stone. It came to me that I had been conflating personality and false personality. It made sense that personality was needed to traverse the unreal world of everyday. It was false personality—the facade we put on to hide behind—that wasn't needed. I desperately wanted to build the bridge now. It was time to come back from the enchantment of the extraordinary. It was time to learn how to be an "Ordinary Idiot" and start over.

CHAPTER FIFTY-FOUR
Judy

Judy, a black pony, lived in the large field across from the gravel parking lot at the front of the manor house. She shared the space with two donkeys and half a dozen brown and white Jacob's sheep. Large old trees provided scattered shade, and the area felt rather like a park. A tree-lined gravel driveway marched down alongside the field to the road which led to Sherborne Village in one direction and the A-40 west to Cheltenham or east to Oxford in the other.

My two passions growing up were ballet and horseback riding. I had been watching Judy throughout the winter, and now I started visiting her in the pasture. Intimations of spring were coming on and it was often warmer outside in the sun than in the house, where winter's chill had permeated the gray stones.

Walking quietly through the greening pasture, I approached Judy slowly until she allowed me to get close enough to stroke her. She was about fourteen hands high, big enough to hold my 110 pounds. She didn't seem to belong to anyone in particular, at least I never saw anyone riding her.

Still in a delicate and sensitive state, I found it easier to be with Judy than to try to deal with the people around me on the course. Yet my Sherborne family shared this magical world with me. We spoke the same language of the Work and shared our experiences in Theme meetings, often recognizing another's personal revelation as our own. In many ways I felt more akin to my fellow students than my own family, with their ordinary middle-class interests and lives.

However, the tendency to say what was on my mind before thinking about it did not always make my exchanges with everyone go well. If I liked someone, I'd want to tell them if the rinse they were using on their hair wasn't having the intended effect. But it might come out the instant I noticed, say in the middle of a group of friends, "Oh man, your hair is purple!"

Bennett had said something in one of his talks about working on one's sensitivity with people through learning to communicate with plants and animals first.

So here I was, in the pasture with Judy. I didn't have to worry about offending her or being misunderstood. We could communicate perfectly well without words. Holding onto her mane at the withers, I lightly vaulted onto her back, my legs wrapped securely around her. Her head came up from munching grass, ears turned back towards me, inquisitive. I stroked her, "Good girl Judy, good girl." I leaned forward, reaching my hand out and grasping her muzzle, gently pulling it to the side as I pressed my legs into her sides, urging her forward. She took a step, turning in the direction I'd pointed her head and began walking. I let my pelvis sink into her, the small of my back following her movement. I intended to learn to ride her without a saddle or bridle, just as I'd done with the black horse I rode in my dream at the beginning of the course.

I let her walk, urging her on with my legs when she slowed, pulling her head up before she could reach down to the grass. Rocking with the rhythm of her movement, communicating through hands and legs, we became acquainted. Bonding with this animal felt right, felt like my real work.

I watched students walk out the door on their way to practical work. I should be going with them, but it seemed more important for me to be here with Judy. Hands entwined in the coarse hairs of her mane, I breathed in the sweet-pungent horse smell. It felt like I was seeing through Judy's eyes as I watched, from the pasture, people disappearing around the corner of the building in groups of two or three—gesticulating, talking.

Suddenly I had a realization—beyond my personality, in some deep recess of myself, a truth emerged. A feeling that Judy and I shared. On a primal level I was afraid of people. I wrapped my arms around Judy's neck and buried my face in her mane. Oh, Judy—Judy. What am I going to do?

CHAPTER FIFTY-FIVE
The Great Prayer

"So does the head come up for one or two counts during the second prostration?" asked Larry to the group of us sitting in the dining room sipping tea and dunking digestive biscuits.

Rachel remained quiet as was her way, Jack looked thoughtful, Lynne was passing the milk to her boyfriend Fish, and I felt left out. They had just finished a Great Prayer practice for the demonstration to be held on our first spring Visitors' Day.

"It's one count on the first prostration, and I think two counts on the second," Lynne said after releasing the milk pitcher to Fish.

"Okay, then what happens with the third prostration?" Larry asked, gazing into his mug.

I picked up my second digestive, a chocolate-coated one, my favorite. Dunk and rush it into your mouth so the chocolate can melt on your tongue. I couldn't answer any of these questions. When we'd returned from Easter break, Mr. B had told me I was out of the demonstration group since I'd missed an important practice by leaving early.

I was devastated. The Great Prayer was the most important Movement of all; performing it was a sacred event, and I had been part of the chosen demonstration group working to present it.

Why had I felt it was so important to spend that day with my parents?

As my friends carried on about the fine points of the head gestures in the Great Prayer, I considered my own questions. Would I have been so ready to run off with mom and dad if it hadn't been for the prospect of a long, cold, silent fast day painting the Great Hall? If I hadn't been afraid of getting paint in my hair?

"At the end of the third prostration," Jack was saying, head bowed and hands on his knees. "The head comes up on the third *ras*, but stays up for the next two counts, *ras, dvá*," he finished, crossing his arms and looking up at the ceiling while sounding the count in Russian.

"That's it," said Larry, finally taking a long swig of tea.

Yes, I thought, that's it. If we'd been doing something that day I hadn't wanted to miss, I would have waited until the break started on Saturday to go with my parents, like Jack had. A feeling I wasn't used to, heavy and sad, filled my chest as moisture welled around my eyes, threatening to spill over as I sat there amidst the earnest conversation. I had gotten my way avoiding what I hadn't wanted to do, passing up an opportunity to struggle against my likes and dislikes. It was right that Mr. B had taken me out of the Great Prayer. The part of me that wished to change acknowledged this with a tear marking its small path down my cheek.

The evening of the Visitors' Day came at last and we were all assembled in the vibrant, deep-red and white of the Great Hall. At the top of the room three marble ledges formed steps up to a raised area that worked well for the audience to view the Movements. Chairs had been assembled for the older guests and staff, while students not in the performance and younger guests sat on the floor and steps. Sitting in the audience, I felt left out, contrite over not being allowed to participate in the performance.

Elan was already playing the long introduction to the Great Prayer. My fellow classmates were dressed in their white tunics and rainbow-colored sashes, kneeling in a horseshoe shape on the floor of the great chamber. Their heads bowed over crossed arms as they counted a slow cadence in Russian, *ras, dvá, treé, chyetírye*, up to eighteen.

Sitting not far from Mr. Bennett's chair, I saw him turn his head, probing the audience for someone. He eventually caught my eye and motioned me over, whispering in urgent tones,

"Do you know how to read music?"

The Great Prayer. Photo courtesy of Alex Daggett, taken by Amy Pollack.

I had taken a few years of piano and voice lessons in grade school but that was all. Something inside prompted me.

"Yes," I said.

"Good," he whispered. "Go quickly down the hall to the back door and slip in so no one sees you and turn the pages for Elan."

I hastened down the hallway having no idea if I could read music well enough to follow Elan's playing and know when to turn a page. Sneaking in behind the piano I stood next to Elan. All my senses were heightened. I had to follow the notes and be ready without being noticed. Sensing myself, I let go of my self-doubt, connecting to Elan in the act of working together. For the duration of that long Movement, my eyes linked the sound of the notes with the black symbols on the white sheets. As I followed the pattern of the music with Elan's moving fingers, it somehow became quite clear to me when to turn each page. Afterwards, I felt assuaged, knowing I had played my part in this great Movement.

Mr. Bennett had said something once that I took to heart that night. "If one finds an excess of energy resulting from one's Work, it is possible to throw that energy out into the future, with the intention that it will be available in a time of need."

That night, with the success of the Great Prayer, the energy from the Visitors' Day, and the remorse I had been feeling, I took the energy that I might have wasted and envisioned throwing it far away into time. Indeed, I could feel energy float out and away from me. I tucked that moment away in my memory bank.

PART FIVE

FINDING BALANCE

> "If one sees hazard as a misfortune rather than an opportunity, one will seek to close the door to freedom rather than keep it open."
>
> —J. G. BENNETT

CHAPTER FIFTY-SIX
Tiptoeing Towards Chief Feature

The trees were now in full bloom, and when the sun pushed through passing clouds, it rained warmth down upon our bare heads as we dug in the garden. The busy chatter of nesting birds filled the air. Once again, I was sitting in Mr. B's study. My questions never seemed to be the right ones.

Mr. B sat back in his chair after having listened in his concentrated way. You knew he could tell you all kinds of things about yourself in these private moments, if only you knew the right question to ask. It never occurred to me that maybe I was being given the answer but couldn't hear it.

"There's another thing, Bobby Jo. I think it would be a good idea for you to map out a log of everything you intend to do each day with time entries, for three days. I would like you to come back and show it to me next week."

Besides our personal schedules, we were instructed to take turns teaching something to each other. Something of our own, that we felt we could uniquely offer, all in preparation for going back into life after the course.

Upstairs in my room I sat on our single mattress and bent over my sheet of paper, my hair twisted up behind my head, fastened with a blue and red, tooled, butterfly-shaped strip of leather, a stick stuck through it. Our cute casement window was open, and a sunny breeze freshened the air. If it was up to me, I pondered, how might I order my day? The course schedule gave me an outline, but still . . .

I mulled over the possibilities for my personal schedule. Writing was one of the things I wanted to do in life, and I hoped the sly offer of "working on Mr. B's books in place of meals" would be accepted. I pictured myself organizing his papers or typing up his manuscripts. Spending time on studying to become Catholic also seemed a legitimate use of time as well as preparing for my teaching project. We were going to take turns teaching something to each other in small groups. I decided to teach basic lessons about horses, using Judy the pony as my assistant.

The next week, I returned to the Bennetts' flat. Mr. B read my proposed schedule and, picking up his blue ink pen, scribbled some notes in the margins. On Wednesday, he bracketed the 11:00 a.m. entry about purchasing pony reins and wrote, "do full morning work on floor." Where I had written to call Father O'Callahan, he wrote: "Zikr 40 min."[1] For Thursday, a fast day, my suggestion to, "Work on B's book in place of meals" was crossed out with the note: *some work in garden is best here*. Another note for 40 min. of Zikr was written in for the evening, after my "work on Movements" and before "read or go to bed early." On the Friday entry he corrected my spelling of "practicle work" and "comission" and added, "40 min. Zikr" next to "6:00–7:00 p.m.—B's book or sewing for fête."

And again, as with the distasteful suggestion to paint Richard Duffel's loo, part of me recognized that my entries to go to Cirencester, call Father O'Callahan, and go to bed early were coming from my own self-will rather than serving my inner Work.

"Thank you, Mr. B," I said, hoping the heat in my face didn't show. I picked up my papers, feeling foolish. *Of course, he wouldn't want me to work on his book, I can't spell, and I know that! Jeez, Zikr for forty minutes? Each time? Damn, I wish spelling wasn't such a big deal.*

I looked up to catch a bemused smile on Mr. B's face as he watched me from his chair. He nodded a kind of "it's okay and you can go" nod as I rose and took my leave.

I knew I would do what he suggested. If I was trying to change myself, I

---

1 Zikr: a Sufi form of prayer utilizing a specific breathing pattern that Bennett introduced on the course, incorporating it into some morning exercises and as its own practice.

had to learn to not always choose what "I" wanted. I just didn't understand how to tell the difference between what self-will wanted and what serving a higher purpose wanted. Unless the clue was the "anything but *that*" feeling I was becoming all too familiar with.

Soon, Mr. B introduced a new concept: Chief Feature.[2] As he spoke about it, we learned that this was the coin of our individuality and flavored everything we did.

"The problem is, our chief features are so integral to ourselves 'tis impossible for us to see our own."

"Let's take Jack, for example," he said later in the meeting.

"How would we describe Jack in a few words?"

Todd spoke up from the center of the room, "When I think of Jack, I think of bounce."

"Yes," Mr. B replied with a smile. "That certainly describes Jack's gait."

Laughter echoed through the room.

"But that doesn't quite get to the core of it."

Other hands went up.

"Light?"

"Slight?"

"Artistic?"

"Likes to perform?"

"These words all describe something about Jack, but they don't quite capture the crux of the matter."

Mr. B explained, "A person's chief feature is often not obviously apparent, but once described accurately, 'tis immediately recognizable to others."

Here Bennett paused, "Learning to discern another's chief feature is a sensitive and important exercise, one best left within the bounds of a student/teacher relationship.

"For our purposes here, we are working our way towards an understanding of what this means, chief feature. I do not expect any of you to be able to accurately name each other's chief feature, but rather to gain some insight into how it is that we go about discovering it."

---

[2] Ouspensky, *In Search*, 226, 228, 241, 266-8.

Small groups of eight or so were formed. My group was meeting in the Horse Parlor on a day when the sun shone bright through the clouds outside, but the stone walls of the house were still holding winter's chill.

A staff member sat in on each group, acting as facilitator.

"Kip, would you be willing to let us have a go with you first?" asked Dick Holland, who looked very small and frail, indeed, sitting in Mr. B's big red chair, despite his military bearing.

"Sure, I don't mind," Kip replied, a sunbeam bouncing off his blond hair.

"Well then, let us take turns going 'round the room with everyone naming what they perceive as a core characteristic of Kip's," suggested Dick.

"Something about a mathematical mind," volunteered Amy, who had been to Kip's teaching session where he explained some underlying tenets of mathematics.

Dick nodded for the next person to take a turn.

"A dry sense of humor," Susan offered.

"Perseverance," Peter threw in, pushing his glasses up the bridge of his nose with a finger.

Dick held his hand up. "We need to look for characteristics or terms that encompass both positive and negative aspects so that we capture all facets of a person's manifestations."

"Calculating?" I enquired, thinking it could be part of the mathematical mind that Amy had started with but could manifest positively or negatively.

"The choice of word is closer to what I am suggesting, however I am not sure that calculating is an accurate description of Kip," replied Dick with a smile.

We finished going around the group with everyone throwing out words or phrases. Then we each had a turn in the hot seat. By the end of the session, it was clear that we hadn't hit any nails on the head, but we were now on a path of wanting to observe each other and ourselves, looking for objective identifiers. I wondered what my own chief feature could be and if it would be revealed.

CHAPTER FIFTY-SEVEN
Essence and Personality

The Theme Essence and Personality had been introduced on Monday. Mr. Bennett suggested we could discover whether a characteristic came from personality by using the Decision Exercise to try to change it. Characteristics rooted in essence could not so easily be affected. Working with likes and dislikes was a good example.

I remembered Jack taking me aside one night towards the end of p.m. service. All that was left was to take the leftover chutney down to the kitchen.

"Hey Bobby Jo, come over here a minute."

Jack was walking towards one of the long wooden dining room tables with a small serving bowl of chutney in one hand and two spoons in the other. He sat down and patted the space next to him.

"Sit with me a minute," he called.

I walked over, a cleaning rag still in hand, and dropped it on the table as I sat down.

"What?"

"Let's work on our likes and dislikes for a minute."

"What do you mean?"

"The chutney," Jack said, holding a dessert spoon out to me.

"You're kidding! You know I don't li—" the rest of the word died on my lips.

It didn't look too bad, sort of like a stewed compote of orange apricots, brown raisins, black prunes and honey-colored figs. It smelled pleasingly of cardamom and turmeric, but we knew the red-hot peppers were hiding in there.

Eyes dancing, Jack scooped his spoon into the chunky, gooey mix and popped it into his mouth, chewing and swallowing.

Not to be outdone, I followed suit.

Laughing and choking, we gulped cold water.

Jack kept at it, so I did too.

"That wasn't so bad," Jack said once the bowl was empty.

"Not after the first bite or so," I agreed, bringing out my handkerchief to blow my nose.

"I can breathe deeper, I think. Must be good for my sinuses," Jack said.

"Yeah, I guess I don't have to worry about not liking chutney being an essence characteristic," I said, taking another big swig of water.

The next time chutney showed up at a meal, we ate it with gusto. We even developed an enjoyment for different varieties, which lasted throughout the course and beyond.

On Friday night during our end of week observations, someone brought up the notion of humility, and trying to be humble.

Bennett railed at him, "You can't talk about humility. As soon as you use that word, personality has already usurped it. A truly humble person does not know they are humble." Bennett looked around. "Who else then?"

Later in the meeting an observation came from Pam, who rarely spoke up in these group settings but whose loud and somewhat gregarious personality we all knew.

"About ten days ago I noticed I had this really fine feeling in my chest which hurt like a physical pain. It felt like this very fine sadness."

Bennett sat with his eyes closed. "Uhmm," he murmured.

Pam continued, "It got really strong, and I realized it had something to do with my mother. I thought I was just working stuff out because for most of my life I was always butting heads with my mother and being mean. We all used to give her a really hard time. But the feeling kept getting stronger and then I felt that something wasn't right. So, I thought, 'Well of course, because we have always been so awful to her. You have to go and make that right.'

"I had this feeling that I had to be with my mother—that it was very important. I dreamed about it three nights in a row, and I knew that something was very wrong. I called up and found out that she's been really, really sick."

Pam's voice dipped and you could have heard a pin drop in the room. Hearing her open up like this was quite unusual.

"And, you just never know . . . I don't know, I thought this might have something to do with conscience. As much as it hurt, it unlocked something that I never, ever would have thought I had in me."

Pam started saying more, but Mr. B stopped her before the moment could be lost, saying, "Yes, yes, that is an essence experience, a genuine essence experience."

Mr. Bennett shut his eyes. Head bent, voice soft, he said, "It does illustrate one thing that I didn't think I would be able to speak about." Opening his eyes and raising his head he went on, "But because you have spoken of this, I can say something about it.

"That is, the real difference between essence and personality is that personality grows from the outside. Like a crystal, it is just picking things up from the environment, adding things on and they're just falling into different places. Essence grows from within, like a child, like a being."

Mr. B spoke slowly, pausing and carefully choosing his words. "The movement of the personality is from without. Personality can only react because it has no freedom from what is outside."

Yes, I thought. That's why personality lives in a false world. It takes its direction from external cues, wanting to make a good impression, wanting to be liked.

"The essence is different in this way," Mr. B was saying. "The movement of the essence is from within. The essence is much more vulnerable to the outside than personality because it hasn't been saturated from the outside. Therefore, it is also more sensitive."

Mr. B stopped talking, his eyes closed again. Then he said from somewhere deep inside himself, "Between mother and daughter there is an essence bond, and nothing that the personality feels can change it."

I was riveted. It felt like we were witnessing a private moment between Pam and Mr. B.

Addressing Pam directly, Mr. B continued. "You know, all your difficulties with your mother are in your personality and hers. But this doesn't change the essence relationship."

It seemed to me that Mr. B was healing a wound that had caused Pam to distance herself from her mother all her life. Her candor had opened a door that he was casting a light into for all to see and learn from.

"Therefore, it happens like this," Mr. B said. "When something begins to awaken in yourself, in your real feelings, you can begin to have essence perceptions. These essence perceptions don't depend on ordinary sensory experiences. On what we see and hear or on receiving a letter and so on. 'Tis different."

After another pause, he concluded, "You didn't know what was causing you this pain. I mean your personality didn't know. It was a very good thing that you called your mother. Having acted from this inner prompting without understanding what it was has allowed your essence to get something moving in it."[1]

I don't remember if Pam ended up flying home to be with her mother or simply spoke to her on the telephone. My hope was that a new relationship would evolve between Pam and her mother, one firmly grounded in essence and not the likes and dislikes of personality.

My own relationship with my parents had its moments, of course. Mom drove me mad by insisting things be done her way (the "right" way), and Dad could be stubborn and old fashioned with his opinions. But I knew they loved me "no matter what." I felt the same about them and was sorry for kids I'd met who did not have that anchor in their lives.

---

[1] From Theme MP3 029 and 030, SHT 138 and 139: *Essence And Personality*. Released 1973.

CHAPTER FIFTY-EIGHT
Chief Feature

Over the course of the next several weeks, little slips of paper with appointment times for individual meetings with Mr. Bennett began to circulate. Word trickled out that Mr. B was revealing our chief feature to us. This was different from any meetings we had ever had with him. We were being given a key with which to take our work to the next level, with which we could begin our own personal work on ourselves.

I had no idea what my chief feature could be or how Mr. B would reveal it to me. All I knew was that I was beginning to sense when I was operating from self-will or false personality. But even after I was told what my chief feature was, I wondered if I'd be able to see it for myself. If chief feature is like the permanent tint of your lens, how can you see yourself clearly?

The appointed hour arrived. With trepidation I knocked on the door to the Bennetts' flat and waited to be let in. Mr. B came to the door himself and ushered me into the inner sanctum of his study. I sat down across from him. He looked at me with a soft smile and said, "You are very much like your mother, you know."

I didn't know, but I could be particular about things, maybe that's what he meant. I was surprised that Mr. B picked up on this from the short interview with my parents. But brief impressions are often telling. I had always thought I was more like my father in some ways and said so.

"No, you are not at all like your father," Mr. B insisted.

I protested, "Oh, I think I am. 'Cause it's my dad who's the one who's artistic and spiritual. My mom would rather bake cookies for the church social hour than study the bible."

Relaxing, Mr. B said, "What it is with you, Bobby Jo, is that you expect everyone else to see the world through your eyes."

I rolled the phrase over in my mind, allowing it to settle in me; aware that I wasn't sure what to do with this information.

For once, no questions popped out of me. All I could do was nod my head and wait to see where all this was going.

He continued, "You must remember the phrase that I have given you and learn to catch glimpses of yourself acting from chief feature. Begin by sensing it in action. Quite often you can recognize it by the negative results it engenders."

Part of me knew this was what I had traveled across the ocean and spent months preparing myself to hear. Part of me tightened up and didn't want to hear it—what was so bad about how I saw the world?

Mr. Bennett was looking at me. He turned in his chair and rummaged around in his desk, finding a scrap of notepaper. Scribbling something on it, he handed it to me.

"I would like you to read *The Life of Saint Teresa of Avila*. You should be able to find it in our library."

Maybe reading about Saint Teresa would give me a clue how to work with my chief feature.

Closing his eyes, he paused, then said, "There is hope for you."

I remembered hope had been the first latifa, or point of contact, to awaken when we were learning to open to our higher feelings. When I had despaired in those early days of the course, Mr. B had said the same, "There is hope for you, Bobby Jo."

It was good to hear it again.

Mr. Bennett looked at his watch. I knew it must be time for another appointment. He stood up, and so did I.

"I would like to see how you are getting on in about a fortnight. Write down what you heard me say your chief feature was today and bring that with you. Ask Zimmy to make the appointment, will you?"

Bennett smiled down at me, and I shadowed back his smile, feeling rather raw inside. As if a light was shining on me, but I couldn't tell what people were seeing. He let me out and ushered in the next student.

CHAPTER FIFTY-NINE
The Key to the Kingdom

It was time for my follow-up chief feature appointment with Mr. Bennett. Knocking on the door of the Bennetts' flat, I held my little scrap of paper with, "I expect everyone else to see the world through my eyes" clutched in my hand. I had been reading *The Life of Saint Teresa of Avila* during the past two weeks. It was a great story about the sustenance Teresa found through prayer, meditation, the Eucharist, and her true humility. But honestly, I didn't see how it applied to me or my chief feature.

I got the connection with my mother, though. She was really nit-picky about things. It seemed like, with her, there was only one way to do things right.

What was it with me? Did I expect everyone to do things the way I did them? Maybe. I thought about how irritated it would make me when Jack set the table as if it didn't matter how you did it. I'd shown him more than once.

Besides, everyone knows the spoon and knife go to the right of the plate, not the left. Here in England the Brits get a pass because they put a soup spoon above the plate since that's considered a dessert spoon for their inevitable "pudding." I had to admit, Jack lucked out on that one, since he got to point out that maybe my way wasn't the only way. Well . . .

Mr. Bennett opened the door, this time with his Cheshire grin, and let me in. We sat down in his cramped study, and I handed him the testimony stating what I had understood him to tell me my chief feature was. He glanced at it, carefully placed it on his desk and closed his eyes.

I tried to let a stream of relaxation drain down through my body as the moment expanded. Even though I had no idea exactly how this information could change my life, it was clear to me that this was the key to my personal work, the denouement of the course. How it was possible for Mr. B to do this for scores of students, hitting the nail on the head for each individual, was beyond me. All I could be was grateful.

But how would I work with this information? I wondered inside myself.

Mr. Bennett opened his eyes and smiled. "Yes, Bobby Jo, 'tis just so. How indeed will you work with this?"

"I am going to give you an exercise to work with when you are confronted with the results from the manifestation of your chief feature. Remember, chief feature can be said to have two sides. It is not so much a matter of turning the coin over, as it is working through to the other side."

Mr. B stopped. I could feel him collecting himself, his presence filling the room. My own sensation of myself strengthened.

"When you find yourself manifesting through chief feature, you must redirect that energy and blend it with the fourth latifa: I Accept. This will prove very useful to you."

Some kind of energy passed to me, but all I knew at the moment was that out of all the lataif, the one I had the hardest time awakening was acceptance.

"One cannot approach this directly," he was saying now. "One must learn to catch chief feature off guard. Catch it in action. Learn what it tastes like, smells like, sounds like."

Quietly he confided, "One comes to recognize chief feature at play. That is the moment to Work." To himself he murmured, "Yes."

After one of his pauses, Mr. B gazed at me thoughtfully, then asked, "We have set up a meditation room by the Great Hall, do you know it?"

I had heard about this small place, almost a closet, under the stairs by the upper platform in the Great Hall.

I nodded, "Yes."

"Well then. I suggest you use that space as often as you can to strengthen your connection with the lataif."

Reluctantly, I accepted the idea of spending time sitting on my own. Being still wasn't my strong suit, and I wasn't feeling very hopeful.

Bennett brightened. "Remember, there is another aspect of chief feature." He glanced at his watch; our time was running out.

"Expecting everyone else to see the world through your eyes can also be a strength. You have the ability to show others what you see. This can be a gift. One can work through one's feature and come out on the other side of it."

I didn't feel like asking questions. Emotions and thoughts were tumbling around inside of me. It was like having been handed a beautifully wrapped gift that, once opened, one wasn't quite sure what to do with. We stood up, and this time Mr. B let me walk myself out as he turned, sat down at his desk, and began writing.

The one-person meditation room began to feel like my personal space. I sat there now, the Great Hall beyond the door quiet, everyone somewhere else. I was in that slightly floaty space reached after the first meal or two are skipped during a fast.

Cross-legged on my cushion, darkness as deep as the quiet, it didn't take long for my muscles to soften and my attention to sweep down through my body, inventorying residual tensions, allowing tightness to melt as awareness moved past. Now filling my feet with sensation, following its movement as it engaged my legs and moved up throughout my body, feeling the sensation connect my face and scalp at the top of my head—relaxed and awake—I begin my zikr.

A deep in-breath, then three equal portions of air to exhale the breath. Attention on the area below my right breast, awakening a feeling of Wish. Not wishing for anything—just a wanting, a longing. Saying to myself "I" with the long inhalation, saying inwardly, *wish, wish, wish* with the exhalation—the fourth beat blank. I began a slight swaying to the rhythm of my beating heart, in time with *wish, wish, wish*, silence.

I did Wish. I so wished. I wished I could not be stuck in my Bobby Jo-ness. I wished I could be something better.

The same with Hope. I felt it as a possibility just within my grasp. Something bright.

And Faith. I did believe. I believed in the Work, I believed that inside myself I was good, that I could be different, that the Work "worked."

But—*accept*? That was more elusive. I breathed into myself and exhaled in three steps, focused on the pit of my throat, waiting. Waiting for it to open, for a response. Waiting to feel something. All I felt was tightness, a reaction to the thought "I Accept." Accept what? Obey whom? I had to let go but didn't know how, or of what.

I *accept, accept, accept,* silence. I let go of trying to have something happen and concentrated on the moment of inhale, the long moment of exhale, exhale, exhale, hold—inhaling "I"—exhaling *accept, accept, accept,* silence. Focus on awareness of throat, not thought.

One day it happened. I simply let go. The tightness melted and a feeling of surrender washed through me. It wasn't about a thing or a person or a concept. It was about opening inside myself.

My private assignations with zikr and the lataif continued. On fast days, zikring instead of eating filled me with a satisfaction that felt more nourishing than meat and potatoes.

It took years of work after the course to recognize my chief feature in action. Let's say Jack sets the table and puts the fork on the right and the spoon and knife on the left. The "everybody knows" attitude in me is accompanied by an upper body tightness, a stiff jaw. I begin to recognize this sense of being rigid, a sour taste in myself. In that moment, if I'm awake to it before I open my mouth, there is a possibility I come to yearn for.

In that split second before I comment, I can choose to bring awareness into myself with a breath, and exhale into my throat, opening to the pureness of acceptance. In those moments a kind of alchemy occurs, the tightness dissolves, replaced by a lightness, the flow of forces having been reversed.

CHAPTER SIXTY
Bhante

The coming of Spring brought soft greening fields and trees, open windows and warm scented breezes—and Bhante, the Most Venerable Samdach Vira Bellong Dharmavara Mahathera.

The story was that Mr. Bennett and Mick were leaving morning exercise one day when Mr. B turned to Mick and said, "Your Bhikkhu contacted me this morning during my sitting. Would you please get in touch with him to arrange a visit?"

Bhante at Asoka Mission, India, 1969/70. Photo by Tim St. Clair-Ford

Mick's elongated limbs must have been floating on air, his dark eyes shining with anticipation as he understood that somehow during the morning's inner exercise, the long sought-after meeting between his two most venerated teachers had been set in motion and would finally come to pass.

Before returning to England at Mr. Bennett's request to manage the kitchen for the courses, Mick had been living and studying with Bhante in India. I'd heard he'd gone to India after having worked for some time with Mr. B's groups in London.

Officially, we students learned that Bhante, as he was efficiently called, would be arriving from his temple in India to teach us how to meditate with healing green light, which we came to know as Green Meditation.

Preparations were made by cleaning up an old cinder block outbuilding behind the back of the Chapel. The internal walls and ceiling were painted a solid vibrant green. The small windows towards the top of the walls were draped in green fabric. The cold cement floor was likewise painted green. A lamp with a green light bulb sat in the middle of the floor, a carpet and settee of cushions arranged on one side of it for Bhante. Another array of colorful cushions fanned out in a semicircle on the other side of the light, ready for students to meditate.

Bhante arrived on a bright sunlit day with blue skies beckoning outside the Horse Parlor windows, where I sat cross-legged on the old Persian carpet with the rest of the student body. We were gathered to meet this slight little man with the long earlobes and shiny bald head. I tried to keep my gaze respectfully lowered because for some reason I had decided that because I was a woman, Bhante was culturally not allowed to look directly at me, or I at him. This made it tricky to check him out to my satisfaction. Under the burden of my premise, which had no basis in reality, I found myself stealing surreptitious glances at him as we listened to his funny, lilting voice.

My first impression of Bhante was of an Asian man with shaven head and bright orange robes. To me, he seemed both old and ageless. His smile was infectious, often accompanied by a knowing chuckle. He ate in his room once a day at noon and then only what was offered to him, never making demands. Mick waited on him with reverence.

We learned that Bhante had become a monk later in life. Inexplicably to me, he had left his wife and infant daughter as well as his career as a judge in Cambodia to study Buddhism. As a monk, he sought solitude in the jungles of Thailand, where he lived for seven years.

Over time, we heard about his years in the jungle. He told stories of being unharmed by tigers and snakes as he sat entranced in meditative states at the foot of a tree, and of levitating off the ground. Despite all this, Mick told us that in his youth Bhante had been quite wild, and he'd even been a sailor. Students reported that they had seen Bhante reach an arm out from under his saffron robe, and there were tattoos on it.

One group of thirty could just squeeze into our new green meditation room. Bhante would sing-song some prayers and then repeat them in English with us joining in. The prayers were short and always repeated thrice.

"May all Beings be Wheeellll and Hoopppeee," was one, in his sing-song lilt.

"Oh, mighty Lord, the sustainer and giver of life, bathe this troubled world in radiant rays of thy compassionate light," was another.

Bhante sat on his cushion in comfort, quite at home with all of us clustered in about him on the floor. We gazed at the bare green light bulb shining softly in the middle of the room and settled down to the business of breathing in the green light of peace, contentment, and wellness, and breathing out negative thoughts, anxieties, and toxins. The light scent of burning sandalwood perfumed the air we consciously inhaled.

Breathe in green . . .

Exhale—toxins.

At the end of the meditation Bhante said prayers again and we repeated them back. While intoning more prayers, he sprinkled us with holy water from a kitchen bowl, sending out little showers from a small branch of boxwood with the flick of his delicate wrist.

Green Meditation with Bhante became part of the weekly schedule. The unspoken rule on the course was that if you were not inside the door by the time a morning exercise or meditation started, you missed it. Timing was important. Transitioning from a practical activity, like gardening, involved taking time to wash up tools and sometimes change clothes.

"You go ahead, Jack, I'll finish putting the tools away."

"You sure? That would be great. I need to go back to our room before Green Meditation."

"Sure, no problem," I said, reaching out to take Jack's garden-fork. I still had to wait my turn at the spigot. I watched him saunter off, flaxen hair catching the breeze as he disappeared through the heavy wooden door by the kitchen and into the stone manor house, my heart floating after him.

By the time I rinsed off the fresh dirt from the tools we'd been using and returned the spade and fork to the garden shed, I realized it was pushing the hour. I ran around to the front of the house and started jogging through the old gravestones at the side of the Chapel. Sweat started moistening my shirt with the exertion and worry about being late.

Suddenly a hand landed on my shoulder pulling me back to a walk. I whipped around, heart jumping. And there was Mr. Bennett.

Bending his tall frame down so that his face was on a level with mine he quietly said, "One mustn't be out of breath arriving for meditation." And he winked at me.

In that moment we were complicit in the pact of misjudging our timing and having to rush. With Mr. B following, I slowed my pace on the path and we both demurely slipped inside the door and found our cushions just as Bhante began chanting the opening prayers. Inside my chest my breath slowed and my heart warmed at the thought of Mr. B and me, compadres.

Breath in green.

Exhale toxins.

CHAPTER SIXTY-ONE
Spring Groups

With the light and hope of spring, the chill in the old stone walls of Sherborne House slowly melted into a shared memory. The rhythm of life on the course quickened with new activities now that the daily dose of house duties like cooking or cleaning and practical work like painting or gardening were routine.

New groups were formed: Meditation, Play, and Morris Dance. The latter was introduced by a tall and lanky older gentleman, Alexander Hamilton. He had come out from London one day with an accordion slung over his shoulder to talk to Mr. Bennett about teaching this ancient rite of spring dance. The play, *Peer Gynt*, would be performed on a Visitors' Day in June, directed by a fellow student who was a professional actor. The meditation group would work with different forms of meditation, culminating in an overnight vigil. My personal poll indicated most students wanted to be in the play group. We had been encouraged to let our preferences be known in order of first, second, and third choice.

"Oh! Is the list up?" I caught up with Jack who was standing at the elbow of the main hallway, the huge bulletin board taking up most of the wall.

"Yeah," Jack replied, holding his forefinger down with his thumb while stretching out his remaining three fingers to scan down the page of names. I loved how he used his hand in that way, brushing it over the words he was reading.

"I don't know, Bobby Jo, I don't see either of our names listed in the play group." Jack looked confused. "The student director just told me yesterday he knew exactly what role he wanted me to play too. I don't get it!"

I squinted at the board, looking down the catalog of names, hoping to see my name under PLAY.

Jack was already looking at the other tacked up pages, "Oh, I see your name. You're in the meditation group at least."

I wasn't sure I considered that an "at least."

Jack became silent. His fingers had paused on the third tally, touching his name. "Morris Dance! What the…"

"Ha!" I wonder if that's because you said you had 'two left feet' on the assessment form we filled out before the course started? But you're so good in Movements, Jack, I wouldn't think that would still apply."

"I don't know, I suppose Mr. B has his reasons—but man, I really wanted to be in the play!"

Jack was crestfallen. Hardly anyone had asked to be in the Morris Dance group, which appeared dorky from the outset to us Americans—a men's only folk-dance waving red and white handkerchiefs and wearing leggings with bells.

Bhante had departed for his ashram in India, leaving us with a new green meditation room and an appreciation for healing green light and soft chuckles.

Sitting now in the meditation room with the others in the meditation group, whom I supposed really wanted to be there, I followed a particle of air as it travelled from the atmosphere into my nose and down my windpipe, branching into smaller and smaller pathways until it popped out into a minuscule air sack in my lungs. Along its course, I thought about Bennett's description of air being everywhere, filling the whole universe, giving itself freely to all without preference. How all living beings share this one thing equally; universally.

Vayu, I inhaled, invoking the Sanskrit word that translates as "wind," or "that which flows."

As I released the particle back into the atmosphere, I made the effort to hold the mantra *Prahna* deep inside my chest, without giving way to thoughts. Thoughts about being in a group that was going to be doing a lot of sitting, not my strong suit. I liked morning exercise but had decided

I didn't care for evening meditation because it put me to sleep. But here I was, so I might as well try.

The meditation group began meeting with Mr. Bennett in the ballroom on a weekly basis. One day Bennett introduced the *sati-sampajanna*, or complete awareness, meditation. As with our morning exercise, we prepared by sitting and coming into a relaxed state, releasing tensions, then filling our feet with the energy of sensation, allowing it to suffuse our body, moving up our legs, filling our torso like warm water, bringing our hands and arms alive, and finally moving up over our face and scalp to connect at the top of the head like an electric grid of energy.

Victor, the fellow student who had become a friend, was a funny, pudgy, little guy who had been a disc jockey in California before coming on the course. He wore glasses, a short beard, and had receding black hair. Totally lovable, he had that familiar, deep, radio-talk voice. To our delight, Victor had composed a tongue-in-cheek song to the tune of the Troggs' pop hit, "Love is All Around":

> I'm sensing in my fingers
> I'm sensing in my toes.
> Sensations all around me
> And so the feeling grows.
>
> There's no beginning
> There will be no end,
> And after meditation
> My legs won't bend.
>
> I'm sensing in my fingers,
> I'm sensing in my toes.
> Sensations all around me
> And so the feeling grows.

Even though I often found myself humming this anthem, I considered sensation and morning exercise serious practices, the two building blocks that set my day in motion and kept me centered throughout it. I came back to sensation now, sitting with the meditation group in the ballroom, Mr. B at the head of the room. With the sati-sampajanna meditation, he was bringing a new dimension of detail and separation to our practice.

Having reached a state of relaxation, my attention went to my eyes. I could sense the lids, feel them close and open, and sense the little muscles in my face surrounding them. I became aware of my eyes looking at the wooden floor of the ballroom a few feet in front of me. I followed my eyes up and became aware of them looking across the room at the men. I followed my eyes down, aware of their movement and that they saw the floor, while a part of me stood aside, observing, impartial.

I sensed my ears, became aware of them listening to the sound of still air, of a bird trilling outside, to a muted cough, a rustle of clothing. Awareness of touch—fabric on skin. Awareness of smell—faint floor wax and paint, dust and bodies. Awareness of taste—metallic sourness in my mouth. Awareness of motion—air moving in and out; the chest rising and falling.

I was aware of the act of standing, the sensation of my muscles moving, of my clothes shifting, of air brushing my skin as I stood. And sat again.

Sitting cross-legged on the floor at the far end of the ballroom, Mr. Bennett instructed, "Now be aware that 'I' am not my eyes and my seeing. 'I' am not my ears or my hearing. 'I' am not my touch, my smell, my taste, my breathing, my moving."

I repeated these words to myself like a mantra but was unable to hold onto any prolonged sense of separation—the separation of an "I" that could operate inside myself from an objective place and not be tossed about on the waves of emotion or imagination. I kept trying.

After some minutes, Mr. B's voice floated down the room again, "Let your mind wander, allowing formless thoughts."

My mind did wander, my stomach leading the charge. Am I smelling onions and tomatoes? How soon is lunch?

"Now put your attention on one thought. Hold the thought as a meditation."

Toasted grilled cheese. Toasted grilled cheese. Toasted grilled cheese. My stomach rolled out a gurgle.

"Put a negative situation in front of you. Observe negative thoughts."

Kippers on toast. Kippers on toast. Kippers on toast. My throat drew tight.

"Now put a positive situation in front of you. Observe positive thoughts; think good thoughts."

Tomato and onion soup with toasted grilled cheese. Served hot. My shoulders dropped my breath deepened. We were two thirds of the way through the course and my "ridiculous I" recognized the balance between taking the Work seriously but not taking myself so seriously.

"Now let go of these efforts and hold an inner stillness," Mr. B said, bringing the meditation to a close.

At our next meditation group, we began to practice sati-sampajanna as a walking meditation. This time when I stood, I followed the same pattern of awareness as my knee slowly rose, my lower leg swung out, and my weight shifted onto my right leg. Following Mr. B's lead, we slowly moved about the periphery of the ballroom in a large circle.

By the end of fifty minutes, we were no longer in a single file but moving freely about the room, each to his own rhythm, her own stride. In slow motion we moved; in slow motion we found our cushions again. Sitting, we continued the meditation and mantra silently. When ready, one stood and continued the meditation walking. With the freedom of choice, a release came. I found myself focusing on how I moved inside myself and in concert with the bodies around me and how tedious it all felt.

Too soon, our big night was upon us. We had begun at 9:00 p.m. and were to continue until daybreak. Our meditation group had worked its way up to this overnight denouement, but I wasn't sure I had.

Hours in and L-I-F-T leg, P-L-A-C-E foot, S-H-I-F-T weight, L-I-F-T leg—*God! I'm so tired of this.* My stomach tightened, and I wondered how many hours lay ahead. *If I lift my arm s-l-o-w-l-y, can I look at my watch? Midnight. It's only midnight? Shit.*

My blood was pounding in my chest, creeping up into my temples. *Focus! Put your attention in your feet. That's it, breathe in—breathe out.*

But my breath was short and tight, my head light. The slower I moved, the faster my thoughts turned. Will they notice if I curl up in the corner? Oh, that would be terrible. All night on the floor like that? Torture. I need to get out of here—but how?

Deliberately, slowly, I sati-sampajannaed myself to the end of the room and out the ballroom door, allowing the big door to swing on its silent hinges just enough to slip through and close with full awareness of my hand guiding it shut behind me. Escaped, I floated upstairs to bed, feeling nothing but relief.

Where was the Bobby Jo who appreciated the art of sitting still in the morning exercise and exploring her inner world? Apparently not the same Bobby Jo that didn't like staying up late at night and didn't want to push against herself. No. If anything, a little tinge of self-satisfaction tickled me. No one had noticed I'd left. But why would they? Each were in her or his own *now*, invested inside the world of their own body. The only person I was tricking was myself.

The next morning, I made an appointment to see Mr. B.

"I just can't do it," I confessed. "Can't I *please* be put in another group?"

"Bobby Jo, this is the work you are most in need of." Mr. Bennett shook his head, "But I will see what I can do."

In the end, I was allowed to join the Morris Dance group with the other unfortunates and Jack.

CHAPTER SIXTY-TWO
Morris On

The men stood in the ballroom waiting for class to begin. Unlike Movements class, they were configured in teams of six, three abreast, facing each other so each Morris team formed a rectangle. But like Movements, they would have to learn rhythmic stepping and how to execute choreographed figures. Alexander Hamilton swung his accordion in a familiar gesture around from his shoulder and onto his chest, fluidly looping his long arm through the strap. He began playing a lively tune and the men started hopping and kicking to the music.

We women stood on the periphery, watching. Morris dance was considered a ritual folk dance, traditionally performed in rural England by men only. Legend had it that the dance held magic power or at least brought good luck wherever it was performed. That was cool, I thought, but I felt ridiculous. What the heck, why were women even in this group? During an interlude, Barbara June asked if we should form our own teams next to the men and at least practice learning the dance.

"Oh no," came the quick reply from Mr. Hamilton's lofty height. "That would not do at all."

He reflected for a moment. "I have heard of women in London trying to do that," he admitted. Then with a sneer he added, "But that is just fluffy Morris!" He turned back to the men, ignoring us for the rest of the session.

The next time a Morris class was scheduled, the women decided to meet downstairs on the ground floor to coalesce their role in this group.

"I'm tired of sitting around watching those guys make fools of themselves in front of us," Trilby led off, her short brown hair setting off her eyes, which were snapping.

"Yeah," Barbara June agreed, musing, "There must be something we can do while they're up there prancing."

Jane, looking every bit the wholesome English country girl that she was—with her wild, strawberry-blond curls and pretty, round face—looked up and stated, "Aren't they supposed to wear some kind of costume? Maybe we should work on that to get ready for the Sherborne Fête. Isn't that coming up soon?"

"Hey Trilby," ever practical Robin threw out, "Could we use the sewing machine in the laundry room?"

Everyone started talking, "Yeah, we'll need to research what the traditional Sherborne Morris Men's costumes looked like."

"We can sew instead of just standing around doing nothing."

"Right. We'll have a proper women's group."

I had been reluctant to be in this group from the outset, but it was better than being stuck doing meditation all day. The notion of sitting around sewing struck me as overtly demeaning, but the fact that we were defining our own role was appealing, "a proper women's group." Whatever that was.

"I'll ask Anna Hodgson if we can use the sewing machine, I doubt she needs it all the time for the laundry," Trilby said.

"I'll look into what the costumes for Sherborne Village used to be like," Jane offered.

"Maybe I can help you with that," said Barbara June.

The rest of us agreed to meet in the sewing room for the next scheduled class with any needles, scissors or thread we might have brought with us to Sherborne. I could at least do that—bring my travel mending kit.

The sewing room was small, painted white, with a little table and single chair for the old sewing machine Anna used. I wasn't sure for what, sheets and kitchen towels? Making Movements costumes? We crowded in on the floor around a pile of white and red cloth Elizabeth had allowed us to purchase with the small budget our group had been allotted. It felt like Girl Scouts to me, but if I couldn't be in the play group, it was the better alternative.

"The Morris Men of Sherborne Village wore white pants and shirts, red bandanas around their necks, a red sash with rosettes sewn onto them, red leggings festooned with bells, and black bowler hats. They waved red and white handkerchiefs, one in each hand," Jane explained. "Some of the dances call for staves," she added.

The room was close, with a faint musk-smell, all of us reaching for pieces of fabric, ripping it in lengths for the leggings or large squares for the bandanas and handkerchiefs. Someone set up the ironing board and pressed hemlines into the torn fabric. Trilby managed the sewing machine, pressing the pedal, guiding red strips of cloth through, creating a background hum as we settled into our tasks of threading needles and whip-stitching hems for the handkerchiefs.

Quiet descended for a time as each attended to her project. A companionable rhythm emerged, the whoosh of steam from the iron, the whir of the Singer, the push of needles and pull of thread.

"Jane, did you or Barbara June learn anything else about the history of Morris Dance, or anything particular about the Sherborne Morris?" asked Robin.

"Well, there are two other roles besides the dancers. One is the Fool, who's supposed to wear a colorful vest and carry a blown-up pig's bladder dangling from a stick. He's supposed to swat any of the dancers who make a mistake or aren't trying hard enough," answered Jane.

"Reminds me of Mullah Nasruddin," said Barbara June, grinning. "You know, the Sufi fool who really knows more than anyone. Oh, and we have to come up with a horse costume for another side character," she added.

"And what about coming up with the bowler hats? How are we going to manage that?" asked someone else.

"Jane, can you ask Elizabeth if we can buy some?"

All eyes turned towards Jane, who was quietly bent over her sewing. She looked up, unhappiness on her usually bright countenance.

"I already asked. The budget Elizabeth gave me pretty much just covered the fabric we have here. She had to allocate most of the available money towards the play, I'm afraid."

"Well, that's not fair!"

"Yeah, what makes the play so much more special than us?"

"And what, the hats are supposed to just appear out of thin air?"

"What about papier-mâché? We might be able to do something with that for the horse head, at least."

"Actually, my mom made a horse costume for me once for Halloween and I think the head was papier-mâché," I remembered. My mind floated back to fourth grade and the black leotard with a horsetail of yarn sewn on the back and a horse-shaped head construction that fit over my head. "It was pretty cool."

"Well, let's do what we can with what we have in front of us. We should concentrate on getting the leggings, sashes and bandanas done at least. The Spring Fête is scheduled for June and that's just a few weeks away!" urged Robin.

Anna Durco taught Women's Movements, another new addition to the schedule. Like Vivien Elliot, she wore costumes. Unlike Vivien's, whose flowing ensembles had a theatrical flair, Anna's seemed unaffected—loose pants tight at the ankle and tunic-like overgarments seemed to be a manifestation of who she was. She was unlike any woman I had ever met. Certainly nothing like my mom, who kept a tidy house, had been a part-time secretary, and liked to organize the coffee hour at church. Anna exuded the dark spice of something otherworldly, her jet-black hair and white skin offset by shocking red lipstick and an exotic accent.

Born to Czech parents in Chicago, Anna had met Gurdjieff as a young child at the World's Fair in 1934 and conversed with him in his native mixture of Russian, Greek, and Asian dialects. This may not have been as strange as it sounds. Jack was convinced that his Slovak

Anna Durco. Photo courtesy of Jane Bulmer Heath.

grandparents were Russian. His aunt once told him that his grandfather was "a real Caucasian," meaning he was from the Caucasus mountains, which divided Russia from Georgia—not far from Armenia and Turkey, where Gurdjieff grew up. Anna was now middle-aged yet still beautiful. None of us students knew her background, except that she had been irrevocably touched by Gurdjieff's aura, remembering everything he had said to her that day.

One week, Anna invited several of the women students to dinner. Some of us were part of the Morris Dance group still trying to find our way where men had center stage while the women sewed their costumes, sidelined in the basement. Going to dinner with Anna felt like being singled out for special recognition. I found her mysterious and alluring.

I have no idea what town the restaurant was in. I remember a long, dark, wooden table draped in white linen in a semiprivate space, maybe set apart with half walls and lattice work. There were uniformed waiters. We were served wine, and the menu was varied, not the usual greasy pork pie or fish and chips. At twenty-two, I felt very grown up.

This was my first ever women's gathering—being with others of my gender without the strictures of fulfilling a role. I don't remember what we talked about. For once, we weren't listening to guys philosophizing.

As the wine took effect, our somewhat stilted initial conversations became animated. We told tales, we giggled. Anna egged us on, attentive, encouraging. I found my voice, gesticulating with wine glass in hand. Probably some story about Jack.

"And so, yeah." My voice rose, my head in a bubble, my hand suddenly raised in salute and *POP!* Wine sprayed everywhere as glass shards rained down on the table.

With my hand still extended, heat rose in me like a pressure cooker, coloring my face, prickling under my arms. Unable to grasp what had just happened, I squeezed my eyes shut and opened them as if that would clear my head.

"My glass broke," I explained, deciding something had been wrong with it. "I need another one."

Anna stood up and motioned to the waiter as she came to stand beside me. He had been watching from his corner, purse-lipped, disdain on his brow. This silly rag-tag group and their oddly dressed matron. Girls who couldn't handle their wine—and now, *look*.

A presence filled Anna and the space around her as the waiter sauntered over, a towel draped over his arm. Plucking the shattered glass from my hand, she presented it to him with a hard look.

"My dear man, it seems this glass was defective. We need it replaced. Another glass of wine will do."

He hesitated, his smirk replaced by confusion, glancing at the bewildered look on my face and back again at Anna.

Never breaking her gaze, leveled at him through dark eyes, Anna dismissed the waiter with a wave of red nail polish, "Thank you."

Yes, madam, right away."

He returned, composure restored, a full round glass of wine in hand and gently laid it on the table at my place, withdrawing with a slight nod of the head.

Anna looked me in the eye and picked up her wine glass. Still befuddled at how the glass had exploded in midair like that, I followed suit, as did the rest of the table. It never occurred to me that I could have been at fault and that Anna chose to step in and support me. Still gazing into my blue eyes, she took a deliberate swallow. Returning to her seat, she began a new conversation with the woman next to her, the table falling back into companionable babble.

The next time we watched the men practice, tying the leggings around their calves and handing out red and white handkerchiefs, we didn't mind their strutting or proudly out-leaping each other. We laughed and cheered them on. I started feeling a dynamic at play, reaching as far back as the pagan beginnings of this dance.

Sap was rising in the trees and so was energy and power. We women were not just standing idly by, we had a role to play. We. We were the reason the men tried harder, strove to outdo each other. This was the stuff of life, of creation, of partnership. Maybe ours was the best of the three groups after all.

CHAPTER SIXTY-THREE
Jack's Decision Exercise

"I was setting up my Decision Exercise this morning and the weirdest thing happened," Jack mused after breakfast.

We were in our room, getting ready to go to practical work. He sat down on the bed and continued, like he was talking to himself.

"I was going through the steps to make my decision for the day, based on what I'd prepared last night. But each time I started visualizing the task I'd chosen, I was interrupted by a little voice saying, 'Make a Morris hat.' I tried to ignore the voice, but it kept butting in."

"Whoa," I said, and sat down next to him on the bed cross-legged, our knees touching.

Jack waited for me to settle, then continued, "Finally, I gave up. 'Okay, I'll make a Morris hat!' I told the voice. I went through the rest of the steps, answering the questions—What? Why? How?" Jack looked at me, his brow furrowed. "I have no idea how I'm going to make a Morris hat. But Mr. B was ending the morning exercise, so I had to finish up and ask the question, 'Am I going to do this?'" He looked down at his hands and said, "When I asked the question, I got a resounding *yes* inside." He looked up at me as if I might have some insight.

"Don't look at me, we're busy making your costumes," I said. None of us ladies knew anything about making bowler hats! Heck, most of us never heard of Morris Dance till a few weeks ago. Besides, this would be the first time in decades there'd been a Sherborne Village Morris team. We'd only had historical records to go by to figure out what the costumes were like, so I doubted there were any Morris hats floating around out there for us to use. "You're on your own with this one, Jack. Sorry," I said, rising and twisting my hair into the quick French knot I was in the habit of fashioning to keep it out of the way while we worked outside.

Jack rose too, a determined look on his face as he pulled on his sneakers. We headed out of the room together, occupied with our own thoughts.

As it turned out, Brian, a fellow group member and a scientist to boot, had created a plaster mold and suggested it could be lined with papier-mâché to form a hat, which could then be painted black.

At the end of the day, when most were getting ready for bed, Jack had made his way out to the old Orangery greenhouse. He lined Brian's mold with a papier-mâché recipe he'd concocted, with no idea how long it would take to dry. He felt like he was going through the motions, driven by an inner taskmaster he didn't understand.

This is crazy, Jack thought. *What the heck am I doing out here, anyway?* He looked around at half-potted plants and seed trays sharing the table with his hat mold. Through floor-to-ceiling windows, cold half-moon light cast dark shadows and then fleeting light, as clouds swam across the sky. Something scurried along the edge of the floor. *This is getting spooky. What was I thinking?* Jack stepped closer to the table, wishing he owned a wristwatch. *How am I going to know if this darn hat is set by midnight? If this decision is not completed today, then I've just been fooling myself. But the "yes" was so strong!*

A long eerie *whooo* echoed out in the woods, followed by *WHO-whoo, WHO-whoo,* quite close, making him jumpy. He wondered how long he could handle hanging out in the spooky Orangery. Having no idea how close to midnight it was, he knew he needed to be patient. He looked up at the cold glass and steel space, feeling the emptiness press on him. He tried counting, as if he could be the second hand and tick off the minutes.

He poked at the hat with a stiff finger. It seemed hard enough. *It must be time.* Carefully, gingerly, he began prying the hat out of its mold, rocking it back and forth. It was halfway out, it was coming! He gave a little tug—the hat tore apart, a portion sticking to the mold. Jack froze, his hands gripping half a hat. Now he could feel the dampness of the papier-mâché.

"If only I'd been more patient," he said, when telling me the story.

At the time, he'd felt an acute sense of failure wash through him. Then frustration. The decision had not been realized. So why had he heard that voice so clearly? Why had he listened to it? He'd stepped away from the table, resolution filling his limbs as he lifted his arms in the dark and held them out sideways until they ached. This was the price his body must bear for saying yes to a decision that had not been made with all three centers. All of himself must learn to be on the same page.

A few days later, during a private interview with Mr. Bennett, Jack brought up the incident again, which he had already spoken of during a group meeting.

After listening carefully, Mr. B opened his eyes, their usual piercing quality softened with thought. "Here is an example of how we interfere with Higher Worlds," he said. "This decision was coming from the world of potential. Yet you lacked the faith in yourself to allow the World of Potential to cross over to the World of Manifestation. You allowed doubt to get in the way of it."

Mr. B's voice was encouraging. "You are on to something, Jack. I want you to continue preparing your Decision Exercise, but when you receive a clear directive, open yourself and allow it to happen. The 'how' is not as important as believing in the affirmation. If you had believed in your 'yes,' the hat would have worked."

CHAPTER SIXTY-FOUR
Spring Outing

On a balmy day in late May, the Morris group loaded up and drove in various conveyances to one of the many villages nestled in the rolling Cotswold countryside. This particular village was hosting an annual fête complete with Morris Dance. Mr. B wanted us to get a taste of how it was done. In a few short weeks, Sherborne would be hosting its own fair.

While still early in the day, we disembarked and began roaming about individually and in small groups. Some proprietors of the booths—rough two-by-fours nailed together and draped with sheets, a plywood counter fronting it—were just completing the setup of their games.

Jack and I stopped by one with several bottles arranged on a table inside the booth. Assorted red, blue, and yellow rings were piled on top of the counter in front. The man in the booth was a bit roughshod and sported a shadow of beard, as if he never quite had time to shave. He wore heavy work boots. I guessed he might be in his forties, and he paid scant attention to us as he went about his business.

The bottles were different colors and sizes, most contained soda. They were sitting upright, fairly close together. Each one had a white paper square stuck on it, handprinted with large black numbers. In the midst of the array stood the prize, a fine deep blue bottle of Harvey's Bristol Cream Sherry. I was not acquainted with sherry, but I liked the look of the bottle. It was pretty. I asked the man if he was open for business.

He looked down his nose sizing me up and said, "Twenty pence will buy you three tosses. If you get one around the neck of a bottle, you get to pick a number out of the bag. The numbers in the bag match the numbers on the bottles. The one you pick is the one you win." He relayed his information in a tone that conveyed anyone-else-but-me would know this.

Digging out my twenty pence, I laid it on the counter saying, "Here you go."

He offered me three rings and leaned back against the side of the booth with his arms folded across his chest.

My first toss landed on the table, sliding between two soda bottles. This wasn't going to be as easy as it looked. My second throw came closer to the middle of the table but still didn't get around the neck of a bottle. My third throw finally ringed a bottle. I had remembered to sense my hand as I threw, aware of its life as an entity and my connection to it. This was a good chance to practice the things we had learned on the course out here in the ordinary world.

The man came forward, shaking a paper bag with folded pieces of paper inside. He held it out towards me, inviting me to get on with it. "Here you go then, Missy."

I decided to try an experiment. Shutting my eyes, I sensed the area below my right breast, awakening the feeling of *Wish*. Blending the feeling with sensation in my right arm and hand, I pictured the blue bottle in my mind and wished that I could win it. The man rattled the bag again, impatient. Holding onto the feeling of *wish*, the sensation in my arm and the thought of the bottle, I reached in and drew out a piece of paper, handing it to the vendor. He unfolded the paper, and his face went red. Scowling, he picked the bottle of sherry off the table and presented it to me. He looked pointedly at Jack and muttered, "lucky dog."

Jack, who had been standing aside watching the whole time, gave me a bemused glance and led me quickly away. Regarding me questioningly, he said, "How did you do that?"

"I used *Wish*," I replied, suddenly feeling that I may have done something inappropriate and perhaps even dangerous. I wondered to myself if there were bad karmic consequences for using the sacred impulses, lataif,[1] for personal gain.

---

[1] The Sufi Naqshbandi order view lataif (plural) as psychospiritual organs/capacities that are potential receptors of Divine energy when activated in those undergoing spiritual development.

Jack grinned and said, "Well, I think you may have spoiled that poor man's whole game plan. I bet he was expecting a bunch of guys to be trying all day for that Sherry."

I looked back at the booth and saw the man rearranging things on the table and kind of thumping them around. Raising the bottle to give it a good look, I had to admit I was still glad I had won it. It would be the perfect bottle for making blue water like Bhante had been encouraging us to do. Other people were already setting colored glass bottles of water outside at Sherborne House to catch the rays of the sun and imbue the water with refracted "color." According to Bhante, different colored water treated different types of ailments, one tablespoon taken as medicine. For instance, blue water was soothing, good for constipation. I let Jack tuck the bottle under his arm as we strolled on.

The Morris Dance was starting around 2:00 p.m. We couldn't miss that, but we were getting hungry. Spotting Victor, we caught up with him. We were standing in the village road which had been shut down to regular traffic for the fête. People were wandering all around, going in and out of artisan shops as well as the game booths.

Trilby, who was strolling by, stopped and said, "If you're looking for something to eat, there's a pub down the street." She pointed behind her. "You'll see the sign over the door. There's steps leading down."

"Thanks Trilby, that's great!"

Victor, Jack, and I located the pub just as a man dressed in white Morris costume darted past us and down the steps. He disappeared into the dark interior. Ducking under the lintel, we followed. Once our eyes grew accustomed to the dim light, we saw several Morris men gracing a number of tables with pints of beer in hand. Jack noticed a cluster of men in the corner throwing darts. "Bobby Jo, can you order me some fish and chips? I want to check this out," he asked and sauntered over. The scene in the pub must have been reminding him of his favorite bar at home in New Jersey where he'd go to find his friends.

Just as we were settling into our lunch, I noticed a woman in an ankle length skirt and colorful blouse in the doorway. She went straight to one of the men playing darts in Morris costume. She said something to him in an urgent whisper. He handed his pint of beer to her and dashed out the door. She followed behind being careful not to spill his brew climbing the steps.

"I think the Morris Dance must be getting ready to start," I interrupted Victor as he was setting up a joke to regale the table with.

"Well, finish up, me lads. We must not be late for the dance!" Victor acquiesced in his best British accent.

We washed down our remaining lunch with what was left in our mugs, throwing a pile of pound notes and pence on the table while gathering our things, then scurried up the steps onto the street.

Bright strains of Morris music wafted from around the corner. We noticed a crowd gathering and quickened our pace. As we passed down the street, I noticed other women pulling men from pubs.

Drawing near, we saw the familiar rectangles of three sets of two, the men standing six feet apart facing each other. Several groups were forming. Some teams stood on the side, waiting their turn. Each group's costume was noticeably different in decoration, although most had the white pants and shirts. I felt a prick of pride that we women were resurrecting little Sherborne Village's traditional Morris costume.

All these men seemed to have a wife or girlfriend standing on the sidelines. Their women were dressed in colorful flouncy skirts and peasant blouses. Most were holding large pints of beer, cat-calling and laughing, nudging each other, and grinning. The mood of light-hearted playfulness, with undertones of sexuality, was contagious. An audience gathered, drawn like fish to a scatter of food on the water. It occurred to me that the presence of women contributed in large measure to the spirit of this ritual dance.

The Fool, dressed in a ragged looking vest with ribbons flowing from his elbow bands, stood on the side. A man hidden inside a leering papier-mâché horse's head pranced and bobbed around him. The Fool announced the first dance as accordion, fiddle, and tambourine players launched into a lively tune.

Dancers, ranging in age from twenty to forty-five, concentrated on outdoing each other with the height of their leaps and the width of their kicks. The women called out to their guys, egging them on. At the interludes, a man might break rank and swallow thirsty draughts from a mug held out by the woman who claimed him, some stealing a kiss in the bargain.

In one of the sets, dancers struck their hefty sticks together in unison, accenting the music. The crowd cheered and clapped. We had not seen a dance using staffs before. Impressed by the percussive choreography, I glanced at Jack and saw a look of admiration travel between his and Victor's eyes.

On the ride home, Jack and I ended up in Mr. Bennett's car. As dusk followed us, we were treated to Mr. B's infamous driving. Barreling down the highway, he pulled out to pass a sixteen-wheel lorry. Despite my recent concern about using the sacred energy of a latifa for one's own purposes, I found myself fervently employed in that pursuit.

Bennett veered back into the lane just as an oncoming car whooshed by us.

As usual, I couldn't help but blurt out, "Mr. B, that's one way to get our latifas going!"

"As long as its *faith* and not *hope*," he gleefully responded.

We arrived back at Sherborne House in one piece, including my deep blue bottle of Sherry.

Late that night or the next, a knock came on our slant-ceilinged attic room door. I was surprised upon opening it to find Sonia standing there with three little cone-shaped sippers. She grinned and invited herself in,

"I've come to teach you how to drink sherry."

Sonia was one of the Alaskan coterie, most of whom were rugged guys with hair-raising stories of their adventures aboard fishing vessels in frigid and dangerous seas. The whole group, men and women alike, exuded a stalwart physical toughness that brooked no nonsense. Sonia was one of these, despite her five-foot frame and blond hair.

Without hesitation, we pulled out our unopened bottle and sat in a tight circle on the floor, as we had no chairs to offer. Sonia set the glasses down while Jack opened the bottle. Without a word she poured the rich golden liquor into the three small conveyances, held one up to the dim light of our one dresser lamp, and passed it under her nose. We did likewise. The aroma was dark and pungent and sweet. Sonia then announced, "Cheers!" clinked our glasses in turn and took an appreciative sip.

The liquid slid down my throat easily and warmed both my taste buds and my gullet all the way down to my belly. We sipped and chatted and poured again.

Sonia told us of life in Alaska—you either learned to be self-reliant, or you left, or you perished. But mostly she told us of group meetings with George and Mary Cornelius and how everyone knew George was a total curmudgeon but loved his big heart—how petite Mary deftly and gently kept him in line. How much the group owed to them as their teachers. How George had encouraged them to make the trip to England and come on Bennett's Basic Course.

As we sat and sipped and shared stories, I realized my *wish* had snagged more than just a blue bottle. We had a new friend; one I would never have thought to approach on my own. I had also acquired a lifelong love of cream sherry.

CHAPTER SIXTY-FIVE
Digging Deeper

Summer was coming. Most practical work in the garden was now planting, weeding, and harvesting rather than digging new beds. All of the salads and vegetables we ate came from our own toil, a welcome relief from the diet of lentils, sardines, and marmite consumed during the colder months.

Today, however, there were a couple of new beds to dig. Each was about twelve by twenty feet. I was working with five other women assigned to one of the beds. Six men were digging the other. Being outside without bulky clothing was a treat. Jane and Rachel wore skirts.

We gathered at the edge of the bed. I thrust my shovel into the hard-packed earth, digging the blade deep with a push of my foot, bending my knee to leverage the mound of dirt up and out of its hole, using the muscles of my lower back. Thrust and dump, thrust and dump—the ground giving up its rich nutty earthiness into smaller crumbles of moist soil, earth worms wriggling free out of the clumps.

With sunshine warming our backs, Barbara June was on my left and willowy Vicky was on my right, her birdlike bones working the soil just as well as my compact frame. Thrust and turn, thrust and turn. It seemed like our shovels were tied together in an effortless motion. Aisha, who had befriended me in the kitchen when I first arrived all those months ago, came abreast alongside Rachel and Jane, their skirts tucked up into waistbands, and their respective black and red hair tied back with bandanas. We worked in companionable silence. I felt the strength of the coming summer sun, heard the joy of birds going about their nesting, smelled the sweat breaking out under my arms, and became aware that all six of us women had come abreast in one horizontal line, working down the bed together as if our shovels were one tool.

Glancing over at the men, I saw them moving down the breadth of their bed. Kip and Steve were in the lead, grunting and thrusting deep, turning their shovel loads over quickly and thrusting again, looks of concentration furrowing wet brows. I could see that they were competing against each other and was surprised to realize they were enjoying it.

Comfortable with our rhythm, we slowly came abreast, then moved past the men in an easy flow. With the guys grunting and straining across the way, we women worked in unison, finishing our bed before the men. It looked well-dug and uniform, I thought.

Steve was leaning on his shovel watching as Kip caught up to him. The other men were strung out behind. The men's garden bed looked uneven, with mounds of deeply dug earth in some quarters but not in others.

Picking up our tools, we walked off to hose them down and wash up for lunch. We women chatted quietly amongst ourselves, still in the glow of connection. The men wiped their brows, exuding satisfaction at the competition, grins and nods joining the camaraderie of having worked hard together.

Growing up I had been a tomboy, wanting nothing more than to be accepted as one of the guys. When Women's Lib hit the scene during my first year of college, I figured, great! We'll all be equal, what's the difference anyway? Since living in England, I noticed European women didn't try to mask their feminine qualities but seemed to have a handle on a subtle art that I was clueless about. They didn't need to wear pants to compete with men, nor did they compete with brawn. For the first time, I noticed that women had strengths that were different from men's—women seemed inclined to work together, men to strive and compete. Strolling with Jane back to the tool shed, it occurred to me that women did not need to mimic men, competing in strength and speed. Cooperation was a far more powerful tool.

The lunch bell rang. I had found Jack and we made our way to the dining room. Lunch was silent, as usual. After the grace—"All life is One and everything that lives Is holy"—we sat, waiting to be served. Working outside in the sun and earth brought a vibrancy to the grace for me: "Plants, animals, and man—all must eat to live and nourish one another. We bless the lives that have died to give us this food. Let us eat together, resolving by our Work to pay the debt of our existence."

The plates came out, mounded high with Welsh rarebit. No, wait. The rarebit sauce wasn't poured over bread, but a head of lettuce. A lettuce smothered in creamy cheese sauce. Yum! I dug in and enjoyed every bite of this crunchy summer fare.

I hardly noticed when some at our table put their forks down and looked quizzically at what they were eating. It was obvious to me what our lunch was. Afterwards I learned that all the lettuce had been hastily picked that morning after Mick, our itinerant iconoclast, discovered the whole crop was bolting into seed in the hotter than usual June sun. This was the kind of on-the-spot emergency we had all become used to dealing with.

I preferred going without my glasses, so it didn't matter to me what anyone else was looking at. As long as it tasted good, who cared? Only later when I heard friends discussing the meal did it become clear. In the rush to pick the lettuce and plate lunch the kitchen crew hadn't enough time to thoroughly wash it, so a surfeit of rarebit had been used to cover up garden bugs hidden deep in the folds of the lettuce leaves.

Maybe it was a result of the constant environment of inner work, but there was no sense of revulsion in me as I listened to the unveiled truth of our lunch. What was clear to me was that I had not known about the bugs and I had enjoyed what I had eaten. It tasted good. My hunger was satisfied. I was content. There was no need to manufacture an emotion or physical reaction that had not been part of my experience and need not be part of it now. A step in the struggle against automatism had been taken.

CHAPTER SIXTY-SIX
The Work at Play

It was a perfect spring day in June. Sweet perfumes floated on the air as a fitful sun played hide and seek, the brilliance of green grass glistening with dew. Today, June 8, was also Mr. Bennett's birthday. A mystical light shone down through the clouds upon the manor house and the grounds. Sherborne was a beehive of activity.

Jack had been chosen House Supervisor for the big day. His role was to see that the house duties ran smoothly. The entire course was gathered down in the Horse Parlor after breakfast. From his seat on the floor, Jack spoke.

"A lot is going on today. We are all going to be busy and there's bound to be loose ends. If you see something that needs to be done, do it."

No one needed to look into the crowd to see who was speaking. By that point in the year, we knew each other's voices. Indeed, we knew each other's coughs.

"No doubt you will see something that needs attention and think someone else will take care of it because you're busy and you're an exception," Jack said. He paused, looking down. "Then everyone is an exception which means no one is an exception." Jack said no more.

After a few minutes of silence, everyone quickly exited the room and moved to attend to their assigned duties.

As I walked down the corridor by the kitchen, I saw Elizabeth and Annette conferring. Annette was dressed in her green kaftan, looking stylish as usual. She had a clipboard in her hands as Elizabeth's assistant event coordinator. Elizabeth was in her everyday dun-colored skirt and white blouse.

How was the food to get out of the kitchen and up onto the back lawn where the guests were to be? There was no direct route from the kitchen at the back of the house to the lawn in front. That was a conundrum. Someone walked up and mentioned a window and they went to look. There it was—a two-by-three-foot opening high up on the wall in the old wine cellar. Brilliant. The food could be passed out from there to the servers outside.

A schedule of events posted on the bulletin board led off with:

11:00 a.m.—GROUNDS OPEN TO THE PUBLIC

and ended with:

4:00 p.m.—PEER GYNT

The play group would perform the final event on a stage that had been built upon the rise of ground under the giant larches.

Chairs still needed to be set up for the audience, and the game booths were not all draped and decorated. Everyone had more than one task to perform before dressing for the event. With too much chatter and buzzing energy, something could go wrong. Two and a half hours suddenly did not seem like time enough to have it all ready. On top of everything, it began to drizzle. But help showed up where it was needed and when guests began to arrive late in the morning, everything fell into place.

Morris women, dressed in skirts and pretty blouses, were the hostesses, offering sandwiches and other finger foods pouring out from the kitchen under Mick's direction. Platters were handed from person to person in a chain of volunteers stretching from just outside the kitchen, down the hall and into the wine cellar. One person stood on a chair by the window to pass the food outside to the waiting servers.

Light laughter tinkled amidst hearty shouts of greeting as local village folk and urban students of Mr. B's London groups began filling the expansive manicured lawn behind the manor house. Savory aromas of sausage puffs and melted cheese on triangles of toast filled the air. Children romped through the crowd, playing tag. Somewhere the pure note of a flute sounded. Game booths attracted families and couples. The Sherborne Fête was in full swing.

Jack, dressed as the Fool with patchwork vest and black top hat, juggled through-out the crowd to get attention. Prancing around him in a huge black papier-mâché horse head, red fabric dangling down, swinging around his body, was our friend Ken Haag.

The men moved into their formations of two groups of six facing each other as we women stood clustered on the sidelines. Following the Pied Piper and his trusty steed, people began gathering round. Lively accordion music drew more of the crowd. I hoped the locals were appreciative that we students had resurrected dances from the Sherborne Morris that had not been performed in Sherborne Village for generations.

I watched the formation nearest me of Brian, Steve, Victor, Paul, Tony, and Kip. Holding their red and white handkerchiefs, they snapped their wrists. Bell leggings tinkled with the stamping and circling of their legs. We Morris women prompted the crowd, calling for higher kicks and snappier steps. In that moment a feeling of connection traveled from deep inside me down into the land below my feet from which my ancestors had sprung. I was happy to be a woman playing my part in this timeless dance.

Jack skipped and hopped around the two teams mimicking their kicks and flapping his arms in mime. If one of the men misstepped, Jack bopped him with the dun-colored, air-filled pig's bladder dangling from his jester's rod. The horse pranced, bobbing his head in time to the frolicsome music. It seemed as if the very earth was laughing and cheering and coming awake. It seemed over all too soon.

The men made their bows and filed off the field as we accompanied them in our flouncy skirts and puffy blouses, garlands in our hair. The illusion of being free to forget ourselves within the entertainment was transmuted into the next present moment of preparing for the play. Slipping away, we melted back into our previous roles of hostessing and setting up.

Sherborne Fête Morris Dancers.

Ten minutes before four in the afternoon, Jack walked through the crowd juggling, drawing the attention of children who began following him and pulling their parents along. Strategically moving towards the stage, he gathered the crowd until they were clustering and taking seats, children sprawling out on the grass. Having disappeared, Jack popped up onstage together with Collins and Jane, who were playing flute and guitar to "Circle Game" the folk song made famous by Joni Mitchell.

Jack juggled in rhythm to the music as Jane sang. The audience participated, their attention focused on Jack's nimble fingers flinging the balls up and catching them again. It felt as if all of us were keeping those hard, white lacrosse balls up in the air for him. As the painted ponies went up and down in the song, two balls went up and down in each of his hands. When the lyric went "round and round" the balls moved in a circle from hand to hand. I felt magic in the air as I followed the balls from my vantage point in front of the stage.

Behind me was Sherborne House. Without looking, I knew that it was quietly humming with work on the inside. I closed my eyes and followed the flow of scented air into my lungs. Exhaling, I opened my eyes, rotating my head to take in the variety of people moving about to find chairs, watch the stage, stroll across the lawn with food in hand. Here were relaxed attitudes, muffled conversations rising and dipping, Jane's guitar and Collin's flute floating overhead. I felt the results of our work, both inward and out, as a palpable ambiance of camaraderie and goodwill amongst all participants. We, the students, were playing our parts to put on this fête, and like the actors in the play about to start, we were performing our roles. The difference was the conscious attention we brought to all we did. I could feel our accumulated energy, like a cloak, surrounding us and our guests.

People were filling up the seats in front of the stage. There was a hush as the Master of Ceremonies climbed up the side stairs and looked out over the seats below. Welcoming the audience, he announced the play, *Peer Gynt*.

Peer Gynt and the Button-Moulder

A student who was a professional actor played the title role of Peer Gynt. Mr. B played the Button-Moulder. For all his experience as a professional, it seemed to me I was seeing this student unmasked. His lines sounded all too real, not like he was acting, but as if he realized his life had come to nothing.

Suddenly the play in front of me had come to life. I saw myself. Like Peer Gynt, the oblivious man, I, too, was going to be melted down and poured back into the mold. Was I just fooling myself and floating along, like Peer Gynt, in the stream of life that flows automatically and ends up in the netherworld? To be melted down by the Button-Moulder to form another soul?

A doubt gripped me. Could I enter "the other stream" Gurdjieff talked about? The stream of transformation that takes work and effort to enter but leads to awakening?

What was my own personal work outside of prescribed tasks and Themes here at Sherborne? I wondered if our actor friend was inwardly writhing under Bennett's gaze as he continued to play his role in the play perforce, carrying on as I had learned to do that day with Elizabeth, when I admitted I didn't understand anything, and she handed me a cleaning rag.

Was he, like me, gripped at this moment by the "Terror of the Situation" which Gurdjieff's words awakened in me? Knowing that this life I was living was a lie unless I could do the work needed to awaken? Yet I didn't know if I was capable of doing that work.

The play ended, according to the script that had been prepared by the actor-student himself. I never heard him describe his experience on that stage with Mr. Bennett.

The fête was over, the visitors leaving as the day waned. Chairs were brought back inside, game booths disassembled, cleanup in the kitchen commenced even as the dinner cooks worked to prepare a meal for the end of the day.

Jack saw Elizabeth walking along the ground floor passage on his way to check on something in his House Supervisor capacity.

As they passed, she commented in her dry way, "You made a wonderful fool of yourself today."

Jack slowed his pace, glowing inside, cherishing the compliment.

At dinner, despite Mr. B's objections, we celebrated his birthday at the end of the meal when Mick brought a cake up from the kitchen depths. Elizabeth had conveyed Mr. B's wishes there should be no fuss, but we sang a rousing "Happy Birthday" to him anyway.

CHAPTER SIXTY-SEVEN
Looking Ahead

Sitting in the Horse Parlor on the warm reds and faded browns of the antique carpet, waiting for Mr. B to enter, I found myself ruminating, thinking Jack's forehead was almost as large and domed as Mr. B's. It struck me how smart Jack was, how he thought about things and had an innate wisdom that others recognized. Surprised, I realized I was not judging his worth by the fact that he'd played the truant in school and dropped out of college, as I might once have done. I gazed at his long, delicate face with the silken golden-brown hair falling on either side of his vaulted brow. So what if his nose had an off-kilter bump? He was happy to own it, as it was a legitimate inheritance from his mother. I had grown to love the whole package.

The door between the Great Hall and the Horse Parlor flew open. Mr. B stood there for a moment, his eyes scanning over us as he took inventory. In three long strides he maneuvered around his chair and plunked down on the velveteen burgundy seat, closing his eyelids in contemplation. My attention came back to myself, aware of my posture, my tensions, my breathing, allowing knotted muscles to soften and let go. Mr. B's presence filled the room, attended by our own, receptive to what was to come.

"I would like to speak to you all today about the world situation. Particularly about what is to come in the next thirty to forty years," Mr. B began.[1]

---

[1] Most of this chapter is taken from JGB's talk entitled "Future Plans: The World Situation," given in the spring of 1973 at Sherborne House to students on the second Basic Course.

LOOKING AHEAD

For Mr. B to tell us about the future was nothing surprising. This was a topic he had studied, thought and talked about for years. He had often proposed the need for an Ark, like Noah's. A community that would be able to weather the coming breakdown of civilization and provide a model for a new society based on self-sufficiency and cooperation.

When he would close his eyes and seem to go somewhere and then reappear to answer a question, it was easy for me to believe he had traveled in time, either to the past or the future. Now he was saying, "It is highly improbable that the world will get through the next thirty years without pretty dramatic events."

There was a pause between *pretty* and *dramatic events*, as though he was seeing it. "Particularly events connected with the workings of our society. Society will come under strains that it's not prepared to withstand because it's so very slow adapting."

"Like dinosaurs," Larry threw out, looking up at Mr. B through his wire-rimmed glasses.

"What?" Mr. B stopped and turned his attention from the place within himself to the room. "What? What did you say?"

Larry spoke a little louder. "Like dinosaurs. Our institutions are like dinosaurs. Big and slow, with little brains."

"Yes, just so," Mr. B nodded once and bent his head again, returning within as he resumed his thought. "Society has built great institutions with extremely complex systems of production and distribution both of the necessities of life and the non-necessities. Because we see that human individuals behave with a certain amount of intelligence, we overlook that human institutions of any size do not work with intelligence. They work according to habitual patterns of behavior and response, with little ability to adapt. And this, this will put them at a great disadvantage as the general climate of the world changes ..."

I could almost see Mr. B floating into that future world, looking around, and coming back to report to us, "... as it will, leading to shortages of various necessities. Strangely enough, the shortages will mainly be in the necessities, while there will be a super-abundance of non-necessities."

Mr. B raised his great head and looked at us while still seeing the future, "There will be a super-abundance of things we can't eat, drink, or clothe ourselves with."

Several seconds of silence ensued and no one filled the gap with a cough or a shift of position. The depth of the silence held our attention.

Then, picking up the thread of current history, he continued in his measured, soft but articulate, voice. "We had political activism in the 1960s where people tried to stop the development of destructive weapons and to stop wars, to promote social justice and combat racism. This ended in widespread disillusion. People saw, without understanding it, the working of the cosmic law of things becoming their own opposite."

I thought about the Enneagram and how, without a shock at the correct intervals, things shift and get off course. Which was why going from point A to point B had to take into account the unseen push and pull of energies. Just like Mr. B was saying.

"How the people who try to liberalize institutions play into the hands of those who want to impose a hard line. Those who want to decentralize power play into the hands of those who want to concentrate power, whether its government or industry or military. Now we're in the 1970s and people are looking for a way of life without institutions.

"The two trends I see are: one, the tendency to group together in small independent communities; or two, to look for quick ways of transformation to arrive at an independence from outer world forces through mass-scale spiritual movements."

Yes, I thought, *people are flocking to Transcendental Meditation and the Maharishi, all kinds of gurus and movements.*

"My own belief is that there will be general disillusion with all of this by the end of the 1970s," Mr. B stated. "I think that in the 1980s we will see the visible loss of trust in institutions. Governments will try to adapt, but it will become evident to great numbers of people that a new social system will have to come.

"However, this is going to involve one thing that very, very few are ready to accept. A change from the tendency to regard expansion as a good in itself to a life attitude which will regard concentration as a good in itself."

Mr. B's voice suddenly grew stronger. "This is so much against the trend of the present time, that it is like a revolution. Every one of us is geared to expansion. How many of us are prepared for a way of life where we live with less rather than more? This lesson can't be learned by common sense. People close their minds to it. It will only be learned by bitter experience. And that bitter experience will come."

I thought about my first experience of preparing breakfast for the course and cutting the bread so thick we ran out of slices of toast because people in the front of the line took two pieces. I remembered how mad Mr. B had been when I'd offered more bread, and if I hadn't, someone might have noticed the lesson that by taking more than you need, others go without. Now he was saying that could happen on a much larger scale in years to come.

"That period, in my mind, will come somewhere in the later part of the 1980's and last into the beginning of the next century. By then either we should have got through or we will collapse."

I did a quick calculation. *The tough times were going to come somewhere between my thirties and my old age, hmmm.* I couldn't imagine myself being sixty or seventy, but I could see myself living in an intentional community somewhere with Jack, raising a family.

"All of you who are young will likely see the great transition. Everyone must understand that this is the greatest opportunity that has existed for many thousands of years in the Work. Because not for thousands of years has there been such a need for people who *could* work." Mr. B paused to let that sink in.

"Why is that? Because it cannot come from polarity—from the passive majority who are governed, nor the active minority who possess power. The transition from one system to another system can only come through the third force, from holding the negative and the positive together."

Sounds like the struggle between yes and no. Holding the negative consequences of institutions and the positive attitude of "less is more" in front of me. The key is holding those opposites without trying "to do" something, because if I do, it'll just turn into its opposite. But where does that leave me?

"The thing is, following our dinosaur analogy," Mr. B gave a nod to Larry and worked the curled ends of his chair as if polishing them with his palms, "during the reptilian age of great monsters dominating the earth, there were little creatures—the first mammals, running unnoticed underfoot. It took two and a half billion years, but they had the extraordinary ability to maintain their inner medium by changing their internal temperature. That power enabled them to survive the change of climate and gain domination over the earth. This seems to me a remarkable analogy of what is likely to happen."

Will I be one of these new "mammals" who is able to make the effort to hold the positive (First Force) and the negative (Second Force) within me without reacting? Is that what will create an opening for the neutralizing Third Force (or Grace) to enter? Is it the effort of not reacting that leads to the Unconditioned World, where there are fewer laws and miracles can happen?

"Whereas it took ten million years for reptiles to lose their position and for mammals to come to the front, now this will happen in a much shorter time—the Law of Acceleration is in full operation, the curve is very much steeper."

Mr. B had just said he thought these things would happen in my lifetime, not his. This was the first time I'd heard of the Law of Acceleration. A sense of urgency, verging on desperation, invaded me. *Am I up to this task? Me?* I wasn't so sure.

"We should talk about what we could be doing in front of this. When you leave here, some of you will be going back to school, some to work. I want you to know it is possible to maintain a balance between providing for the needs of life and an intensive inner work activity.

"There are already the beginnings of small communities that are trying to experiment with new ways of life, but most of them are failing. This conversion of reptilian to mammal, to use our analogy from cold-blooded to warm-blooded communities, is as much beyond human power as the last conversion was.

"But I have no doubt it is being directed by a higher power. Our part in it is one of cooperation rather than innovation.

"The societies of the last few thousand years have been based on egoism, the satisfaction of personal desires rather than the desire for service. For the first time in a very long time, mankind requires a new structure, a new way of life.

"According to the Shivapuri Baba, 'This civilization has failed mankind and two-thirds of the human race will perish. It will be swept away because it cannot give what mankind needs.'"

Mr. B looked up and brightened, "But I don't say this, I don't even think it probable."

Then his face clouded up in thought as he added, "I can believe that the majority of the human race will cease to be significant because they will belong to a perished world and will be unable to adapt themselves to the new."

Someone coughed, I straightened the small of my back, which was beginning to sag. Refocusing my attention, I recognized my discomfort was with the future being laid out at my feet.

"So! Coming back to our immediate problem in front of us. Some of you will be able to join a group effort to form a community along the lines we are talking about. Others of you may be able to offer what you have learned here to the many around the world looking for a new way of life. In either case, in the course of time something begins to grow.

"That is why we are spending these last six weeks together to reprise what we have learnt and in practicing and showing one another.

"Unless this course has failed you completely, you will have by now learnt that you can't do it."

A titter of laughs ran around the room. *Yes, like how I can't do a Movement, but if I put myself in the right alignment with myself, the Movement "does me."*

"At least you will not go away with the idea that you can set yourselves up as first-class gurus. Or even second-class gurus," he said with a grin.

"But what you will have learnt, is that we cannot work alone. The nature of this work is that it cannot live without being shared."

The meeting came to an end and people rose and began filing out. I hesitated, feeling still inside. Mr. B had also remained in his chair, watching the room. There was a question in me, but I didn't know what the words to it were. All I knew was that I desperately wanted to know some truth about myself, and I felt Mr. B could tell me. I waited. Eventually it was just the two of us left. I was still sitting on the floor.

As if he knew what I wanted, Mr. B began to speak, "Bobby Jo, do you want to hear the truth?"

"Yes," I whispered, swallowing.

"Well, here's the thing. If you are not careful, you are going to end up a selfish old woman."

He said this not unkindly, but he did say it with certainty.

I didn't flinch. In fact, I relaxed. Finally, I had heard the truth about myself.

But he was not finished. After a pause, while I was still rooted, he added, "You know, altruism is the truest form of egoism. Helping others gives the greatest self-satisfaction of all. A true egoist discovers this for himself."

It was as if he was speaking from self-knowledge. I tucked his words away as a warning and a touchstone. I did not want to end up a selfish old woman.

"Bobby Jo, what you need is an irksome practice." Mr. B's face lit up with his Cheshire grin. It no longer frightened me.

CHAPTER SIXTY-EIGHT
Nature

One day we were weeding the garden beds under the enormously long evergreen hedge that lined the grounds behind the house. A warm July sun nudged its head in and out of drifting cumulus clouds as if it were playing hide and seek. My hair was tied up in a loose French knot to keep it off my neck and out of my eyes. I was wearing it this way a lot lately. Plucking weeds out so as not to disturb the flowers, I inhaled a riot of fragrance from fat pink, blue, yellow, and white blossoms. The bees were busy too. Another good reason to pay attention and work with presence.

There seemed to be one busy bee in particular that couldn't stay away from me. I didn't want to tangle with this fellow but also felt a symmetry of purpose. We were both interested in the well-being of the flowers. As long as I continued working my trowel in the earth, the bee was content to buzz in and out of blossoms, gathering nectar nearby.

The gong outside clanged. Time to pause and stand to collect ourselves. I stood up. Immediately I heard buzzing near my head. Forget the pause!

Quickly moving away from where I had been digging, I ducked my head to lose the bee. It didn't work. The buzzing sounded louder and even more frustrated. A sinking realization came to me that the bee was caught in the mess of brown waves pinned up with my leather and stick fastener. The fear of getting stung gripped me. Blood pumped, heart thumped, skin prickled.

Just as my body gathered to break into a frantic run and yelp for help, it occurred to me that the bee needed help too. A warmth invaded my breast that soothed my rising panic, slowed my racing heart. The poor little thing!

It had just been minding its own business after all. Carefully I reached up and slid the stick out. Bending and throwing the thick mass over my head I gently shook my hair loose, using my fingers to fluff it out, holding onto the feeling of empathy for the captive. The bee worked itself free, content to fly off and resume its task amongst the flowers.

Up to that moment nature had been something outside myself, an outdoor task to perform, a duty to complete. I had never encountered a partnership with nature. A world now unfurled for me with a magical dimension. Just as carrying a Theme in my head opens me to a new understanding, something in my emotional center had softened to connect me to nature in a way I had never experienced before. Instead of being afraid, I felt sorry for the bee and wanted to help it. In return, it didn't sting me.

CHAPTER SIXTY-NINE
Where's the Love?

Where's the love story going in this tale? Since so much of my attention was on my inner process, romance seemed secondary. I'd come to Sherborne to understand myself and grow into a "real" person, one with presence and wisdom, one who knew things rather than one who asked. Jack had been my ticket and companion into this world of inner work. As a friend and a lover, I felt our connection was preordained. Hadn't I "known" I had to transfer to Livingston College, where we met on the first day? Hadn't I "known" at Mr. B's talk in New York that we would come on the course? It seemed obvious to me that Jack and I were meant to meet and come to Sherborne. I assumed that my sense of a shared destiny was just as obvious to Jack. But my Chief Feature of assuming that everyone saw the world through my eyes caught me out.

One day I was going for a stroll outside after lunch and came upon Larry and Rachel. I joined them. I began complaining about some issue with Jack, my way of processing thoughts. Rachel was the kind of friend who was silent but listened. Larry was a sympathetic listener and a natural counselor. Our discussion was fueled by the ever-looming event of our return to life after the course.

Reflecting on his own relationship with Rachel, Larry casually asked, "Bobby Jo, do you think you and Jack will get married after you get home?"

I didn't realize that Jack, who happened to be hidden by the side of the house when we rounded the corner, had quietly fallen into step next to Larry as he was speaking.

"That's just the problem," I replied. "He hasn't asked me."

In a halting voice Larry said, "I'm in a position I don't want to be in."

Drawn by the odd sound of his voice, I glanced over and saw Jack just as I was answering Larry's question. Hearing my own words and seeing Jack there, something in me cleft open. Like that surreal day of the fire drill, I felt myself falling backwards into a yawning chasm. A primal scream welled up from my depths, bursting forth:

"NNNOOOOOOOOOOOOOOOOOOOO—"

I was as surprised as anyone, at the piercing sound arising from deep within me and the anguish I felt. As if my being was expressing something I was too young to comprehend. The desperate wail of a woman realizing she has entrusted her soul to a man who has not committed.

Larry put a supporting arm around my limp shoulders and guided me back to the house.

When my relationship with Jack had started getting serious, I had put the question in front of myself, "Do you love him?" An image had formed, as if in answer. I saw a thin steel rod, flexible yet unbreakable, running through Jack. It symbolized a backbone of strength despite his gentle nature. What I felt was an immense respect, and I knew that was a sound foundation on which to build a lifelong relationship from which love would grow. Jack and I had already built a relationship based on the value of the ideas and practices of the Gurdjieff work. We shared so many experiences from the course and the deep understandings those had generated. We shared an essential understanding that made intimacy natural and right. Thankfully, we were small and nimble enough to fit together on the narrow foam mattress that was our bed on the floor of the attic room we called ours.

When we joined completely in the physical world, I became aware of a conduit between our breasts much like the magical floating umbilical cord we had experienced between us in the Horse Parlor last fall. Even deeper and stronger than our physical union, this energy carried the sensation of completion on an ethereal plane. It infused me with ecstasy. At the same time his love-making felt smooth and full and liquid, as if my depths were drinking up a vanilla milkshake. I was complete and satisfied.

I knew that our union was forever. It was obvious to me; how could it not be to Jack? With a very deep part of myself I needed him to acknowledge that he knew it too. The scream taught me that.

I began to understand that Jack would express his feelings in his own time—and how hard it was for me to allow him the space to do this. The course was teaching me that.

CHAPTER SEVENTY
Washing the Walls

The place was getting a thorough wash down and clean up. Loose ends from practical work projects were completed. The kitchen was scrubbed and organized, wood and stone floors cleaned to a high polish. It seemed unreal to think we would be leaving this home for far-flung countries and activities, returning to a life I could hardly relate to anymore. Yet there was more than an undercurrent of anticipation in the air as the last few weeks of the course slipped by.

"Geez, can you believe it? Only three days left," I said, prying thumbtacks from *The Wind in the Willows* poster and laying it on the bed.

"This isn't how I thought we'd spend the last days of the course," Jack said, pulling the mattress away from the wall.

"What were you picturing?"

"You know, hanging out, sharing memories, saying goodbyes. That kind of stuff."

Jack stood there, his arms limp at his sides.

I felt sensation filling my hands, warm and prickling as I held the sharp tacks. A presence was here in this room we had shared. It wasn't memories that came to me but the fullness of my being, of NOW. We fell silent and went to work. I placed the tacks down on the dresser and Jack pulled it away from the wall. He disappeared, going downstairs to the kitchen as I finished pulling our little mementos off the wall.

"Here you go," Jack said, reappearing and setting down a bucket of water. He handed me a sponge.

I soaked the sponge and wrung it out. "So, are you just going back home to West New York?" I asked, taking a section of wall and swiping a high arc, then pulling down and up, scrubbing in much the same way as I had learned to paint across and then up and down the day I arrived here, thinking I knew so much, then discovering how little that was.

"Yeah," he said, wringing his own sponge out and setting to work. "Part of me wants to get as far away from here as I can, the other part is disappointed I wasn't one of the students who was asked to stay on."

"Well, my ego would have loved to be asked to stay, but I'm not sure about the rest of me. I think I'm ready to go out into the world." I dipped my sponge again. "Besides, Mr. B did say we should take a six-month break from the Work. Ya know, to let it settle."

"I know, and I have every intention of doing that. Besides, I'm anxious to see my family again, wondering how they're doing, especially Michael. I worry about him, being the youngest and all."

"Yeah, you kind of had him under your wing before we left, taking him to the Pinnacle to meet Mrs. Popoff and all. He's such a cute kid. How old is he now?" Michael was my favorite of Jack's brothers, and I felt he'd looked up to us. I had taken him to the park when he was eight and taught him how to climb a tree.

"Twelve, I think. But, you know, I want to see my mom and dad again too, not just my brothers." Jack dipped his sponge and moved to another section of wall. "I used to be mad at my mom for getting on my case, but I realize now that she was doing that out of love. Even if she did lock me out of the house when I was staying out late and getting stoned all the time."

We worked in silence again. I sensed the room starting to feel less full of us, more neutral, as if we were washing our vibrations off the walls.

"What about you?" Jack eventually asked. "Your sister Stevie, is she coming?"

"Yeah, Mom and Dad are paying for the two of us to travel around for two weeks after the course. I think they feel bad that I got a whole year abroad and she's never been."

Jack didn't ask, "Am I invited?" And it never occurred to me that Jack might wish he could see more of Britain too.

"I'm meeting her in London, and then we'll rent a car and drive to Wales and the Lake District in Yorkshire, where Daddy's ancestors are from, and end up in Edinburgh, Scotland, before coming back to London to fly home. That's a whole lot better than the ten-city, ten-day European package Mom started out proposing. At least this way we'll be able to take our time and do what we want along the way."

The fact that Jack had struggled to earn the money for his round-trip flight and contributed the remainder towards the course, while my parents paid for me, was something I took for granted as our given lots in life.

"Sounds great," Jack said. "What about after that, when you get home?"

"I don't really know. It's hard to even imagine being home, let alone what I'll do," I said, standing back and inspecting the wet wall, looking for spots I'd missed, hoping he'd say something about us. But then jumping in again with my own thoughts, "At least I got my BA from Livingston, so I don't have to go back to school. Mom said they mailed me the diploma last January, remember?"

The BA made me feel less guilty about having tricked my dad into paying for the course as if it were a senior year abroad program connected to my school. The only connection was the private arrangement between my professor and me. Ten credits to graduate in exchange for sharing the journal I would keep. Thank goodness my professor had heard of Gurdjieff and had become intrigued about my adventure.

Jack was finishing the last wall, and I went to get the broom. The scrubbed hall and stairs felt strange, almost unfamiliar, like I didn't belong here anymore. It was hard to imagine myself anywhere else but here. Each person I passed—Emily on the stairs, Victor in the hall, Rachel at the broom closet—felt like immediate family, so it didn't occur to me to ask for addresses. If it had, it would have struck me as superficial. How could we possibly not stay connected? I felt that way about Jack too.

Our bags were packed and ready to go, just like the Peter, Paul, and Mary song. Jack and I had been offered a ride to London. It felt surreal. Jack would catch his plane home and I would meet my sister arriving from the States. We didn't discuss our relationship. After all, our parents' houses were only half an hour apart in New Jersey, so it would be easy enough to see each other.

"Mr. B is in the library," Mick told us as we stopped to bid him adieu. He was on his way down the hall to the kitchen. It didn't seem possible we'd not see his lanky frame and those irreverent pursed lips somewhere in our future.

We headed for the library.

"I don't know if I want to say good-bye," I equivocated to Jack, not sure of my feelings now that the moment had come.

"Oh, come on, we have to say good-bye," Jack insisted, dragging me into the room. "What if we never see him again?"

And there he was, sitting at a small square chess table next to the windows, for all the world like an ordinary person. Opposite him was a student, a professor from Massachusetts. They were the only two in the library. Sunlight glinted off the ivory and ebony pieces. The relaxed atmosphere was disarming.

"Mr. B, we've come to say good-bye," Jack said, walking up to the table as Mr. Bennett looked up from examining the last move on the board. Jack held me firmly by the hand. "We're leaving for the airport now."

"Well then, we shan't say good-bye but safe journeys," Mr. Bennett smiled softly, no Cheshire grin this time.

Inclining his head towards me, "And I must say, Bobby Jo, I have to admit even I have changed during this course."

Looking at me with bright, curious eyes, he said in a conspiratorial tone, "You know, when I first met you I did not care over-much for you." Then he lit up even more and added, "But now I can honestly say that I have grown to like you!"

I stood there, warmth flooding into my chest with his words, a grin creasing my face. I felt a shift inside, a realigning of my relationship with him, the joy of recognition. He understood me. I had graduated.

To both of us he concluded, "Please give my warmest regards to Mrs. Popoff."

Nodding thoughtfully to himself, he then turned his full attention back to the game at hand.

A car was waiting behind the kitchen. We piled our luggage into it just as we had unloaded it so long ago. I don't remember who else squeezed in to drive to the airport with us. The trip down the driveway and up the lane onto the A40 proceeded in silence. I must have been looking out the window because I can still see the tree-lined gravel drive and the pasture shaded by large oak trees with the donkeys and the pony, Judy, contentedly munching grass.

CHAPTER SEVENTY-ONE
Re-entry

Jack and I entered Heathrow Airport, lugging our stuffed suitcases. The concourse echoed with quiet voices, clicking heels, and rolling carts. It seemed odd to be saying goodbye to Jack as he gathered himself to follow signs to his terminal.

"Well, have a good flight. I'll get in touch when I get home," I said, resting my bags at my feet. I hoped he'd say something to encourage me.

"Yeah, I'm sure it will fine," he said, departure ticket in hand. He grinned. "I can't wait to see Dennis and tell him about Sherborne. It's cool that he's been working with Mrs. Popoff and is signed up for the next course."

I pictured Jack having long discussions about the Work with his best friend at the On Tap bar in West New York. I waited. He said nothing about wanting me to call him as soon as I was back. Instead, he asked, "When is Stevie's flight arriving?"

"Oh, it's not for a while. I'm just going to hang out here until it's time."

Jack looked up at the clock next to the departures board. "Well, I guess I'd better go then." He picked up his old canvas duffle bag. "See ya on the other side."

I raised up on my toes and gave him a quick peck on the cheek. "I'll call you," I said again. He swung into his long easy gait, bell bottoms flapping around his beat-up tan sneakers with the loose shoestrings.

I waited at the gate for my sister's plane to taxi to a halt, eager with anticipation as I watched the passengers walking down the staircase and out across the tarmac. She was one of the last to disembark and I was surprised, then chagrined, to see her athletic bare legs striding towards the gate in khaki shorts. She was wearing a bright green L.L.Bean vest and carrying a dayglow-orange nylon backpack. She might as well have been running across the asphalt shouting, "I'm an American Tourist!"

We hugged each other and went to find the incoming luggage. She was telling me about her trip and asking questions in a voice way too loud for normal conversation by British standards. I was surprised at how embarrassed I felt. This was my older sister, Stevie, whom I revered and hadn't seen for over a year!

I had been careful to book us a room in the Continental Hotel recommended by my British friends as opposed to the Americanized International Hotel.

The halls in the Continental were narrow and dark. We had to walk up two flights to get to our room after dinner and I had an uneasy feeling about the guy following behind us. I fumbled getting the key into the lock, my hands trembling.

"Move!" I said, giving Stevie a little shove so I could fit in behind her before slamming the door shut.

"What was that?" Stevie turned in surprise.

"Didn't you notice that guy right behind us in the hall?"

"No. What guy?"

"Oh, well, there was a guy, and I couldn't tell if he was really going to his room or not."

I looked around at our two single beds, aware of my thumping heart. I sensed my feet, taking a long breath in and exhaled, allowing relaxation to wash down from my head to the bottoms of my feet as they sensed the floor. It was unusual for me to be paranoid, and I wondered how accurate my sense of danger had been. All my senses seemed to be on high alert in this new world. I couldn't tell if this was a sign of acquired awareness or of unease with what felt like dissonant surroundings. After ten months of tranquility and intentional speech and movements, I found London's honking cars, scurrying people, and mixed aromas of exhaust and grease and fish—disconcerting. I was used to high ceilings and wide hallways. This hotel's dark narrow halls with a stranger at our backs had set up alarm bells which I couldn't be sure were justified. But I had come to trust my inner sense. I hoped this awareness was a sign of maturity.

Stevie was already unpacking her toothbrush and heading for the sink in the corner of the room, unperturbed. The thought that just because she was older, she might not automatically be wiser, occurred to me for the first time.

After three days in London, we struck out for the Cotswolds in a rented car, learning to drive on the wrong side of the road.

"Bobby Jo, I wish you'd put on your seatbelt," Stevie said, as we bumped down a twisting lane, barely wide enough for one and a half vehicles. I wasn't used to the belts, which seemed gratuitous.

"Why?" I said, watching each bend, anticipating a car popping out at us and wondering what happens then.

"Because they're for your protection and it's recommended."

"Oh, for goodness sakes. This isn't an airplane!"

"Really. You're supposed to wear them."

"Stop telling me what to do!" I snapped, surprised at the anger in my voice but even more surprised that I felt secure in sticking up for my point of view. I'd always acquiesced to my sister before. By virtue of being two years older she'd conveyed a superior authority. My newfound self-assurance made me feel like her equal, like I could be her friend and not just her little sister.

Taking turns driving, talking about home and our impressions of Britain, I began to feel like an American again and eventually stopped criticizing my sister for being one.

One day we were heading up through Yorkshire where we believed my father's side of the family came from. A Yorkshireman we met in a pub reminded me of my father. I was struck by how this gentleman's tall, rectangular build resembled that of my father's. Somewhere along the line I had heard our surname, Flather, had originally been *Flathee*, "He who flails the wheat." I pictured our ancestors wielding huge scythes, their tall, lean bodies brown and muscular, chopping down golden wheat stalks with long arching strokes, their sweat-stained peasant shirts open to the waist.

One particular day, driving farther north towards Scotland on empty roads along rising elevations of bright purple heather, I had a moment. Despite Mr. B's instruction at the end of the course to let go of inner practices for six months to allow things to settle in us, or perhaps because of it, I found my inner state suddenly detached. As if another veil had lifted.

I was aware of the wind blowing in the car window as the two-lane pavement sped by, the scent of purple heather floating on the currents. But another part of me felt suspended somewhere above my head. I had the distinct sense that this other part was new, growing—fed by the efforts I made to be present, to sense, to not react in my habitual ways.

And then I felt my personality. Greedy, hungry, ready to take credit and gloat.

No! I thought. *You can't have this.*

I pushed the new awareness away from my consciousness, wishing it to fade, quick, before I could think about it. But a little glow remained, like an aftertaste, a comfort of knowing that efforts did accrue. I let go of this too, wishing this embryo of being to stay hidden from my sight so that it could grow, unmolested.

EPILOGUE

Years have passed, my life unfolding in and around Claymont, the Society for Continuous Education, an intentional community in West Virginia. The society and community have survived, led for years by Pierre and Vivien Elliot, with efforts of inner work guided by what was learned at Sherborne and the legacy of Mr. Bennett and G. I. Gurdjieff. Pierre and Vivien are no longer with us, but the Work continues. Many at Claymont practice physical presence, relaxation, transforming the energy of negativity along with working in the natural world. Over the years my work has filled my internal garden shed with tools I can use to till the soil of myself. A work that needs to be done for oneself, but can't be fully accomplished without others, the results of which are greater than the sum of their parts.

Jack and I married two years after the course in an Episcopal chapel. My parents' Episcopal Minister and Jack's favorite Catholic priest from West New York performed a joint ceremony. I was five months pregnant. Our immediate families and several Sherborne friends attended. When our son was ten months old, we moved to West Virginia and joined the newly forming community at Claymont.

Kip, Steve, and Barbara June also came to Claymont, as did many others from Sherborne courses. Even more came to live there who attended one of the thirteen courses held at Claymont, most under the guidance of Pierre.

Our children grew up going to the Claymont Children's School from preschool through sixth grade. Our son later told me that it was the Claymont Children's School that had prepared him for college. He also confided that he had grown up assuming that when he graduated from high school, he would then go on a course at Claymont. Alas, by the time he graduated high school, courses were no longer held at Claymont due to changing times.

Forty-seven years later, our children now grown with families of their own, Jack and I are still married and still involved with Claymont, which has become a seminar center and is exploring ways to expand its educational mandate.

But I am no perfected being, as I thought back then I should be by now. My personality is not expunged of annoying characteristics, nor is my self-centeredness erased. When I am taken to task for this—indeed, when I cry out inside myself, "How is it that after thirty, forty, almost fifty years, the same traits remain? Why do I make the same mistakes, like blurting things out without thinking, only to regret them later?"

You may well ask, "Why do you want to follow this teaching then?"

And I will answer. I follow this teaching because I know—with all of my bodily sensation, the curiosity of my mind, the response of my feelings—that this is my path and it is right for me. When the world throws curve balls, be they political events or personal ills, I have tools I can use and support from friends who share my language and expand my understanding. My children have grown up surrounded by people who value the intangible gifts of nature and inner growth, rather than the material world.

And even though Bobby Jo still sees her selfishness and knows she can rub people the wrong way, she can also attest to this: That it is possible to consciously follow one particle of air into the nose, down the airways, into the lung, and then to exhale with the awareness of "something" remaining behind. That a second breath can be traced, with warm gratitude radiating in the breast, carrying a wish. That something hidden within grows, and that our personality and our animal nature are necessary parts of ourselves. For without these, there is no compost with which to grow the garden.

Taking a third conscious breath—inhaling impressions of sound, light, temperature, and scent, following the flow into the lungs as the impressions are filtered through the head like effervescent particles that are then directed towards the solar plexus—one knows with certainty that one can make the effort to "work on oneself" again, again, and yet again.

Until The End

ACKNOWLEDGMENTS

My first thanks go to Emunah Herzog, who gave me a weekly ear with practical questions and encouraged me to keep working. Emunah, you've never steered me wrong, especially when you suggested I check out Gotham Writers. Those ten-week online courses proved invaluable. Thank you, Gotham, and all my wonderful classmates for your thoughtful, provoking, and encouraging critiques.

Then there's my close friend from Sherborne House, Rachel Altman, who offered to line edit. Rachel's edits made me feel like that part of the job was "done," an important phase of my process. Bless you, Rachel.

Of course, I can't leave out Jack Chromey, whom I sometimes think of as my memory-checker but who also added important insights and tidbits that made their way into the story.

My new friend, June Loy, generously offered to read the "finished" manuscript and posed important comments, questions, and suggestions that were much appreciated. Thank you, June!

Mindy Lewis, my official content editor, has been a gem and a teacher, not to mention invaluable with her corrections, suggestions, and coaching questions. But I would not have had the courage to seek an editor if it had not been for Jane Bayers, a Gotham classmate, who offered me the introduction that eventually led to Mindy.

My depth of gratitude for Cynthia Bourgeault cannot be measured, as she not only agreed to read the manuscript but enthusiastically opened the door to publishing with Monkfish Publishers. Of course, that leads to Paul Cohen, who accepted an unvetted author and showed faith in the project. Finally, many thanks to Dory Mayo, who as copy editor, made sure my commas and caps and spaces and details were attended to. Another sympathetic reader whom I count as a friend. Of course Colin Rolfe can't be left out, as he has administered the finishing touches of layout and design, plus welcoming the cover designed by my love, Jack Chromey.

To all who have enthusiastically agreed to let me read the work in progress, or use their photos, or spin vignettes with their names and descriptors that may not be completely accurate but thus is memory—Thank You! A special thanks to Regina Roman, who did an impromptu photo shoot at Claymont and gifted me the use of a professional profile photo.

It's been a long and winding road, but hardly a lonely one. Thank you, Team Book!

ABOUT THE AUTHOR

Roberta J. Chromey is a memoirist, a life-long journalist, and a recent blogger who shares her insights based on fifty years of inner work in the Fourth Way of George Ivanovich Gurdjieff. At seventy-one, Roberta continues to practice Gurdjieff Movements and lead morning-exercises developed by John G. Bennett. As a young adult, Roberta's teachers were Irmis B. Popoff and John G. Bennett, both of whom worked closely with Gurdjieff. The diary Roberta kept while attending Bennett's esoteric school in England from 1972–73 became the basis for her memoir, *Real People*.

Roberta was born in Washington, D.C., and grew up in Bethesda, Maryland. She attended University of Maryland and Livingston College, a division of Rutgers University, receiving a BA in English and Education in 1973. In 1976 Roberta moved with her young family to become a member of the Claymont Society in West Virginia. She earned her CRTT credentials as a Respiratory Technician in 1981 and became a Registered Respiratory Therapist in 1991, working in West Virginia and Virginia hospitals for twenty-five years. For eighteen years she helped her husband, Jack Chromey, run a printing and marketing business. Now retired, they have two children and four grandchildren all living in Asheville, North Carolina. Roberta has enjoyed experiencing the cultures of Uruguay in South America, England, France, Italy, the Netherlands, and India. Roberta and Jack divide their time between their homes in West Virginia and North Carolina. They are both active members of the Claymont Society for Continuous Education in Charles Town, West Virginia.

www.ingramcontent.com/pod-product-compliance
Lightning Source LLC
Chambersburg PA
CBHW030134170426
43199CB00008B/59